Sing A Pretty Song...

Sing A Pretty Song...

THE "OFFBEAT" LIFE OF EDIE ADAMS, INCLUDING THE ERNIE KOVACS YEARS

Edie Adams and
Robert Windeler

WILLIAM MORROW AND COMPANY, INC.
NEW YORK

Recognizing the importance of preserving what has been written, it is the policy
of William Morrow and Company, Inc., and its imprints and affiliates to have
the books it publishes printed on acid-free paper, and we exert our best efforts
to that end.

Library of Congress Cataloging-in-Publication Data

Adams, Edie, 1927–
    Sing a pretty song . . . : the "offbeat" life of Edie Adams, including
the Ernie Kovacs years / Edie Adams and Robert Windeler.
        p.   cm.
    ISBN 0-688-07341-7
    1. Adams, Edie, 1927–   . 2. Singers—United States—Biography.
I. Windeler, Robert. II. Title.
ML420.A25A3   1990
782.42164'092—dc20
[B]   90-5739
                                                                            CIP

Printed in the United States of America

First Edition

1 2 3 4 5 6 7 8 9 10

BOOK DESIGN BY BERNARD SCHLEIFER

For my son
Joshua Dylan Mills
and my daughter
Mia Susan Kovacs

$\mathcal{A}$CKNOWLEDGMENTS

A SPECIAL THANKS TO:

Lenita Hughes, my assistant, for her help in all areas of my life: research, organizing, editing, proofreading—and when I'm stuck, just schmoozing helps.

Henri Bollinger, my friend, whose guidance and expertise have pulled me through many difficult periods of my life.

Josh Mills, my son, for his constant encouragement.

Sheldon Enke, my brother, who remembers much more than I.

Nan Burris, who is always there for me.

Lisa Drew and Bob Shuman, for their incredible patience.

Rachelle Bienveniste and my constructively critical UCLA writing classmates.

Steve Atha and Marvin Moss, whom I miss very much.

Thanks also to: Patricia Boyd Brady, Aurelia Bremner, Lynne Honus, Bert Kingsbury, Mrs. Tom Kovacs, Jack and Felicia Lemmon, Mary Adams Jacques, Carol Matthau, Andy McCay, Jim Moreland, Ruth Adams Scheffler, Laurel Spira, M. Wilson and Raymona Vorbeck, Hugh York and George Zachary, Esq.

Acknowledgments

A SPECIAL ACCOLADE GOES TO:

Robert Windeler, my teacher and co-writer, for his heroic efforts in cutting the original fifteen hundred pages I presented to him.

—EDIE ADAMS

Without the unstinting support and encouragement of my assistant, Stirling Nix, and my friend and business manager, Hugh Dodson, I could not have sung this particular song. They always inspire me to do the best I know how, and I am eternally grateful.

—ROBERT WINDELER

Sing A Pretty Song...

$\mathcal{P}$ROLOGUE

THIS WAS IT. The big day. Ernie and I were finally going to dinner at my parents' house in Tenafly, New Jersey. I called it the inspection dinner and had carefully dressed in my suburban Bergen County clothes. I had hoped that Ernie would wear something quieter, but here he was in his loudest sport shirt, brown voile with huge sunburst splashes of bright yellow dots. "Hmm, interesting," I said of his outfit.

"Look, it's a hot, sweaty day. I just *had* to wear voile; besides, it matches my cigar."

It *was* one of those heavy, wet eastern seaboard hots, with the temperature and the humidity the same: two evenly matched ninety-eights. Ernie had the top down on his snazzy white Cad-Allard, so the oppressive heat, together with the steady stream of exhaust from bumper-to-bumper traffic on Manhattan's West Side Highway, had us both mopping our faces. When we got to the George Washington Bridge, a clear sweep of untrapped air kept us dried off for the three miles of bridge entry and across the Hudson River. But, once we had turned right in New Jersey, onto Route 9W going north, traffic slowed us down, and again we started to drip.

Ernie was a little nervous about having Saturday night dinner with my mother and father. He'd met them, of course, at the studio when they had come to see one of the crazier,

11

chaotic daily shows we did live at CBS earlier in 1952. Even through their bewilderment about Ernie's brand of show business, he couldn't help noticing their coolness. "They don't like me," he had said, and he was right.

My mother and father, Ada and Sheldon Enke, those two conservative native Pennsylvanians, did not understand Ernie's brash manner of acting or dressing. They had carefully pointed out to me that he was nearly ten years older than I, *divorced*, had two children, a cigar, and a mustache. What they didn't have to say was that he was Hungarian and a Roman Catholic to boot. They knew, however, that for the past year now I had been seeing him exclusively; no matter what they thought or said, he was not going to go away. So they had finally thawed enough to ask him to dinner on this sticky July evening at their house, where they could examine him close up on their own highly structured turf.

When the holiday traffic brought us to a near standstill on the New Jersey side, Ernie started in.

"God, this heat.

"I'm thirsty.

"Whew, would I like a nice cold drink.

"I'd like a nice ice-cold gin and tonic.

"I'd like a nice ice-cold *big* gin and tonic, with lots of ice and gin and lots of tonic with a lot of fresh lime juice on top."

He licked his chops, then repeated, "A great big icy cold gin and—"

"The only liquor in our house is cooking brandy, and it's only used to light the plum pudding at Christmas. The only tall cool one you're going to get is a big, frosty glass of Lipton's iced tea."

Silence.

Then Ernie suddenly made a sharp left turn off the highway, down the hill into Englewood, New Jersey. I said, "Ernie, you're one town too soon. Tenafly is the next turnoff."

"I have to buy something," he said.

"What?"

"You'll see."

He drove into town, parked, scanned the shops, then went into a pet store. I couldn't figure that one out. Shortly he came out carrying a large brown paper bag, folded on the top so that I couldn't see what was in it.

"What's in the—"

"Just a minute." He walked a few doors up the street and into a liquor store; after a few moments he came out carrying an even bigger bag and grinning from cigar to ear.

"Now direct me to that park with all the trees that you said was near your house."

By now he was grinning wider, puffing deeper, and driving faster. He screeched to a halt under a huge shady tree, opened his pet shop bag, pulled out a goldfish bowl, and put it in his lap. Then he reached into the other bag for ice cubes, which he proceeded to pour into the fishbowl. Then he opened a bottle of gin, poured half of it over the crackling ice, and added a giant bottle of tonic that fizzed up. "Mmm, the bubbles do tickle your nose," he said. He topped off his concoction by squeezing the juice of two limes on top. He swirled the bowl around a few times, then picked it up with both hands and took one long pull. Then, with eyes rolled back and the most beatific smile on his face, he said, "Now *that's* a gin and tonic."

With a little help from me, he finished most of it, then drove the short distance to my parents' home, at 91 Sunset Lane, a fortified, mellow, and happy man. Had I known what awaited us, I might have finished the giant G&T for him. At that time my usual drink was a claret lemonade.

Even though it was a record heat for July, Mother had done her ever-popular special dinner for us: *hot* crab casserole served in individual seashells to start, followed by pot *roast* with *roasted* potatoes and carrots. Then came the salad—lime Jell-O quivering on a lettuce leaf, topped with shredded carrots and a thick dollop of Hellmann's real mayonnaise—*hot* rolls, *hot* coffee, and *warm* chocolate cake for dessert. Of course, there was iced tea throughout.

The table was set in full Victorian regalia. Each place had a service plate with a doily on it, surrounded by every piece of turn-of-the-century bric-a-brac known to man. The center-piece of cut flowers clattered on its epergne. Everything else on the table was a tiny booby trap, tinkling, rattling, or squeaking and much too small for Ernie's large hands to negotiate.

The dining-room table was a drop leaf, and my mother had carefully placed Ernie where he had either to straddle the two close-together legs or to try to tuck both legs of his six-foot-two-inch frame between them. Any movement of his legs would set off the tintinnabulation on the table. Since most of the "good" dishes had come out of the spindly glass and china closet, the few that remained there resonated even louder on their nearly empty shelves when anyone walked by. And Ernie was always leaping up and wandering around, looking for an ashtray for his cigar, the bathroom, or any other excuse to get up from that table.

"Everything makes a noise in this house," Ernie said, and it did.

The living room had nests of rickety tables topped with wobbly knickknacks that also made noises when anyone passed. He later used the sounds of my mother's house as the basis for his silent character Eugene, but he moved the setting to a stuffy library. Ernie struggled through that dinner with the most puzzled look on his face. He seemed to be studying the table and its contents, while politely answering my parents' questions in that soft-spoken voice of his, all the time desperately trying to avoid eye contact with me.

I was just beginning to think that the gin and tonic had completely mellowed him when my father said, "Here, Ernie, you've got to try this horseradish; I grow it myself in the backyard."

"Is it strong?" Ernie asked.

"Milder than most times. I cut it back with cabbage today. Try it."

Through a mouthful of pot roast I tried to warn Ernie about my father's ideas of strong and mild . . . too late. Ernie had just popped a teaspoonful of the horseradish on a blackened piece of pot roast and into his mouth. He was chewing on it when his eyebrows froze up in the middle. He stopped chewing, and his eyes filled with tears. He spit it all out on the plate and tried to suppress "Ishtanem" through teary eyes. (He always swore in Hungarian when he was really mad.) He continued with a stream of filthy Hungarian expletives that, luckily, nobody understood except me. His whole life Ernie never did get over the fact that my quiet, conservative father had slipped him a horseradish mickey.

Throughout the rest of the meal Ernie managed to move all the food around on his plate without eating much of anything. When we were clearing the table and bringing out the coffee, he whispered to me, "Let's get the hell out of here and get some dinner." We said our polite good-byes and raced back across the bridge to the newfound comfort of New York café society Billy Reed's Little Club—our new "home"—for a late supper.

$\mathcal{O}$NE

ERNIE KOVACS AND I were as different as our upbringings and heritage could have made us. The two things we shared were our great love and admiration for each other and an irreverent sense of humor about almost everything else. We spent only eleven years together, from early 1951 until his death in January 1962. But we seemed to pack several lifetimes into that short span.

Ernie was an off-the-wall mad Hungarian, older than I, who had dedicated his life to staying a child. He never seemed to take anything seriously. Here was a fully grown man, at least to all outward appearances, with a soft voice and the mischievous vulnerability of an active ten-year-old. Since I spent most of my childhood trying to be an adult, this combination was irresistible. I have since spent a lifetime trying to recapture and imitate his off-center, impulsive life-style. His name was not the only thing foreign to me. Ernie taught me to have fun, to play and be a kid, for the first time in my life.

I was born old, just on the cusp of the Depression, in a two-story stucco apartment on Wyoming Avenue in Kingston, Pennsylvania. My father was a partner in the Enke-Oliver Hardware Store at 627 South Main Street, in Wilkes-Barre,

Pennsylvania. The store prospered for a few years, and we moved to a large house with a screened-in porch and a big lawn, in Shavertown, Pennsylvania. Then, very suddenly, we moved into a tiny house on a dirt street in Trucksville when my father's hardware store partner declared bankruptcy. My father eventually paid back every cent owed to their creditors, an important early lesson for me. It would never have occurred to him to do otherwise. My father also worked several jobs throughout the Depression, to pay back debts incurred by his brother-in-law. My father was the classic care giver, on his white horse, saving the world. At least I know where I get it.

Throughout my formative years I don't remember childish pursuits. I remember most taking care of daily mundane things that made everything work and everybody happy. When my father, who became a traveling salesman after the bankruptcy, was gone, I felt it was my role at home to take on the responsibility of seeing that "everything went smoothly."

My mother, Ada Dorothy Adams (born 1893), was a brilliant woman with a lovely, trained dramatic soprano voice. She did what all good second-generation Welsh girls from Pennsylvania did: She went to college (East Stroudsburg State Normal School) and became a high school teacher of both English and music. Her going to college to become a teacher was not to pursue a career but to have "something to fall back on" in case the man of the house was incapacitated. Her strict Welsh male chauvinist upbringing had discouraged her activity as a doer, at least on the surface.

I always felt that she should have been a senator, or a newscaster, or, being Welsh, a writer. She must have realized it, too, because she never seemed happy with her lot as wife and mother. During her lifetime I never knew directly from her how she felt about anything; I had to pick up clues even after she died.

Somebody described Brahms as "a gypsy lady dancing in a tight whalebone corset," and I always thought of my mother that way—outwardly calm but boiling inside. The rigid Victorian life she was born to couldn't stop her from thinking.

Even as a child I knew that when I grew up, I did not want

to be like my mother. She was two years older than my father; I thought maybe that was the reason the balance was off on their relationship. She was seemingly the boss, constantly complaining, and he was the appeaser, trying to make everything right. I made a mental note to myself, as far back as I can remember, to marry only a man who was older than I. Maybe that way I could avoid the conflicts my parents had. According to my Freudian friends, I've been looking for my father ever since.

My father, Sheldon Alonzo Enke, was on the road a lot. I adored him, but I didn't see enough of him. He often worked until late at night but would wake my brother and me up to give us ice cream or other treats when he returned. I always thought of him as "my poor father." He seemed to be constantly working, yet he always had a kind word and something good to give us, like a few cents for Pepsis. My mother was moody and volatile. She could rule the house with her eyes. While she was the screamer, my father was the quiet rudder within the family. My brother, Sheldon, vividly remembers waking up to screaming one early dawn in the middle of a snowstorm. He looked out the window to see my mother, without a coat on, running after my father all the way to the car, yelling through the blizzard about money problems. It continued while my father packed the car with his samples. My brother, who had never heard this sort of thing before, put on his coat and galoshes over his pajamas and ran out to the car as my father was pulling off. Sheldon knocked on the door and got in, crying. He wanted to know if Dad was coming back at all. My father hugged him and said, "Don't worry. She's just going through her change of life. I'll be back."

He always did come home, but his temporary escape was to run away as a salesman. After his hardware store failed, he was always traveling, it seemed, selling scrap iron, tires, Pennzoil, or real estate.

My father played the piano but not often, because my mother was the expert. I guess that's why I never played the piano either, even though I took lessons all the time. He read Zane Grey westerns and gave me the works of Whitman and Thoreau. He read me to sleep a lot; many times it was with

"Beautiful Joe," the story of a dog that was treated cruelly. I sobbed out loud each time, even though I knew it by heart. I never heard my father raise his voice, but he sometimes expressed a low-key kind of anger. One of my most vivid memories of him—I must have been about four—was our standing outside my aunt Eve's house in the snow, waiting for my mother, to go home. He was upset about something but silent. I must have asked him what was wrong. He looked down at me for a long time and said, "Edith, don't ever get married." I can still see the pain on his face. It was the first time I was aware that all was not well between my mother and father.

As alike as they may have seemed to those who didn't know them well, my parents also came from very different backgrounds. One of my father's ancestors, Edwin Fuller, had come over on the *Mayflower*. His son Samuel married Jane Lathrope in 1625, and their daughter Hannah Fuller married Nicholas Bonham. The Enkes had fought as Hessian mercenaries, hired by the English, in the American Revolution. That made me both a *Mayflower* Daughter and a member of the DAR. The Enkes disappeared into Pennsylvania Dutch territory after the Revolution, to surface again in Sweet Valley, Pennsylvania, in 1840. My father's family were the poor relations of thirteen generations of Bonhams, Fullers, and Wolfs; he talked proudly about how one of his relatives had owned a farm that started in what is now Central Park, well above Fifty-ninth Street, and extended down to what is now Fifty-seventh Street in New York, but I never knew much about my father's family. My mother's second-generation Welsh immigrant family was dominant in my life.

Ada Adams and Sheldon Enke married, in Wilkes-Barre, Pennsylvania, in 1921. My mother had the first of her two children, Sheldon Adams Enke (born in 1922), just before she was thirty, and her second, Edith Elizabeth Enke, me, when she was almost forty. Not only did her mother also have a last child when she was nearly forty, but her grandmother, my great-grandmother Griffith, had a change-of-life "surprise package," at a time when most people were dying in their forties. My mother thus had an aunt, Eve, who lived with her parents and was only two years older than she, raised like an older sister. I guess we Adams women were late spawners. I had my two children at ages thirty and forty, although mine were carefully planned. It must have been part of the heritage because it simply was not done in my generation either. My son, Josh, missed being a baby boomer. I keep telling him he was born in the cracks, in 1968, with no generation label of his own.

I don't remember seeing or spending time with any of my father's family, other than obligatory visits to my grandfather, Ralph Waldo Enke, and his second wife, the hated Aunt Mae. He had been born on a family farm in Sweet Valley, Pennsylvania, but left home early. He was a retired railroad engineer by the time I knew him. She had been the nurse present when my real grandmother had died. Mae had short dyed black hair with bangs, like a flapper. She was tough, talking with a cigarette hanging out of her mouth. Because she smoked and swore, the family didn't like her; my father especially couldn't stand her.

I vaguely remember my father's brother, Uncle Paul (head of veterans' affairs in Pennsylvania), and his wife, Aunt Irene, another perennial flapper, according to my mother. They had no children, so I had no cousins on my father's side. It was if my father's family didn't exist.

In contrast, the family I grew up with was on my mother's side: the Adams, Thomas, and Samuel clan, and I do mean clan. We saw first and second cousins daily and even fifth and sixth cousins weekly. Everyone on my mother's side sang; we never asked if anyone sang, only what part: soprano; alto; tenor; bass. The Jews, Italians, and Hungarians are the most visibly clannish, but the Welsh really live as one unit no matter how many bodies are present. They always sang together, laughed together, cooked together, ate together, went to church together, spent every holiday together, funeraled and birthed together. They needed no outsiders, no money, props, or extraneous anything. All they needed was one another, music, poetry, *The New York Times*, and for the men a Dobbs hat. This was an expensive New York hat, a kind of dressy homburg, that all the men in this family had to have to complete their sense of self, even if they worked in the mines.

The houses of my childhood were packed with relatives on my mother's side. When I was seven, we moved from the tiny house in Trucksville to my grandfather John Jay Adams's large three-story house at 377 State Street, in Nanticoke, Pennsylvania. Catty-corner from my grandfather's kitchen door was my aunt Bert and uncle Art Kingsbury's back door, no more than thirty feet away. Aunt Bert always had coffee and cake, no matter what time of day or night. It was like open house; nobody locked the doors. Later in my mother's papers I discovered that Grandpa Adams had sold them the property for one dollar. My cousins Bill and Grace Bailey were two blocks away, within running distance, and my aunt Eve and uncle Stan were a block away in the other direction. She baked heavenly cookies and pies, which she'd learned to do living at my grandfather's.

I had always had the impression that my grandfather had a lot of money since he lived in such a big house and always had a maid. A standard family joke for years was the time my grandfather had told one of the maids, Annie, to hang his Dobbs hat on the tree, and she had gone outside and hung it on a real tree. Coming from that cramped house on a dirt road in Trucksville, I was very impressed with my grandfather's roomy house and the maid. He was now retired, but it was a surprise to discover much later that he had been a mailman, I guess one of the few people who had steady government paychecks during the Depression.

My grandfather was an austere cartoon, stiff and with red hair and a handlebar mustache. He had been born in Wales. His second wife, Aunt Gussie, was a wealthy woman in her own right, thanks to the work of her fine German hands. She had been my late grandmother's seamstress and had a dress-maker shop with four people working for her. Aunt Gussie's succession of maids in those days lived in and worked for just room and board. Aunt Gussie needed help cleaning the house because it was always full, but the kitchen was her domain. It was spotlessly clean; you could eat off the floor. Two sets of aunts and uncles and their children lived in a suite on the third floor, at different times.

There was always a crowd of people in the house, mostly

adults. My cousin Bill Bailey was really the only one my age, and we were often paired off together at family gatherings. His older sister, Grace, was beautiful and always immaculately dressed in clothes made by her mother, also Grace, and Aunt Bert, Aunt Grace's sister. They had a new outfit for her for even the tiniest occasion. Any excuse to dress up young Grace. I always inherited her hand-me-downs. I hated that.

Every night twelve to fifteen people sat down at our dinner table. Nobody ate until my Victorian, Republican grandfather, in his three-piece dark suit, celluloid collar, and watch fob, sampled the soup. Conversation stopped as he was presented a small portion to test. If it was hot enough and seasoned correctly, then everyone else was served. If he said, "It needs more salt," or, "It's not hot enough," we all waited patiently until it was brought back to his liking. We children never spoke to him unless he spoke first. The family lived by those old saws such as "Children should be seen and not heard."

In Welsh households the women were supposed to wait on the men. Most of the women I saw seemed to be much stronger than their husbands. However, they did as they had been taught without complaining. I remember my uncle Stan, who had the first car in town, sitting at breakfast reading the paper as his wife, Aunt Eve, presented him with a boiled egg in an egg cup. "Eve, crack my egg," he called. "Eve, Eve, crack my egg." I remember thinking how funny it was that a grown man couldn't crack his own egg; I was only nine, and I could crack my egg, and do my older brother's homework on top of that.

Typically Welsh, my grandfather Adams liked cheese in every dish, on it or in it, and soup with every meal. It didn't take me long to notice that my mother hated soup and wouldn't eat cheese in any form.

The other classic Uncle Stan Welshman story occurred soon after. Some relatives had been visiting, left, and, realizing that they had forgotten something, returned and rang the doorbell. Uncle Stan was lying down on the sofa with his head resting on the arm, maybe a foot from the front doorknob. His wife was all the way down in the basement, washing clothes. He called down, "Eve, Eve, there's someone at the front door." She came all the way up from the basement to open the door when all he would have had to do was reach over his head without even getting up.

We children answered everything my grandfather said with "yes, sir" or "no, sir." Since I was usually the youngest person in that household, I began my career as a peacekeeper, trying to please everyone. The adults always had a lively discussion going about almost anything. Sunday afternoon was the big time. All the relatives gathered on my grandfather's front porch to argue politics, music, poetry. The men listened to sporting events on the radio and smoked cigars. The women brought out the refreshments. I did what all the adult women did: waited on the men hand and foot and tried always to create a pleasant atmosphere. I never gave them a bit of trouble, and I felt that my role in this big family was to keep peace.

State Street in Nanticoke saw the real blossoming of my good girl syndrome and a training ground for my marriage to Ernie Kovacs. Just as I was attracted to Ernie's freewheeling ways, he seemed to depend on the qualities I had acquired in small-town Pennsylvania. He told an interviewer in 1956, "Edie has a high sense of right and wrong, and the children are very conscious of it. They listen to her. They try to imitate Edie's mannerisms, her looks and her talk. I'll be happy if my daughters turn out to be the kind of person she is—nice and good." At that time, I guess I was.

Grandpa's house had a large kitchen, dining room, and living room, plus a large parlor that I saw only once, when Aunt Gussie's German mother had died and was laid out in black Victorian funeral weeds. As I think about it now, it reminds me of the clothing the two sisters wore in the play *Arsenic and Old Lace* when they held their basement funerals for the gentlemen lodgers they had poisoned with spiked elderberry wine. *Arsenic and Old Lace* was the first play I ever saw on Broadway, and in 1988 Dody Goodman and I played the two sisters in a production in Florida and New Orleans. I remember our "sort-of" relative's foreboding presence while she was alive, now an even scarier sight laid out in Aunt Gussie's painstakingly stitched, elaborate funeral weeds, placed in a heavily draped coffin. I remember even more vividly that my cousin Bill Bailey dared me to touch the corpse. I took his dare, and the feel of one cold, hard finger made me jump and run from the room. I hadn't known that dead people would feel cold and different from the living.

Living in someone else's house was interesting for me, but I didn't realize until much later, when I had both my mother and my mother-in-law living with me, how difficult it must have been for my parents. I knew that my mother was unhappy, and my brother later told me that my father was, too. It was during this period that he traveled even more as a salesman, perhaps to get away from all those people and surely, as I found out later, to pay everybody's bills. At first he worked as the manager of a Dunlop tire store; he gave my mother's brother Jack his first job there. Aunt Gussie made onion sandwiches for them to take to work, by trolley, to Wilkes-Barre. Later Dad was a cashier at the Polish National Bank in Nanticoke. He got another of my mother's relatives a job at the bank, from which he absconded with several hundred dollars. My father paid that debt back, too, and the amount was deducted from the relative's share of my grandfather's estate and given directly to my father.

Jack left the tire store to get a job on the New York Stock Exchange and put himself through New York University, with much help from his brand-new wife, Ruth Bize, from an old family of French Huguenot settlers of northern Florida. She sold her jewelry to put Jack through NYU, while holding a job as first a toy buyer at Macy's and later head of all the store's personnel, a big job for a woman in the 1930's. I looked forward to her visits to State Street because she was gorgeous, chic, beautifully dressed, and well spoken with a cultured southern accent. "It's not an accent, Edith; it's merely a rhythm of speech," she told me. She was educated, charming, refined, sophisticated, and nice, everything I wanted to be. Aunt Ruth recently told me that she always felt that my mother didn't like her. I told her, "That was because at the time you were everything she wanted to be and didn't dare."

With so many people living at my grandfather's house the only room left for Aunt Ruth and Uncle Jack was on the third floor, where the snow blew in through the cracks in the windowpanes in the winter. She was used to a little more comfort, so she tried to come visit only in the summer. One summer Jack and Ruth brought me a dog from the Bide-a-Wee shelter in New York. He was a pit bull that I quickly named Spot, and he looked just like Spuds MacKenzie.

Mother's brother Jim became the night manager of a Bickford's cafeteria in New York and married the hostess, an English lady, Ethel Atkinson. I liked Aunt Ethel and inherited her hand-me-downs; unfortunately they were dark crepe dresses for greeting customers at work, not for every day. In fifth grade I heard some of the kids mocking me: "Where did you get that, from your grandmother?" I finally figured that my only way to be dressed as I wanted would be to learn to make my own clothes, and from then on I did.

My first self-made dress was a pale blue dotted swiss with large pinafore ruffles, wrong for two reasons: It was too young for me, and the ruffles were too overdone for someone my size. At least it was my first non-hand-me-down.

Aunt Ethel was also beautiful and very chic. I thought it was great that she had a full-time paying job. These working New York women really had something special. Their home lives were democracies, not dictatorships, as I saw at my grandfather's house or even in our family, where my mother was clearly the boss. The two Adams brothers and their wives shared an apartment in Greenwich Village, one pair working at night and the other during the day. They also shared a black cleaning woman named Edith. Aunt Ruth tells me that when I, at age four, first met the other Edith, I couldn't take my eyes off her. I kept peeking around the corner at her all day long. Apart from my fascination at sharing her name, I had never seen anyone with dark skin before; there simply were no black people in my part of Pennsylvania. I didn't know any others well until we moved to Tenafly, New Jersey, when I was sixteen. There was one black family in Tenafly, the Harpers, with two kids; their son, Willy, was captain of the football team, and his sister, Gracie, was one of only eight cheerleaders.

My father changed jobs yet again and was gone even more, leaving me to cope with with my mother's moody outbursts. These seemed to increase; she would run out the back door to Aunt Bert's and complain about all her troubles, with Aunt

Bert trying to calm her down. By the time she got back, she had retreated into stony silence. Sometimes she would go for several days without speaking. She would go into her bedroom, close the door, and leave me to handle any motherly responsibilities. With even more time on her hands than most women, it would never have occurred to my mother to do anything more than substitute teaching. Grandpa's lessons had been well learned. Even though she hated her life and wasn't needed to wait on the men in Aunt Gussie's house, she still was incapable of bucking the Welsh credo that had been instilled since birth. With all her talent and intelligence, she still had no outlet. I've often wondered what would have happened to my life if she had been the first working Welsh mother in our family instead of me.

Even though we were living in the same house, I remember her absences. This retreating was a habit she was to keep up until my father died and she came to live with me in Los Angeles and suddenly blossomed, wearing pastel colors, even pale pink. But back then she wore somber or neutral colors, black, beige, gray, or navy, tailored suits, and hats (with no flowers on them); she dressed like a horsewoman. She wore sensible shoes and no rouge or makeup of any kind.

Later, when I was growing up in Grove City, Pennsylvania, my mother was not available to me. Either she was out singing in church or at a war bond drive, or if at home, she was in her room with the door shut. Briefly, in between, when she was visible cooking, I remember not words but her constant heavy sighs cutting through the silence as she stood at the stove.

When she did speak, I never knew what to expect. The one thing consistent about her was her inconsistency. She was likely to change lanes and come up with a new set of rules for me to deal with or to send a mixed message. Her one constant nonverbal message was: "Don't end up like me." I "heard" that one loud and strong; I did not want to end up like her. I always expected to do something special with my life. Her credo, for my life to be happy and fulfilled, was to do exactly as she said—"sing a pretty song and wear a pretty dress." In the face of adversity of any kind, if I did that, all would be well.

27

If something displeased my mother and there were non-family members present, she could shatter me or my brother with a Welsh evil eye, the "look" that would crumble a marble statue. My brother, Sheldon, to this day calls her Inglés from the character in Hemingway's *For Whom the Bell Tolls*, who could stop an escaping prisoner with a ray gun glare. It sure got attention when she was a substitute teacher in my third-grade class. I was always singled out; as her daughter I had to be more than perfection.

She would walk up and down the aisles of the schoolroom, giving the lesson, seemingly not noticing who was acting up. All of a sudden she would deliver a sharp knuckle rap to the upper arm, between the bicep and the shoulder, of anyone who offended her and thought he or she was getting away with it. Aimed accurately (as it usually was), the rap triggered an almost electric shock "crazy bone" (as we said in Pennsylvania) kind of pain. No one ever forgot it; I know I never did when she hit me. I wonder how she knew where the exact spot was.

Mother was a nut on perfection. I asked her later, when she was about seventy-five, what was the worst thing that had ever happened to her in her whole life. She thought solemnly for quite a while and finally said, "When I was about five years old, I was on my way to Sunday school with my new Easter clothes on. I tripped and skinned a hole in my stocking and in the palm of my new white kid gloves and scuffed my new patent leather shoes."

Throughout my life I have always tried to be the "perfect" girl in all my activities: social, school, and work. If I couldn't fit my mother's image of perfection, very early I realized that the problem was hers, not mine. Recently, in a UCLA course called "Breaking Free of the Good Girl Syndrome," the teacher, Leslie Eichenbaum, explained that most of the women of my generation were sentenced to the same fate. We have wasted decades on sows' ears, trying to live up to our mothers' or society's images and expectations of silk purses.

My daughter Mia's and my relationship was always stormy but loving. But at least she knew what I was thinking during our endless, and I now realize senseless, arguments.

Did I take on some of my own mother's perfectionism in dealing with my beautiful, talented, funny, brilliant, and strongheaded daughter? Did I expect too much from her, push her beyond her own boundaries? I will never know. Mia died in a car accident in 1982, just as we had almost become full-time friends again. Of all the traumatic events that can happen in anyone's life, there is nothing worse than the death of one's child. I still have trouble talking about Mia, in spite of grievance counseling and many trips to the cemetery to talk to her. Even now, I think I see her whenever a beautiful blond girl drives by with the top down on her car and the radio turned up, smiling just because it's a nice day.

As a younger woman my mother had dark auburn hair and a bearing as spectacular as the cavalry horses she rode with my father when they were engaged. (He was a cavalry officer in the U.S. Army.) She had one blue eye, over which arched a blazing white eyebrow, and one green eye, capped with a dark auburn brow. In later years, when her hair was gray, the eyebrows just seemed to blend in and you had to look closely to see that her eyes indeed were two different colors. She had been an active suffragette in her youth and remained well versed in world politics, thanks to her beloved Gothic-shaped table radio. She told me in high school not to take French as a second language but Spanish because half the world would be speaking Spanish very soon. She could answer any world history question but actually tried to believe that the best thing women could do to help the country during the Depression was to keep out of the job market. If women stayed home and bought appliances, it would create new jobs for men and put the economy on the road to recovery. As a former suffragette, how could she come out with something as ridiculous as that, sighing over her cooking pots? I never thought for a minute that deep down she actually believed it.

A Republican who voted Democratic, she maintained an interest in the League of Women Voters. My father was a Democrat who voted Republican, so I remember heated political discussions from early in my life. In 1936 my father took off from work in the middle of the day to see Franklin Delano Roosevelt, who came through Nanticoke by train on his reelection campaign. I was hoisted onto my father's shoulders to wave to this important man, who gave a speech from the caboose. At school the slogan I heard was: "Landon and Knox will land on the rocks." My parents always told me to vote the man, not the party; later, in Tenafly, I cast my first vote (and his only one in the town) for Socialist Norman Thomas for President. This appalled my parents; in their minds, this was neither the man nor the party. Thomas was simply not in the running.

My mother could be hard and hurtful. I can remember her trying to get me to stop crying, pointing a finger at me and then at the dreaded red and gold can of dry hot Coleman's mustard that was at my eye level on Aunt Gussie's kitchen counter. "Don't cry," she said, "or I'll put mustard on your tongue." I tried very hard to stifle my sobs . . . my whole life.

Another time, when I was about eight, again I was trying not to cry out loud, but I was sobbing quietly in my room after a friend had said something that hurt me. Mother came into my room, held me close, patted my head, and said, "You should worry." I remember the incident partly because I'd never heard that expression before, but mostly because it was the first time I could recall my mother's comforting me. Surely it was one of the first times I could remember any hugging or physical contact other than an obligatory good-night peck in the air. Maybe she was so absorbed with her personal internal war that she found it hard to deal with my needs.

All her life my desperately unhappy mother kept sending me double messages: "Don't learn to press pants, or you'll press pants all your life. . . . Don't learn to clean fish, or you'll clean fish all your life. . . . Anyone who can read can cook." She could do anything but didn't feel comfortable about it. She learned to cook passably and even bake bread, although she hated to do it. I've tried not to end up like my mother, but constantly through the years I'm surprised to find myself doing so many of the same things she did and still struggling inside with some of her demons.

At my mother's funeral in Hanover Green, Pennsylvania, in December 1975, I was overwhelmed by the number of her former high school English students, now at retirement age, who told me how she had given them hope and great encouragement to be whatever they wanted to be. These doctors, lawyers, architects, and other people whose lives she had touched dramatically came to pay their respects to a "great lady" I had never known. One Polish immigrant, who had arrived in this country at age twelve years, had found trying to learn English overwhelming. He was about to quit school and work in the mines when my mother took him in hand, taught him English, and encouraged him to continue his education. He was now the head of psychiatry at the University of Pennsylvania Hospital in Philadelphia.

It was only in going through her ironically named hope chest after the funeral that I even glimpsed Ada Dorothy Adams Enke, the sensitive, artistic woman who had never realized her ambition or potential. In the margins of a Madame Schumann-Heink recital program, my mother had written beautifully phrased and insightful comments on an artful lieder performance, her reactions to the meaning and magic of the soprano's music. She had even sketched the gown Schumann-Heink was wearing and made comments on how to improve it. All her life my mother had told me that she couldn't draw.

My stepgrandmother, Augusta, "Aunt Gussie," who never had children of her own, picked me as her favorite. This was a little difficult because she was not one of my mother's favorites. In fact, they ended up not speaking after a fight over who was to be executrix of my grandfather's estate. Aunt Gussie was a reserved woman who was uncomfortable expressing her feelings. She spoke with a German accent and taught me quite a bit of her native language and how to sing "Silent Night" in German. She took me on and taught me everything. From her I learned about such exotic foods as Rindsroulade, Spätzle, Kartoffel Pfannkuchen (potato pancakes), and even rye bread. My life until then had been strictly white bread, lamb stew, and boiled cabbage. The Welsh boil everything. Aunt Gussie showed me how to roll German pastry dough with a milk bottle filled with ice, so that the dough would slide, and not to handle it too much because that would make it tough. I was the only member of the family she allowed into her kitchen. Everyone else she literally chased out with a broom.

My bedroom was Aunt Gussie's sewing room, with its own private screened-in balcony. She taught me all the basics in that tiny room we shared. During the day she was busy there, making dresses, tablecloths, and curtains while I was at school. Since I slept there and was eager to learn how to sew, when I came home, Aunt Gussie took me on as an apprentice, teaching me how to use her sewing machines, both the "good" one in my bedroom and the older treadle machine in the basement. She couldn't have found a more eager student.

She also taught me how to fit clothes the German way: by putting a dress on the living person for whom it was intended, inside out, rather than on the dressmaker's toille, a canvas dummy. This way the person's own body imperfections could be easily corrected, with the garment on. For instance, if she stood up very straight, the back of her dress would have to be cut shorter and the front longer, or conversely, if the person naturally slumped, the front would be shorter, the back longer. Most dressmaking manuals have you take the excess out equidistant from the front and back, thereby providing a bad fit. Aunt Gussie taught me the turn-of-the-century German way, which I've seen English and Italian tailors also use for a custom fit.

Now when I'm having a problem with a dressmaker or tailor and insist on being fitted that way, I'm usually given an argument. However, as the apprentice who learned from the mistress, I want a perfect fit. One time later, in Italy, when Ernie was having several suits made in a hurry, I saw that the back was clearly too long and had to be made shorter right under the collar. I pointed it out to the tailor, who said, "Oh, si, we do." The next day Ernie tried the suit on, and it was a little bit better but not exactly right. So when the tailor went out of the room, I pulled off the hand-stitched lining thread and pulled back the lining to reveal that the tailor had not made the back shorter but had simply steam-pressed it and hoped the problem would go away. It didn't, and I showed him how much to take out and where. He was furious, but the next day Ernie was delivered three suits without a wrinkle in the shoulders that fit beautifully.

Aunt Gussie started me on doll clothes, which I made with set-in sleeves (unheard of for a seven-year-old). Usually dolls' fabric clothes were like paper doll clothes, made of two equal pieces. Instead, I was turning them inside out on my doll and fitting them like people's clothes. Soon, by age ten, I started making my own dresses. Most girls in my sewing class at school were hemming dish towels. By the time I was sixteen, I was making interlined winter coats with set-in sleeves and matching the plaid in Pendleton shirts for my boyfriends.

Any housekeeping I know I learned from Aunt Gussie. I don't remember doing any of these things with my mother, who actually was doing me a big favor. I feel she was trying to warn me somehow. She didn't want me to end up doing the mundane things she did daily any more than I wanted to. She truly did not see the need to teach me domestic chores. I was expected only to dry the dishes, to make my bed and clean the bathtub after myself, and to dust on Saturday. I was not allowed to do any daily cooking, not even eggs, never mind the dreaded roast. My mother was making me into a little Welsh princess. She carefully trained me to keep out of the kitchen and go into the world and fulfill what she dared not.

Despite his absences, in this period I remember most my father's praise and love. I was his favorite. Sheldon was a loner; he did not communicate much with anybody, at least at home. He stayed in his room a lot, flew model airplanes, and participated in soap box derbies. From an early age it seemed to me as if I were taking care of these two loners, my mother and brother.

A grape arbor stood in the backyard of my grandfather's house, along with a couple of large lilac bushes, almost trees. There was a big dog up the street, Laddie, that everyone else thought was unfriendly. He got along with me just fine. Laddie carried my books to school (about four houses away) and pulled my sled up the hill in the winter. He was my best friend.

Spot from New York, my own first dog, got his tail caught in the antique washing machine in my grandfather's basement. The dog somehow backed under the primitive washer's open machinery and got his tail caught in the cog. I was working on the treadle sewing machine a few feet away, and

I'll never forget the dog's screams. My father had to take Spot to the riverbank and put him out of his misery with a World War I Army .45.

My first day of school in Nanticoke was a nightmare. I was entering second grade. My mother had taught in the high school there about twenty years before, and my principal, Mr. Dieffenbacher, had known her as Miss Adams; therefore, my name to him was Miss Adams. I didn't know then that I was nearsighted, so when the bell announced recess, I just ran with a pack of children in a beeline to the bathroom. I was so nervous I really had to go. I was almost inside the door when I heard the principal shouting, "Miss Adams, no, Miss Adams, not that one!" I was jerked back into the hallway by a firm hand on my shoulder. I was devastated and turned beet red. I had been following the boys into the boys' bathroom. I was so mortified that I can still remember what I was wearing, a brown pinpoint polka dot dress with a white collar, and my hair was in braids.

My innate shyness got even worse, if possible. I was a chubby child and was horrified to get on the school scale on weighing day, with my shoes off. As long as I can remember, I have been concerned about my weight. Aunt Gussie's good cooking wasn't helping. Also, I had a strawberry pink birthmark on my right forehead that looked like the British Isles. The birthmark was even more noticeable with my hair pulled back and seemed to get much more attention in Nanticoke than it had attracted in Trucksville. I used to tell people that a dog had bitten me or that I had fallen down when I was three years old. My self-consciousness about this birthmark was to have a profound effect on my trademark hairdo throughout most of my career; the slanted dip over the right eye was to hide that blemish. I have it still.

I tried to have the birthmark removed at age seventeen by an electric needle, but the man's hand shook so coming toward my eye that I decided against it. It was easier to change my hairdo and try to cover some of the birthmark with makeup. Later, when I had established what is still called the Edie Adams Hairdo (Bergdorf Goodman featured it one week in their windows) and was doing all those cigar commercials in slinky gowns, I had to stand firmly on my right foot and have all my skirts slit on the left side so that the left leg could provocatively peep out of the slit, with the knee bent and only the toe touching the ground—modified cheesecake. (The left side was the one that photographed well.) All that posing and standing around on my right foot took its toll, and slant boards between takes didn't help much. Peter Gennaro, who was choreographing one of the commercials, noticed that I was in pain after standing around on my right side for a few hours. I took my shoe off, and when he pressed the bottom of my foot, I screamed. He said, "Edie, you have a neuroma," a tumor made up of nerve tissue that can't be seen by an X ray. It's a common condition among dancers, but doctors are reluctant to operate on it because it's not visible. You have to sign a release for the surgery; if the neuroma isn't there, it's not the doctor's fault. I went to the orthopedic surgeon for the Los Angeles Rams, who took out a neuroma the size of my finger, from between my third and fourth right toes. Even with a cane and a slow recovery, it immediately felt better. I had a second major operation on the same foot in 1988, to correct a painful condition still caused by constant standing on my right foot. All this from a birthmark!

From age eight on I had great marks in grade school. (I was also to do well in junior high and high school, until my last year, when I discovered boys and almost flunked algebra.) Although my brother was five years older than I, I could do his English homework for him, diagramming long, involved sentences; one of them was at least a page long. English and languages were always easy for me. Math was not.

Sheldon's daily entertainment was to tease me unmercifully, and I could never get a straight answer from him about anything. He once gave me a paper bag, saying, "Here's a present." I was so excited, but he had put a little blind black snake in the bag. The snake wasn't poisonous; but I didn't know that, and I was scared. He also unknowingly did other things that hurt me, like cheating at cards, which he thought was hysterically funny. When I played with him, I was always the Old Maid. I may have taken it too seriously; he remembers it as teasing. I remember always trying to please him, to have him like me, and how much it bothered me when I felt he didn't.

EDIE ADAMS

When I was in fourth grade, we moved to Grove City, Pennsylvania (population six thousand). This was a big move; my mother, father, brother, and I had our own house again. I had my own room. I got a new dog, a purebred black female Boston terrier named Queenie. She and I did everything we could to keep out of that big dark house with the clock ticking. I taught Queenie to sing, entered her in the town's first annual Halloween costume parade, and won first prize. I began to indulge my lifelong penchant for extracurricular activities; I took piano lessons and joined my first choir.

But the quiet college town was sleepy, full of Presbyterian gothic architecture. Life was structured. No liquor was allowed in the town, nor any bicycle riding on Sunday. Lots and lots of church and music, music, music, that's what I did to fill time. One bright spot was that Paula Kelly of the Modernaires with the Glenn Miller Band had lived up the street when she was a child. Her parents were still one block away from us, at 310 Poplar Street. She had sung in all these choirs, and look where she was.

Grove City did have great musical training; we learned to sight-read music in the same way most kids learned their ABC's. We would get our coats from the cloakroom and go back to our seats to wait for the bell. On top of every blackboard was a music staff. The teacher drilled us on key signatures, notes, and sight-reading while we waited, just as other teachers might spend the time on multiplication tables. We were drilled in basic solfeggio (do, re, mi, fa, sol, la, ti, do). You *had* to take sight-reading.

I had choir practice on Wednesday, Christian Endeavor on Friday. But that's all I had. The strict Presbyterians have no props. The Catholics have candles and wine; the Jews have candles and wine. We had John Calvin, a bare bench, and plain bread and water, not even grape juice. And our minister? He preached the classic hellfire-and-damnation sermon in a swallowtail coat. The man droned and yelled about the terrors of hell up there in the pulpit; he was so loud I never heard one word he said. Instead, I read my Sunday school lessons or next week's Presbyterian catechism (this was a strict Presbyterian church). Later, when I joined the choir as a swing singer, doing the soprano, alto, or tenor part as needed, we had to sit through as many as three services on Sundays. Having tuned out the sermon, I would go through the hymnal, inserting "between the sheets" in all the hymns. ("Jesus loves me, between the sheets.") It was a contest each week for all my classmates, to see who'd get through the service without giggling out loud. After all those hours, I memorized most of the hymns—all four choruses.

In late 1989, when I returned to Grove City (after picking up the Slippery Rock University Award of Achievement), I revisited the Tower Presbyterian Church. Indeed, it was not only as big as, but much bigger than I remembered it, seating twelve hundred people. I sat in my old chair in the choir and met the new minister, who was young and mustached and approached me wearing blue jeans, sweater, and sneakers, certainly not what I'd remembered from the Reverend Charles H. Williams some forty years before. The current minister took me to see Williams's photograph in the vestibule, and he was exactly as foreboding as I remembered him. Things really have changed. The new reverend, Clark Olson-Sawyer, does his preaching not from the grand pulpit with hellfire and damnation but more conversationally on the radio every Sunday morning.

My first trip alone to New York City took place when I was eight or nine. We went there to visit my aunt Ethel and uncle Jim Adams. They took me to Radio City Music Hall and changed my life. In Grove City I wasn't even allowed to go to the movies. At my grandfather's in Nanticoke I had been allowed to go with my cousin Billy to Saturday movie serials, which we called chapter pictures, such as Buck Rogers, or to westerns. For eleven cents we could spend the whole day there, and my uncle Tom, Billy's father, always dropped us off at ten in the morning and came back at five in the afternoon to pick us up. The serials were cliff-hangers; they'd stop in the middle of a life-threatening situation, and we'd have to go back the next Saturday to find out how it turned out. For instance, at the end of one chapter you would see the hero falling off the cliff. The next week you would find that hero had not fallen off as we had seen the previous week; he was safe and riding off into the sunset. I always thought that was unfair, but that was my movie education up to then—B movie cliff-hangers.

My mother had one adamant idea about Hollywood movies and the people who made them: They were the lowest of the low in her mind—beneath even burlesque. She might take me to a movie starring one of the classical music girls, Jeanette MacDonald, Deanna Durbin, Lily Pons, or Helen Jepson. But then she'd say, sniffing, "Who *is* this Judy Garland? What's all this fuss about? She doesn't even have a trained voice." Another of my aunts did manage to sneak me off to see *Pygmalion* with Wendy Hiller and Leslie Howard when I was about eleven. Wendy Hiller became my first takeoff. I went home and started imitating her: "Eeeeowww, Oye washed me fice and 'ands before Ah come, Oye did."

That was an attention getter. I was suddenly on; everybody noticed me, whereas before that I had just been one of the crowd, always in the background. Now they said, "Edith, do Wendy Hiller, do *Pygmalion* for them." Getting laughs and applause was heady stuff. For my mother and father I still had to wear that pretty dress and sing that pretty song. But for the other people in my life I could begin to play the clown.

Then I went to Radio City for a real movie on a big screen and a two-hour live stage show. It opened with a man playing a giant organ; then came a complete corps de ballet, a choir singing, and a full symphony orchestra playing. In between were soloists, tumblers, and jugglers. Then came the line of thirty-six Rockettes high kicking and precision dancing, all dressed alike and looking exactly the same height. Everybody was in a dazzling costume.

I knew there was a place for me somewhere on that stage; I didn't know exactly where, maybe even as the costume designer. I didn't dare hope to be in a "trashy" movie. But right then I knew exactly what I was going to do the rest of my life. I said to myself, "This is for me! Show business." I didn't dare tell anyone; but from then on everything I did was aimed toward that goal.

I continued my piano lessons with a new purpose and sang anywhere people would let me. M. Selkirk Burgess was a rigid choirmistress who introduced me to complicated harmonies and dissonances in music. She taught us girls to blend as we sang quietly together by listening to one another. She pushed us way beyond our three-part choir singing, sometimes to eight parts. We were very advanced for our years and sang in frequent contests with other female double octets.

I also joined everything else at school that had to do with drama, music, or just being seen. I always came in second in the forensic contests, on such subjects as temperance, valor, morals, kindness, and goodness. The contests were usually won by Jeannie Allen, in her Shirley Temple curls, who spoke very dramatically. She also was an experienced tap dancer who, in partnership with Patty Sproll, shared World War II bond drive stages with my mother at Crawford Hall on the Grove City College campus. This was our local version of Carnegie Hall; if you appeared there, you'd made it. After Patty and Jeannie did their stirring "Poet and Peasant Overture," solemnly tapping in black velvet short outfits and hats trimmed with white fur, Mother always closed by singing "God Bless America," wearing her only floor-length patriotic blue silk velvet concert dress.

Because my best friends, Clair Adsit and Anne Augustine, and I joined everything, we also landed in the Loyal Temperance League. At those meetings we would duly report, in shocked tones, such things as "We saw a billboard and on it was a lady smoking!" We also memorized little lectures on the clean life to deliver to other children of our own age. How did I ever get to cigars?

I started hearing my mother complain about how my father was staying out a lot and "drinking." But neither my brother nor I can remember him coming home in the least intoxicated. When I put it all together today, it's clear she was the dysfunctional one, the one we were always trying to please. He was the placater who never raised his voice. I was grateful whenever he was at home in Grove City (that wasn't often, mostly weekends) because he was supportive and loving. He made great doughnuts and sometimes gave me the holes to cook. Instead of going to church with us, he cooked dinner on Sundays, which was served at 1:00 P.M., after my mother and I came home from our last choir appearance.

He was an avid fisherman (as was my grandfather), and

he cooked potatoes in the fire when we camped out. Maybe that's where my food fixation comes from. I still can't put on a kettle of soup without thinking, when it's a cold, dismal, rainy day, if I can smell food cooking, everything will be all right. Today realtors selling million-dollar houses or condominiums in Beverly Hills put pieces of bread dough in the oven, so the heavenly smell of bread baking will make the potential buyer feel he is home.

While we were living in Grove City, only seven miles from the Ohio border, my parents bought a cabin (with no running water or electricity) for fifteen hundred dollars at Lily Lake, in eastern Pennsylvania. It was just over the mountain from where they both were born, and they had gone to the lake as kids. The address was RD 1 Wapwallopen; the nearest town, with maybe forty people, was Pond Hill. The lake was on land that my friend Patty Boyd's father's family had bought from the Indians many years before. The grant deed read "from the center of the earth to the skies above"; the Boyds had the legal right to stop a plane from flying over their land. Lily Lake was a six-hour trip on macadam-topped roads, back and forth, from western Pennsylvania. With my father's maroon Hudson loaded with everything we were going to need for the summer packed into the car, I don't know how four people and a dog fit in.

The cabin had only one room downstairs and one upstairs, with two beds back to back and a slanted roof. That's where where my parents and I slept. (My brother was on a couch downstairs.) The people next door, the Swanberrys, had a well with a hand pump, from which we had to carry our always cold springwater. Out back was a path to the john. In the kitchen were an oil stove for immediate cooking and a coal stove for roasting and baking and for heat on rainy days. Into this cabin we put a lot of my mother's Victorian furniture. In the fall, going back to Grove City, we had to hogtie anything upholstered, including the mattresses, to the ceiling, so the squirrels wouldn't tear it apart and make nests in it, and remove all matches because they liked to chew on the phosphorus tips. We had a communal trunk full of bathing suits that were old-fashioned even then; I remember my uncles wearing 1920's suits with tank tops and open circles in the sides.

This was serious Depression time, so no one had much money. I remember my uncle Art, another salesman, coming out to the lake with his portable pump organ in the trunk of his car. He'd set it up in the yard, and all the relatives who had gathered at my grandfather's house now came to our cabin with even more relatives on the weekends. All of us would sing, even our next-door neighbors on the other side, the Reillys. Charlie Reilly, in 1988, told me that my father was the first man he ever met who fished for sport. Everybody else up there did it to eat in those days. I think we must have, too.

Patty Boyd's father, Forrest, was a salty man whose ancestors had bought the land, except for one small corner property that had access to about one hundred yards of shoreline. This was owned by another local family, the Yokums. Forrest tried to keep the Yokums at their end of the lake, sometimes rowing down with a shotgun resting on his knees. When the Yokums insisted on fishing the entire lake, which he considered his, Forrest had a log boom (logs chained together) made and put at the property line, so the Yokum boats could not fish the Boyd part of the lake. It became a real old-time country feud, like the Hatfields and McCoys. We used to sing, "Oh, the Yokums and the Boyds, they was feudin' mountain boys." Before my time they even shot at each other in true mountain feud fashion.

At Lily Lake my father taught me to swim, starting with the sidestroke. He would say, "Lie down in the water," as he stretched his arm way out, looking as if he were going to sleep but doing a strong scissors kick with his feet. "The water is your friend." He taught me to relax with each stroke. Mother didn't go in the water; she couldn't swim and was fearful. I eventually learned to swim long distances, sometimes as much as five miles; any sport in the water came easily to me. I earned my Red Cross lifesaving badges, learned how to ride an aquaplane, the forerunner of water skis, a kind of skateboard towed behind a speedboat, and even won a canoe race at a neighboring lake, Nuangola.

41

I also learned to paddle a kayak and a canoe and row a boat without a ripple, so that my brother could skidder (short jerky movements of the pole) or troll for fish. I had to paddle carefully so that the tip of Sheldon's bamboo fishing pole stayed within a foot of the lily pads' intricate pattern, where the pickerel or pike were waiting. If you hooked the minnow bait onto the lily pad, it dislodged itself and the fish got a free minnow without the hook; you had to start all over again.

The only time I ever impressed Mia was when she was about eight and we had gone directly to Lily Lake together for a vacation after a Las Vegas engagement. I remember arriving at the lake with a trunkful of sequined gowns. We walked down to the dock, I in my spiked heels. There a real farm kid, complete with overalls and a straw in his mouth, about Mia's age, was sitting, fishing. We watched for a while; he wasn't having much luck and kept losing the bait. He was putting the bread dough on all wrong, so I showed him how to do it right. Within a minute he caught a fish, his first of the day. Mia's mouth fell open. She had never seen that side of her mother before. She was absolutely flabbergasted.

I finally learned to do the jitterbug at Lily Lake, where there was a dance pavilion with a jukebox, my overdue introduction to popular music. A large community of Italians living at nearby Mocanaqua were regulars. They were the best. They taught me complicated double-time jitterbugging, complete with gymnastic tosses in the air, lifting me up by the hips with my heels straight up in the air and finishing with a crossover around their back. Later, in Tenafly High School, I won a jitterbug contest. Local Polish people from Schickshinney taught me peasant dances and polkas done side by side with intricate double breaks I've still never seen even on *The Lawrence Welk Show*. My brother, Sheldon, learned the double-time lifts and would do them with me. It was one of the few times I can remember that he and I did anything together as teenagers. Surprisingly, he was an excellent dancer.

This social activity during the summers at Lily Lake represented my first break with my strict upbringing. I could stay at the pavilion until 9:00 P.M. if I was walked home in a group. But since I wasn't allowed out much, most of the time the gang was at our house, playing Monopoly, Sorry, pinochle, hearts, bridge, even poker. At Lily Lake they didn't worry about "devil cards." We even did card tricks. I had fun there.

On the slanted ceiling of my bedroom I had pasted pictures of movie stars, such as Betty Grable, Lucille Ball, Ann Sheridan, Linda Darnell, and my father's favorite, Jean Arthur. I loved John Payne in anything. I liked Gene Tierney's looks but still wanted to sing like Jeanette MacDonald. These photos were the last thing I saw at night and the first thing I saw in the morning. Patty Boyd, my summertime best friend from ages seven to seventeen, who now teaches English in Pennsylvania and still owns property at Lily Lake, reminded me in the summer of 1989 that we would lie on my bed for hours, looking up at the roof. We would "walk" up the wall with our bare feet, point at the stars with our big toes, and sigh, giggle, and dream. My initials were EEE (Edith Elizabeth Enke), and Patty would say, "If you marry someone whose last initial is K, you'll be EEEK!" And so I did.

Patty and I both were movie nuts. I still hadn't seen many movies; but I could buy the magazines, and I was seriously set on looking for a way out. In one of the movie magazines I was always reading there was an ad for a sharkskin skirt you could send away for. I wanted it badly but couldn't afford it, so with my ingrained work ethic I figured out a way to make it without sharkskin.

It was important to me to be well dressed and color-coordinated and to have my nails looking good, and I spent a lot of time on my appearance. I saw a picture of Juliette Marglenne, who later had a line of nail beauty products, in *Life* magazine with two-inch-long clawlike fingernails. I didn't want them that long, but I now knew they didn't have to cut them to the quick. I began to have trouble with my mother over my nails. I wanted to grow them long, and she wanted me to cut them short so I could do the correct curved hand position for my piano lessons. Alice Reilly, Charlie's sister and one of the many Reillys, told me in 1988 that I was always pulled together and color-coordinated with nails always perfectly done. I remember feeling chubby, and I could wear only a hint of makeup; but I was even then determined about my appearance.

43

I remember my mother cooking for as many as thirty-five people on weekends at our cottage. I never knew until after her death that she had charged room and board to some of the relatives who visited us at Lily Lake. When I was a child it never made sense to me that she entertained all those people when she obviously didn't enjoy cooking. It was because we needed the money.

There were always more boys than girls up at Lily Lake, so it was perhaps inevitable that it was there, in our last summer, that I met my first boyfriend. He had the unlikely but prophetic name of Chummy Yokum. He was sixteen, gorgeous, a tall, tanned, and handsome farm boy, who looked just like Li'l Abner, only with blond hair. His body was muscular from farmwork. He was also an excellent swimmer who could stay underwater for minutes at a time. I was sixteen. He walked me home from the pavilion one clear, starry night, paused in front of the Swanberrys' cottage, took my face in his hands to give me a light, friendly good-night kiss; but something happened, and it grew into a full-blown, passionate, electric charge that swept through my body. I was crazy about him but didn't see him again after that summer. I went back to high school; he went into the Army and sadly was one of the first boys from that area to be killed during World War II. He was one sweet, handsome, sexy guy. I saw his uncle, who still runs the general store in Pond Hill, on a visit to Lily Lake in the summer of 1989. Patty Boyd Brady is now one of his best customers. I guess the Yokums' feud with the Boyds is finally over.

$\mathcal{T}$WO

BY MY FRESHMAN YEAR in high school, still in Grove City, I had begun to blossom a bit and to see some possibilities beyond this little Pennsylvania town. I had become an expert sewer and could imagine a career as a clothing designer. I continued to take piano lessons just before dinnertime, with Miss Harshaw, whose stomach rattled louder than the piano, but I could not see myself making a living as a pianist ever. I was president of the freshman chorus; contributed to the *Grover Star*, the school newspaper; and worked on the yearbook, the *Pine Knot*, which said, "Edythe Enke loves to dance, and let me tell you she can really cut a rug." (Along with my new adolescent spelling of Edythe, I was also dotting my i's with little hearts that year.) B. F. Marshall, the music instructor, encouraged me to perform as a singer. Now that I knew I could make people laugh, I entertained my Scarab Club, of which I was treasurer. This was put together to create more interest in the art of drawing, painting, and sketching. For the whole school assembly I would do my humorous chalk talks.

I'd draw two rounded African huts with a palm tree on the side. As I talked, I would keep sketching; the two huts became eyes, the palm leaves became hair. I finished my African native face with a nose and a mouth, then pulled a banana out of my pocket, supposedly off the tree, and skipped off eating the banana. That was hot stuff in Grove City when I was thirteen. Or I'd sew outrageous gag bloomers with stripes and weight them with shower curtain weights. I would put them under my skirt, then deliver a straight speech, only to have the bloomers fall down on cue at the end. You could hear the weights hit the floor. Another knee slapper. At least I was on.

Anything lighter than the usual fare of forensic competitions or serious music concerts was eagerly welcomed in Grove City, so I could perform any day or night. I, in turn, would do anything to get in front of the public. My ability to do funny skits brought me the kind of attention I had been missing at home.

Grove City winters were long, dark, and smoggy, like the local soft bituminous coal and its by-products. (In the eastern part of Pennsylvania the hard anthracite coal did not create a heavy atmosphere.) This was worse than anything I later saw in London or Los Angeles. Industrial smoke from our own Cooper-Bessemer steel, plus the overflow from Pittsburgh, forty-five miles away, and the rest of the steel region, hung over the town for longer than I remembered a winter should be. Grove City had a beautiful but a very short spring and fall. In the winter frozen rain came down in sheets; we ice-skated to school many times.

Every spring there came a bit of housekeeping that I had never come across in Eastern Pennsylvania at Aunt Gussie's. We all had to help. We were given a paint can full of pink wax, which we kneaded into softball-size lumps with which to wipe every inch of the wallpaper in the house, to pick up the visible balls of soot that had accumulated from the furnace. If you left the soot there and brushed it with your hand, it made a permanent stain. My brother usually got the top, from the high ceiling down, with the ladder, and I did the lower walls. Thank goodness we did the ceilings only every other year. When each pink ball of wax turned black, we simply threw it away and dug into the pail for another handful of this Play-Doh-like substance. I've never come across this before or since. Even people in Grove City younger than I don't remember it. When I was recently in Pittsburgh, I couldn't believe how beautiful and clean the city and its buildings were. We had gone to Pittsburgh from Grove City every Saturday to shop, and it was filthy. If they could clean up that Pittsburgh, there's hope for L.A.

I had full run of the house, with my mother in her room, my brother in his room making airplanes, and my father gone. Friends would come over to make fudge. My specialty was peanut butter spread on top of regular chocolate fudge, my homemade imitation of Reese's peanut butter cups. Not a good idea for my figure. I still wasn't allowed to wear makeup, although everybody else did. I simply left my lipstick, Revlon's Raven Red, at my girl friend Ginger Harvey's house and put it on when I went to pick her up on my way to high school. At Ginger's house I played piano duets with her very happily—"Elmer's Tune," "Chopsticks," and "Heart and Soul." I even got to play a mean solo on "Beer Barrel Polka," something else I couldn't do at home. I put my hair up in a pompadour I'd seen in my movie magazines. It was Ginger Harvey's mother who said to me at the time, "Edith, you always walk like you know where you're going." She imitated me walking. I didn't know what she meant then.

One place I wanted to go, desperately, was the dance that Cooper-Bessemer was giving with the USO for all servicemen at the plant. My parents would absolutely not hear of my going to a dance where there would be older men. I had to stay in groups, traveling with my special friend Homer McDougall. I was fourteen and certainly not dating. I pleaded that it was in aid of the war effort and that the school had said we all were supposed to go. Finally, it ended up with my going but with both my parents chaperoning on the sidelines. I danced with the servicemen all night long, being a great jitterbugger and in demand as a dancer.

Late in the summer, before my sophomore year of high school, my life changed abruptly and beautifully. In fact, it seemed to begin. The clouds parted, and the sun came out. My father announced that we were moving—not only away from Grove City but to New York City! At the time it was every dream come true, but in a recent trip back, western Pennsylvania looked very good to me; it felt as if I were coming home. I hadn't realized all these years Grove City's honesty and simplicity were what I had been seeking all my life.

My father had gotten a job at Cooper-Bessemer as a steel expeditor, searching for scrap metal that could be converted to munitions for the war. His territory included Pennsylvania, New Jersey, New York, and New England. He could have lived anywhere within the territory, but he chose New York City. It was centrally located, so he would be spending more time at home. In retrospect, I'm sure that he picked it for me. He understood my needs better than I realized at the time. My mother wasn't very verbal about the move, at least outwardly. Underneath she, too, must have been thrilled.

I don't even remember the possibility of our moving's being discussed, but suddenly there we were, living at 312 West Seventy-fifth Street, in an old brownstone that had belonged to Alexander Graham Bell. My brother was in the navy, so there were just the three of us in that large, airy three-room apartment. It was on the third floor and reached by a creaky old elevator. There was a big sitting room with twelve-foot-high ceilings, a bedroom, a large bathroom, and an eat-in kitchen. I slept on the couch in the living room. Being used to the privacy of my spacious bedroom in Grove City, I found it a little cramped. But I scarcely noticed; I was in my beloved city, New York.

Everything I'd ever dreamed of was here. Now I was in the middle of the great show business mystique that I had only glimpsed half a lifetime before on my fateful trip to Radio City Music Hall. Now, at fifteen, I wanted to absorb the city and its culture in any way I could. I went to the opera for $1.25; granted, I'd sit in the "nosebleed balcony," watching tiny spots move on the stage below, but I was there. Finally my mother gave me her opera glasses. I went to see *Life with Father*, *By Jupiter*, and *Arsenic and Old Lace* and to the ballet. To my mother, ballet was "silly"; only social dancing (the Viennese waltzes of her beloved Franz Lehár, in particular) was acceptable. After all, I could "wear a pretty dress" for that. My mother's image of heaven was to hold the train of her ball gown in the same hand as her full dance card.

School was a bit of a problem at first. I had just left Grove City, population six thousand, and enrolled in Julia Richman

High School, with six thousand *girls*. In Pennsylvania I had been used to flirting in the hallways, at the lockers, expanding my social life between classes. But now there was no one to flirt with, or so I thought.

The first day I sat down in Spanish class, diagonally across from a beautiful, well-dressed, seemingly older and more sophisticated girl. She turned around to me when the teacher was at the blackboard, gave me a long, seductive stare, and then winked at me! It was a decided come-on, followed up by a suggestive move with her mouth and some shoulder action. At the time I knew nothing of females flirting with other females and was quite flustered. In the back of my mind I knew that in New York City I was going to have to "keep an eye peeled," as my father would say.

It was difficult to make friends in the big city, after being brought up in tiny towns where everyone knew everyone else. Mother was fearful (and rightly so) of where I was going and with whom. Even though I didn't meet any boys at school, she was completely paranoid about my every movement away from the apartment. When I did find a girl friend, it always threw me that there was no backyard for private girl talk about boys and clothes. You always had to go to the formal lobby of an apartment building on West End Avenue and up the elevator to sit in those darkened apartments, monitored by parents, servants, or siblings. There was no place to get off by yourselves and giggle. I missed that, and the grass and my English racing bike. (I'd kill for it today, but at the time I was upset that my father had bought my brother an American bike with balloon tires.)

The other thing I really missed about rural Pennsylvania was the family doctor, a friend you knew, visiting you at home. It didn't happen in New York City in the 1940's, and it doesn't happen anywhere now. You went to the doctors. It seemed as if I always had a sore throat, but the fashion then was *not* to have your tonsils taken out. (It changed every five years; my brother had had his out five years earlier.)

One of my sore throats just wouldn't go away, even after three weeks of a liquid diet. The good thing was I lost about fifteen pounds, but I didn't seem to be getting any better. My temperature was fluctuating around 102. When I looked at my face in the mirror, one side was twice as big as the other. We went to a neighborhood doctor, on West End Avenue, who examined the swelling at the back of my throat and solemnly pronounced it "quinsy." As I sat in his dentistlike chair, he said, "Open your mouth." Then, without any warning, he proceeded to stick a curved surgical tool, like a small sickle, into my mouth and lanced the swelling in my throat. Even with my high pain threshold, I'll never forget it. I can still remember the agony of that curved knife as it hit the center of the pulsing lump at the back of my throat, like lancing a boil. I thought he had hit my brain. "Look at that," he screamed as he gleefully drained the source of my pain, without any anesthetic.

Because by now America was actively in World War II, we had to keep our apartment windows blacked out. Mother even became an air-raid warden. We lived about only half a block from the Hudson River, and the ships lined up for weeks, from Seventy-second Street clear up to Eighty-sixth Street. Then, suddenly, one morning you'd look out to the river and they'd be gone. We were warned not to mention this ship activity to anyone, even at school. "Loose lips sink ships" was on posters at every street corner and on my mother's lips at home. She finally had an outlet, however small.

Mother was as excited as I was to be in New York but, of course, more guarded in her enthusiasm. She never once thought about taking a paying job in the city, even though it was wartime and many women who never had before worked full-time. No Rosie the Riveter for my mother. Grandpa Adams's lesson about women doing only charity or volunteer work had been well learned. So she volunteered at the Police Athletic League (PAL). She had knitted many Bundles for Britain before the United States had officially entered the war and continued long after the war was over. Knitting soothed my mother, while it drove me crazy; I needed to see a garment come together fast. That's why I preferred sewing.

My brother, now in officers' training school and wearing his first self-purchased officer's uniform, sent home his old navy bell-bottoms from boot camp. Each leg of the pants was one piece, with one inseam. When I took them apart and spread them out, I could see that the two pieces could easily make a narrow skirt for me. Doing the same thing with another pair of pants, I could make a tailored, sleeveless waistcoatlike top. I had sung the song "Greensleeves" often as child, and it suddenly occurred to me that if I could put bright green sleeves with this navy blue and wear the whole thing with his discarded pea jacket, I would have a three-piece matching outfit. It was a very chic look, and I got lots of comments on my dress at school. I was becoming a pretty good designer or at least scavenger.

My father was now home most of the time. The trips he did take were shorter. For the first and only period in our lives my mother, my father, and I became a threesome when it came to going out. That had never happened before. Perhaps this was why there was much more harmony in our household than ever before and a much better understanding of one another, even though our quarters were a bit more cramped. We went out to eat a lot, and money seemed to be less of a problem. My mother was happier.

Although I wasn't allowed out on my own except to go to school, both parents took me to such diverse places as the Hayden Planetarium, the Statue of Liberty, the Battery Aquarium, and the Empire State Building and to concerts and matinees. Finally, after much pleading, I even got to see the forbidden FRANK SINATRA, the first big teenage idol, at the Paramount Theatre. I actually went into that screaming crowd of bobby-soxers and some fainting females, accompanied by two somber, disbelieving parents, who looked like two dark dirigibles floating in to anchor. Their eyes never saw the stage; they were aghast at the "wild banshee" audience. Both wore their usual black, with hats and gloves. These two middle-aged *parents*, who had spent a lifetime hiding their feelings, couldn't understand the screaming teenagers dancing in the aisles. The screaming teenagers, in turn, looked over at me as if to say, "What are *they* doing here?" By that time I didn't care. I was just happy to be there at the Paramount in New York, instead of back in Grove City, Pennsylvania, waiting for choir practice.

In the school year that we lived there, I learned the subway routes, bus lines, and streets of the city by studying maps. I quickly became a native New Yorker. Of course, I still had to account for everywhere I went, and if I was going to be more than fifteen minutes late, I had better have called home. If not, my mother, worried, would be waiting outside the apartment building. I then couldn't imagine what her fears were for me. I wasn't alert to the dangers of the city in those days. I am now.

I felt only one discomfort of city life, the freezing winds from the Hudson River up the hill on Seventy-fifth street. I never could get myself warm that winter. But before the summer heat hit West Seventy-fifth, my father found us a fairy-tale house in Tenafly, New Jersey, across the George Washington Bridge. It even had a storybook address: 91 Sunset Lane. Again he simply announced it. His business had improved, he felt we all had absorbed as much of the big city as we could in one school year, and it seemed time to move on. It was the first house we owned; we had rented since Trucksville. I felt we were settling in—this was going to be permanent. I would spend my junior and senior years of high school in a small town again and have more personal freedom and mobility than our apartment had allowed. In this lovely Dutch-founded settlement (Tenafly means "built on the swamp") I could have my bike and green grass again. When I went back to Tenafly in 1988 to get the high school's graduate of the year award, I saw that the town had hardly changed at all.

Our dollhouse, with its curved roof extending down over a colonial door and small brick stoop, stood right across from third base at the Tenafly High School baseball diamond. Sunset Lane was unpaved and shady. Today it's paved and even shadier. I visited the house, now owned by the Mike Robins, in 1988, it had not changed. The same boards squeaked as had squeaked so many years before. It was perfect. I felt I was living a dream in a dream house. Yet it was really an unprepossessing two-story white shingled house. My parents had the front bedroom upstairs on the right, and my brother had the bedroom in the rear, which he used infrequently on leave from the Navy. We all shared the one bathroom upstairs, where I had my own bedroom on the front left, facing the athletic field. This was perfect for checking out my new boyfriend, Ray Thomsen, the captain of the football team and a seven-letter sports star. All his sports were practiced on this field so highly visible from my window. Also, once I had joined the band and practiced there, I could call to my mother to bring us hot chocolate when it was cold.

It was at Tenafly High School that I realized that not only was I going to be in show business but I was also going to be good. I just blossomed. I joined even more after-school organizations, sang in the church and school choirs, wrote the music column for the school paper, was on the yearbook (the *Tenakin*), and acted in school plays. The town inaugurated a teenage rec hall, and I won the contest for naming it: the Tiger's Den. The head of the music department, E. Brock Griffith, was an inspiring teacher, the kind of man who put everything into his work. I sang the role of Buttercup in my junior-year production of *HMS Pinafore*. Thanks to "Griff," we were able to tackle such tough operettas as *The Vagabond King*, in which I sang the lead my senior year.

Because I could read music, Griff steered me into the high school band. At first I played a snare drum, anything to be on, but my mother put a stop to that when she looked out the window and saw me chewing gum. The thought of her teenage daughter playing drums and chewing gum at the same time was more than she could take. During the football season one of the drum majorettes moved away. Since I was the only one who could count eights, I promised Griff I would learn to twirl a baton in order to take her place. In a few weeks I knew all the formations and the simpler spinning routines. By the end of the year I could do the higher tosses. I had never marched before, and as was the case with all marching bands and military units, the downbeat at Tenafly was on the left foot. This was to prove another roadblock in my effort to dance passably; every choreographer I have ever worked with since has choreographed a march with a downbeat on the right foot. It's almost impossible for me to do.

Having everyone's eye on me was fun but made me nervous. Never having held a baton before in my life, I had to practice twice as much to catch up. Being the center of attention also made me conscious of my figure. I thought twice before eating marshmallow sundaes or drinking double malts. Of course, I made my own majorette skirt, like everything else I wore. My regular school outfit was a plaid pleated skirt with bulky sweater to match. I sewed the plaid skirts, and my mother knitted the sweaters. I had them in every color. The hottest fashion statement that year was to wear a white man's shirt over your gym shorts with the two front points tied together.

Life was looking up. I began writing humor in Tenafly High School as well as performing it. I wrote "push-button radio" sketches, starting on one subject, perhaps a heavy soap, and changing to a cooking show on another button: "Darling, don't leave me until . . . I parboil the parsnips." I also wrote my boyfriend's funny campaign speeches when he ran for class president. This was the beginning of my comedy writing career. Getting the kinds of laughs I was now getting in the school auditorium from my peers would have made any comic happy. These were not polite giggles, but all-out solid belly laughs that I was getting in the "outside world."

Recently, rereading my diaries of this period, I was appalled to see that I carefully wrote down *not* what I was really feeling, but what all nice girls wrote in their diaries, which might be unlocked and read. It only reinforced a lifetime of holding back my true feelings while putting on a bright face for the world.

At home my mother's mood swings were fewer, but still there. One incident in my senior year at Tenafly High proved to me once and for all that the problem was hers, not mine. This realization kept me sane. One day, after I had given a party for the cast of our operetta *The Vagabond King*, Mother refused to talk to me for several days, giving me only her "look." I had no idea what was bothering her, no clue, no warning, just a lot of those looks. Finally, maybe five days later, it came out that I was going to turn out to be a "gutter girl." I didn't even know what she meant by that. Bowling? I finally found out that my sin had been to serve the cookies I had freshly baked not on a silver tray with a doily but left, horror of horrors, on the wax paper to cool; I had told all the guests to help themselves. This clearly proved that all her training, those years of ever-correct table settings with very little food on the plate, had "gone for naught."

My mother and I continued the battle of the fingernails. I was in my sixth year of piano lessons, which I now hated because I still had to file my fingernails down below the quick. My mother insisted that there was no way to master the piano without cutting the fingernails all the way down. I simply refused because it was painful. (The quick of my fingers grows live skin halfway up the nail on the inside.) I had to file into the flesh of my fingers to get her correct piano-playing length. One day she came into the bathroom while I was in the bathtub and cut my nails herself. The result was not only unattractive but also bleeding. That was an inappropriate shame-provoking thing for her to have done. Again, for the last time, I concluded the problem was more hers than mine. I never had a confrontation with her again. Looking back, I see that from then on I treated her like a patient. No more mother-daughter struggles between us.

Here I was the original Golden Girl, the Barbie doll living out every American girl's dream, the image of what everybody else wanted me to be. Everyone loved Edythe except my poor mother and maybe Edith herself. Ada was just so depressed about being "just a housewife" and not using her brain and talents that she took out her destructive rage on the one closest to her—me. According to most schools of psychoanalysis, our strongest personal need, after food, is the need to repeat our childhood. Later in life I saw myself doing in different ways some of the same things that she had done. And like her, I just turned my anger inward. Oddly, in my choice of men to marry, like my mother, I inadvertently picked those who needed my help. Also, I repeated her pattern by living my life contrary to what I felt I was destined to do. I had to make a living as a cartoon sex symbol when like my mother, I have always thought that I should be doing it with my brain.

From this point on, I was a people pleaser. Although I now spent all my time at school, church, anywhere that was outside the home, and constantly planned my imminent escape from my mother's world, I was still locked in the good girl syndrome, striving for my mother's and the world's image of perfection.

Once a week six of us "perfect" senior girls began to meet at each other's houses (depending on whose parents were out that night). We called ourselves the Buzzin' Half Dozen. We told our parents that we met to try to solve the problems of the world. What we were dedicated to do was to learn to smoke. We would sit around and try to inhale. I tried as hard as I could but never did master it. It made my throat red and interfered with my singing. I did learn to blow smoke rings, however; for those you didn't have to inhale.

My boyfriend, Ray, gave me his seven sports pins to wear; I proudly displayed them in three rows across the left side of my chest and carefully transferred them from sweater to sweater each day. Ray, who was my first big love, a tall, blond, quiet, sweet, muscular, and sexy Swede, gave me a silver ID bracelet I still have. It was engraved "Edith" on one side and "Love, Ray" on the other. Our innocent romance ended when he was drafted (he was a year ahead of me in school). I missed him terribly, and we tried to keep in touch.

But amid all the rehearsals, weekly music columns for the school paper, and homework, I soon found another tall, handsome boyfriend in my senior year. He had dark hair. Ken Marden also had a great athletic build and stood about six feet four inches. He could fix anything. One day he took my bike and somehow hooked it up to his to make a bicycle built for two. We went together on picnics on our makeshift tandem bike. I wasn't allowed to go on a date in a car until my junior prom, even though I'd learned to drive at age fourteen up at the lake. I managed Ken's big campaign for class president; he lost in spite of my funny speeches. I liked him a lot. My parents and his, who were close weekly bridge-playing friends, and even his dour Down East grandmother, who didn't take to anybody, enthusiastically approved of Ken and me as a couple. I began to feel crowded into something I didn't want. I was going to be a star. Marriage and 2.5 kids in the suburbs was not for me. We drifted apart. He went to the University of Maine, and I to Juilliard. I visited him once at the U. of Maine, but he married someone else. Then I never saw him again until I played the Kenley circuit in *Bells Are Ringing* after Ernie's death. Ken came to see me in Dayton, still fantastically handsome but also still very much married.

$\mathscr{T}$HREE

It had always been a given that I would go to college; every-body, even the women, had on both sides of my family. My parents assumed that I would go to Gettysburg College, Grove City College, or even my mother's beloved East Stroudsburg State Normal School (later Teachers College). But small-town Pennsylvania, from which I had so recently escaped, was the last place I wanted to spend my salad days. My dream was to be accepted to the Juilliard School of Music, just forty-five minutes across the Hudson River from Tenafly, in *my* beloved New York. I'd had my taste of life in the big city, albeit under the watchful eye of my mother and father.

You couldn't pre-enroll at Juilliard; you had to audition the semester you planned to enter. It depended on what your voice was doing at that moment. You had to have a backup choice in case you didn't make it. My parents were happy about Juilliard because they assumed I was going to be a music teacher. But I knew that I would be on a stage somewhere singing, even if it was only a student concert hall at Juilliard.

By 1945 my father's steel expediting business was going well, so he could have afforded to send me away to school. But my good grades and spate of extracurricular activities meant nothing when it came to getting into Juilliard. In those days it was even tougher than now. The school was strictly for classical music; no acting, dancing, or comedy courses (they came much later). Contemporary music at Juilliard meant twentieth-century classical music, such as that of Alban Berg, Leoš Janáček, or Arnold Schoenberg. Music as an art form was to be experienced internally, with no facial expressions, much less any tapping of your toes. I have always thought that jazz musicians should study classical music and chord structure and that every classical musician—however advanced—should first learn to tap his toes.

The entrance exam consisted of one aria from the *Italian Anthology*, Part I, in Italian, and a contemporary art song in English. In the Italian you sang only the five vowel sounds —ah, eh, ee, oo, ou. English, with its complicated diphthongs, is the most difficult language in which to sing. So with the pure vowel sounds they could get an accurate reading on your natural voice and the degree of your training so far, and with the English they could better assess your technique. You also had to be able to do advanced sight-singing.

I had a good natural voice relative—not positive—pitch, and I could read music, at least Martin Luther's four-part choir harmony, but at nowhere near the sight-reading level that Juilliard required. My examiners gave me an atonal mass by the Hungarian Zoltán Kodály, and I was in no way ready for sight-reading its complicated harmonies.

For the contemporary English art song, I picked "Oh, Tell Me Pray, What's in the Air Today." To prepare, I began studying voice with Mrs. Williams, our next-door neighbor on Sunset Lane, a local soloist who was very big on the Chautauqua circuit. She taught me as much as she knew, but I was still a bush-league soprano.

But as a sewer I was ready for the World Series. I could have taken a job apprenticing in any major fashion house as designer/cutter, based on the quality of my self-designed clothes. I was able to take a bolt of material from the remnants table and make any kind of outfit I wanted. I had great ideas, color limited only by the best remnant fabrics available. I was always dressed to the teeth in the latest fashions, far above my budget. Little did I know that, in 1981, I would have my own Bonham line in the couture department at all twelve Neiman-Marcus stores. So my backup plan, in case I didn't get into Juilliard, was the Traphagen School of Fashion Design on Fifty-seventh Street.

I did manage to get accepted at Juilliard, but only as a part-time extension student for the first six months. I couldn't enter the real school until I improved my sight-reading. I took "Introduction to Sight Singing and Elementary Harmony," in order to move into the diploma course. I believe that my only qualification for Juilliard was my good natural voice; the rest I would have to learn, studying overtime just to catch up to the basic entrance standard. The school site (now housing the Manhattan School of Music) was then on West 122d Street in Manhattan, near Columbia, so I could easily commute by bus No. 84, or carpool on the ferry, from 91 Sunset Lane in Tenafly. I did, for the next five years.

Since I was taking only two courses at Juilliard, I had a lot of free time to cruise the city. I also enrolled in the John Robert Powers School of Modeling. There I learned to walk, stand, sit, and pose. Most important of all, I lost twenty pounds. I learned to drink my coffee black; there were no artificial sweeteners then, and every calorie counted. I learned that it was possible to alter your tastes rather than substitute something else that was equally harmful. I watched my rounded face take on angles and my features become more clearly defined, even without makeup. Powers sent his models to top photographers, who shot our portfolios for free. Now I had a set of pictures of my new slim figure, dressed beautifully in my four-dollar remnants outfits. At age eighteen, I began to look like those people I had seen in the movie and fashion magazines of my youth.

At Powers, I took a crash course in personality. Fresh with all its enthusiastic ideas, I got off the bus one day and burst into my parents' living room, where my father was talking to a man I didn't know. I decided to try out my crash course right then and there. I met the man, sat down, and began a very animated conversation. I could hear my ebullient teacher telling me, "Be vitally interested in everything your guest has to say." The poor guy didn't know what hit him. I kept saying, "Oh, that sounds wonderful," to everything he said and looked expectantly into his eyes, smiling constantly. If my teacher had been there, I would have gotten an A +. I personalitied the man to the door, and after he left, my father quietly asked, "What was that all about? That was an insurance salesman I'd been trying to get rid of for two hours." I just smiled and shrugged, so full of myself and my newly acquired "charm." My father didn't get angry. He never did.

In the spring of 1946 I switched to the full-time diploma course at Juilliard, taking my English classes at Columbia University, so that I could also use its theater department. Milton Smith was the department head. His constant cigarette dangled from the corner of his mouth as he spoke in a rasping voice. He gave each direction, punctuated by a tremendous clearing of his throat and a cough. I got to sit in on my idol Suzanne Langer's class in "Philosophy in a New Key." By then I had read most of her work. I was on the Columbia fencing team, competing against other colleges. At Juilliard we had no teams, but great bands. The only exercise we got was walking to the practice room. That summer I auditioned for the title role of *Junior Miss*, at the Chapel Theatre in Ridgewood, New Jersey, right next to Tenafly. One of the students in Milton Smith's class at Columbia was doing the stock company production of *Junior Miss* and suggested that I try out.

I did, dressed in my sophisticated black New York outfit with an electric blue bow trim on my seductive black hat. Thus, instead of landing the title role of *Junior Miss* I got offered the even more challenging part of Elvira, the urbane, funny, ghostly first wife in Noel Coward's *Blithe Spirit*, I guess because of the way I was dressed. (Later I learned that auditioners didn't have the imagination to see you in the part they had in mind, so from then on I carefully costumed myself into the precise image I felt they needed.) Julia Meade, not yet a regular on her uncle Ed Sullivan's *Toast of the Town*, played the second wife in this, my first play before a paying audience. In rehearsals I was in awe of Julia, a real actress who had even done Shakespeare. Her mother, a well-known actress, was there, coaching her, in a beautiful flowing dress and a big hat. Julia knew what she was doing and had her mother to coach her. I was dressed for the part but had no idea of the kind of acting stretch I was in for, playing Noel Coward.

Sing a Pretty Song . . .

More than forty years later, in the summer of 1989, at the Montclair, New Jersey, State College Theatrefest, Julia and I worked together again as costars of Neil Simon's female version of *The Odd Couple*. I played the messy roommate (Walter Matthau in the movie), and Julia played the prissy one (Jack Lemmon). In both plays, and every one in between, I had a problem rehearsing. I would always stand around a lot, not doing much, until I got the complete underlying structure. I have to understand the spine of the whole piece before I can understand or perform any of its components. Once I get this overview, carefully arrived at, I never lose my place or anyone else's. I can always paraphrase the other actors' lines if they forget them. This has been troublesome during any rehearsal I have ever had all my life. The only time it wasn't a problem was with Ernie Kovacs, who didn't believe in rehearsal. When he said, "Don't rehearse, just go on," I knew exactly what to do. Ernie also cleared the stage for me; I never had to fight for center stage. When he told me, "Kill three minutes," I knew it was up to me and me alone. The passing years have taught me that most actors have to scramble for every inch toward center stage. If the director doesn't do it for me, I don't know how to do it myself—at least in rehearsal.

I was having trouble understanding Noel Coward's comedy; it was way beyond the girl from Grove City. So, during rehearsals, I went to see *Blithe Spirit* playing somewhere else; suddenly the entire piece became clear. While I didn't copy the actress playing Elvira it gave me my overview. The English accent was no problem once I'd heard it. Then I learned the role with a dictionary on my lap. I only dressed and looked sophisticated. I couldn't wait to be truly sophisticated inside and leave the Pennsylvania and New Jersey girl far behind. When Ernie finally introduced me to Noel Coward, who acted with him in *Our Man in Havana*, and he became our friend, I knew I'd come full circle. I was listening to the real Noel Coward and bantering with him for real. By then even I was so blasé that I wasn't shocked to hear that the main thrust of his conversation was about the endowments of the chorus boys he was auditioning for his latest show. I wasn't thrown. I just said, "Oh, Noel!"

Because I was playing a ghost, my stage outfit had to be

ordered from a costume house; all the others in the play were wearing their own street clothes. On the day the production photographs were taken, I was told I couldn't be in them because my costume wasn't due to arrive until dress rehearsal, two weeks later. I said, "No problem." I asked props for a white bed sheet and wardrobe for a darning needle and the thickest button thread. In fifteen minutes I had taken the sheet, shirred it up the front, and, with six giant safety pins, pinned it tightly down the back, giving me my first form-fitting pre-Muriel dress. (Later the live TV wardrobe people, who had to do everything in five minutes, called safety pins their fine Italian handwork.) I pulled two points of the sheet from the floor and pinned them to my bustline, forming two caplet sleeves and a flowing Grecian scarflike drape down the back. Not only was I in the production pictures, but when the costume rental house delivered my outfit, it was almost an identical design to my ad-libbed bed sheet. There was no way I was going to miss being in that photograph. Julia reminded me, in 1989: "You wore a sheet!"

I also devised my own luminous, ghostly body makeup for Elvira, mixed with nontoxic aluminum powder. It was hard to take off at the theater, so I enjoyed driving home to Tenafly with it still on, especially since my father had bought a used black 1939 Packard Phaeton four-door convertible with red leather seats. It was a gas guzzler during World War II rationing, so my father had gotten a good price on it. With the top down, I was a black-and-white driver in a color movie, scaring other motorists at midnight on my way back to 91 Sunset Lane.

Later that same summer of 1946 I appeared in *Goodnight Ladies* (subtitled "Ladies Night in a Turkish Bath"), at the Grove Theatre at Lake Nuangola, Pennsylvania, just a few miles from our cabin at Lily Lake. The theater has since been restored back to a church. Since the play took place in a Turkish bath, my costume, again, was a sheet and an elaborate high-fashion hat I designed—nothing else. My outfit must have appalled some of my father's distant relatives who had finally come to see me. I never saw them again.

In both of my sheet shows, *Blithe Spirit* and *Goodnight Ladies*, I got my first big audience response. I heard belly laughs on my slightest movements, intonations, and especially the pauses. It was an exhilarating experience. George Abbott later told me that no matter what part you're playing, the audience makes up its mind when you first step onstage, before you speak, whether it likes you or not. It doesn't matter if you're playing the hero or the villain. They liked me. I communicated with them easily. The audience has always taught me more about acting than anyone or anything before or since. Later I would ask Ernie, "Why are they laughing?" He would say, "Don't think about it; just do it. You have natural timing."

For my next live performance I also designed and made my outfit. It was for the fall recital at the Juilliard concert hall. I appeared in an elegant but somewhat reserved Renaissance green crepe dress with a sedate V neckline and prim long cover-up sleeves. No sheet.

I went to visit my brother on a fraternity weekend, now that he was back at Gettysburg College on the GI Bill; he was an Alpha Tau Omega, as my father had been had been at the same school thirty years before. That, and a Princeton weekend with Ronald Wittrich, who was captain of Tenafly's football team my senior year, convinced me that I had been right about typical college life. It was not about learning; it was about parties, tennis, liquor, and having a good time. I couldn't wait to get away from it and back to the sanctuary of the Juilliard practice room. Of course, since my schoolmates were artistes, a lot more went on in the practice room than rehearsing music. I remember going to what I thought was my assigned practice room. It was five minutes past my appointed time, and I could hear very loud dissonant-chord clusters out in the hall. I felt it was time to assert myself, so I breezed through the two doors without knocking, to find a happy couple doing it right on the piano keyboard, not the least bothered by my "Time's up." Never missing a beat, one of them said, "Right with you . . . half a second," as I, very embarrassed, backed out to the hall. In a very few minutes two very serious students came out discussing the technical difficulties in playing Bach, not the slightest bit flustered by my earlier intrusion. These people were a lot more sophisticated than I. I was still middle class enough not to engage in the free-love life of an artiste. It was okay for them, but not for me, Miss Goody Two Shoes from Tenafly. Since I had failed miserably in my desperate attempt to learn to smoke in high school, I didn't particularly pay attention to the odd-shaped cigarettes some of the musicians were smoking or to the funny voices they used before they exhaled. I'll never forget when one of the jazz musicians I'd seen rolling his own cut loose in the student lounge with one loud, energetic scat chorus in what he called be-bop. He wasn't worried about not tapping his foot or showing any facial expression. He looked and sounded like Sam Kinison in the middle of his act. I'd never heard anything like it.

I switched from the diploma course to a Bachelor of Science degree program, again with a voice major and a piano minor. B.S. didn't stand only for the degree apparently. I became even more insufferably serious, according to my diaries. I wrote an atonal string quartet for my "Literature and Materials of Music" course. My teacher, composer Roger Goeb, gave me an A+ on the string quartet, which was the only one played in class. This was heady stuff on a different plane because now I was in an advanced class with older arrangers and composers, who were further along musically than I could ever hope to be. Goeb was asking me in front of everyone why I had put an A♯ instead of a C♭ in a particular place. "I don't know"—I sighed—"I guess I just hear it that way." Groans from the real musicians. In a serious music school, singers were always considered the worst musicians. I didn't care. I just wanted to get the class over with and get on with my performing plans.

I did try as hard as I could to be part of the intellectual core of Juilliard, clearly the avant-garde thinkers and poets. After seeing *Toplitzky of Notre Dame* on Broadway, I wrote in my diary that it "wasn't bad, for a musical comedy." Musically I had now become one of *them*, the Juilliard artistes. I discovered very old people, some of whom were attending Juilliard until they were thirty, collecting degrees and doing everything possible to avoid the real world. I was writing theses on "The Five Schools of Modernism" and was heavily into Roger Sessions. Although they seemed old to me, hanging out with them, I, too, became a pseudo-intellectual snob, discussing the poetry of T. S. Eliot and the existentialism of Jean-Paul Sartre. At Columbia I played in *No Exit*. A few years later I also played in *The Whipping Boy*, by William Happ, which called for me to wear a severely tailored woman's suit. I didn't have time to make it, so I borrowed freely from my new sister-in-law, Barbara, who was an executive secretary and wore beautifully tailored clothes every day. I temporarily adopted my mother's view that movies and television were beyond the pale; working in either one of them would be selling out.

Politically, during this period, some of the students were Communists, who affected Russian peasant costumes in drab colors. Being a chameleon who could always dress for whatever part I wanted, I went along for a month or two, also dressed in earth tones and a babushka, on a corner of which I had embroidered my initials. Even then I couldn't really be part of a group. I had to stand out. There was no way I was going to wear those drab clothes for very long, and I discovered that I was doing more than my share of the "communal homework." Karl Marx's theories worked well in books but not real life, as Gorbachev has found out. At a student assembly I attended near election day, three candidates appeared to talk on the arts. The Communist preached equality in the arts. (There is no equality in talent!) The Democrat avoided the issue. Jacob Javits, the Republican who was then a councilman, promised government subsidies to truly talented artists. It was no contest. I dropped my fast Communist friends and immediately went to work on the Javits campaign. I still have one of the pencils I passed out in front of the New York Public Library for Councilman Javits. I put the drab peasant clothes into the back of my closet and permanently changed back into my snazzy pretty-girl outfits. I later became friends with Senator and Marion Javits and campaigned for him whenever I could.

The perpetual students suddenly became the type of negative role models that have been important my whole life: If you want to lose weight, have a fat person live with you. One of my schoolmates in particular, an older classical pianist who had been a child prodigy, defined for me what I didn't want from my Juilliard education. He was the more educated, expert concert pianist (he'd been going to Juilliard since he was eight). He wanted to marry me, but the aunt with whom he lived in Montclair said to him, "If you want to see how this girl will look in later years, take a look at her mother." I took that as an insult. At any age my mother looked to me like everyone else's grandmother. She was ten years older than the parents of most of my contemporaries, but her attitude seemed to be even a generation older than that. I knew it was really over for me when I heard him trying to borrow money from an army buddy I had thought he was genuinely glad to see. This was his way of surviving, certainly not mine; I couldn't understand why he wouldn't take a job in a music store rather than borrow money from people to live on. I gradually started to phase him out of my life. Last I heard, he was still at Juilliard, taking classes.

The one lingering lesson well learned from this period was that if you make classical music your life, it is your sacred duty to bring good music to the masses. Later, in my own TV show, *Here's Edie*, in 1962, and every nightclub act I've ever done, I included an aria or a vocalese, a wordless musical form, done in my best coloratura voice, whether the audience wanted it or not. Even when I was forced to sing such contemporary numbers as "Honky Tonk Woman" in nightclubs in the early 1970's, the act always concluded with a Gershwin vocalese.

Some of my teachers at Juilliard made a lasting impression. Frau Braun, an elderly German ex-actress who wore big, elaborate hats, would get so carried away that she would stand on her desk acting out Schiller. No one in her German diction classes ever forgot her; she was famous among her alumni in the concert field. She once told a joke on herself, about the time she was in a restaurant with one of her wild hats on. She glanced at another table and saw a lady wearing the exact same hat. "I caught her eye, smiled, and pointed to my hat," Frau Braun recounted. "The voman looked at me as though she didn't see me. Again, I pointed to my hat and gave her an even bigger grin. At zis point she leapt up and vent to talk to the maître d'. It vasn't until I gott home that I realized I had changt my hat und hat anuzzer hat on."

She thus inadvertently gave me my comic German accent

that became the basis for many of Ernie's German sketches, such as Wolfgang von Sauerbraten, in addition to the classical lieder German accent she was supposed to teach me. Frau Braun was one of the first to provide me with the time killers I later used on Ernie's show. Some mornings I could do her reciting Schiller or telling a "Cherman choke" for six minutes.

Madeleine Marshall taught us impeccable English singing diction (much tougher than German or French), although she herself "tawked" in the harshest New York street accent. In opera or concert, anywhere you are not miked, you have to trill your Rs; if you didn't, instead of, "Whisper sweet nothings in heR Ear," what the audience would hear would be: "Whisper sweet nothings in her rear."

The concert singer Nora Fauchald, my singing teacher, clearly thought I was someone special. She taught me the more obscure Erich Wolff, while everybody else was doing the usual Hugo Wolf. She even taught me Edvard Grieg songs in her native Norwegian. I still know more obscure classical songs than most singers in any area of the singing profession. I was never happy with just what everybody else was doing. I always had to go one step further.

All my life I'd sung, with my mother's Welsh family, oratorios in church, gatherings at home, but always with other people. I never did solos until I was in high school and played leads in the operettas. My mother had been the classically trained lieder singer, singing not only her war bond drive solos but most of the church solos. I remember finally singing alone for my relatives in our Tenafly living room. After polite applause at the end one of my aunts turned to my mother and said, as if I weren't there, "She'll never have a voice like yours, Ada," meaning to compliment her but devastating me. I've never forgotten the moment. To this day I cannot sing in small groups, at private parties or in someone's living room, although I'm quite at home in the Hollywood Bowl. Whenever I'm forced to sing at a party, I sing a joke verse to a mismatched chorus and get off in ten seconds with a laugh.

It was typical of my mother's family to stick up for the adults in their family and ignore the children. It was as if my father, brother, and I were in another family. My mother always seemed to me to have been a better sister and daughter than she was mother and wife. Her big family I never felt part of. Reading Margaret Truman's poignant biography of her mother, I couldn't get over the similarities. She wrote that her mother was usually unavailable to Margaret when she needed help. Even Harry, as President, begged Bess in a letter to come to Washington because he desperately needed her help; she stayed in Missouri to help her older brother with some minor problem. Ada and Bess were contemporaries. Both had been in the suffragette movement and had been seriously athletic, Bess in cutthroat tennis, Ada with spirited cavalry horses, something I could not imagine in either case. The similarity of their actions toward *their* families at first struck me as generational and female. But later, in 1969, George Burns asked my then husband Marty Mills, "How's the family?" Without skipping a beat, he answered, "Oh, Dad's fine, Mom's great, my brother and sister are just terrific." George said, "no, I mean *your* family. How're Edie, Josh, and Mia?" So the role of permanent son or daughter and sibling is a problem that's obviously more prevalent than I thought.

It has since crossed my mind that in true Freudian style, in order to re-create my childhood, I married my mother—rather than my father. Oddly, the one member of the large Mills family who made a real effort to make me feel part of the family was Marty's mother, Grandma Estelle.

My mother seemed to be frozen with her Lehár operettas and *The World's Best-Loved Opera Favorites*," while I was now mad for Bidú Sayão's recording of *Bachianas Brasileiras* by Heitor Villa-Lobos and starting to learn to sing Alban Berg's *Lulu* in *Sprechstimme* (half-spoken, half-sung) style. Throughout *Sprechstimme* portions of the score the half-sung notes have a line through the stem; notes totally spoken are indicated only by X's. My mother's pretty songs were now replaced with delicious dissonance.

The next season I made my debut at Carnegie Hall—with 124 others in the Robert Shaw Chorale, singing Beethoven's Ninth Symphony. Serge Koussevitzky led the orchestra. He conducted the mini inner beats with his eyebrows. Since I wouldn't wear glasses and couldn't see that far without them, I relied on the soprano standing next to me for the difficult entrances. Recently, when I was acting at the theater in the Tampa Civic Auditorium, Robert Shaw was conducting the Atlanta Symphony and his own chorale there in the concert hall. When we came out of our respective theaters to the shared dressing rooms, I reintroduced myself and reminded him that as Edythe Enke I had sung for him at the Koussevitzky Carnegie Hall concert while still at Juilliard. "That was you! I didn't know," he exclaimed. "I've been a fan of Edie Adams for years."

That fall my classes got even more serious; there were several stiff requirements looming for the B.S. To my dismay, I learned that I had to take acoustics, and I did, reluctantly, for almost a solid year. It did not come easily to me, and I spent more time on acoustics and its math equations than I did on most of my other subjects combined. I didn't want to build concert halls, I just wanted to sing in them, so I never finished the course.

My summer jobs during the Juilliard years helped lead me away from serious music and toward show business. They included a stint as the combination dramatics and fishing counselor at Camp Waterford, in Connecticut. I put on *The Pirates of Penzance* with the same twelve-year-old boys I taught how to fish. The next summer I taught an exercise and cosmetics course for women, designed to sell Madame Bovary's products, at the Balsams resort in Dixville Notch, New Hampshire. The Balsams was noted for its food, second only to its breathtaking view of the White Mountains. Its brochure touted the resort as "the Switzerland of America," and it was a beautiful spot.

Madame Bovary was a Hungarian with gorgeous skin and a heavy Gabor accent who came once a week to check on sales, with her husband, Prince Van der Riis. I would talk on the microphone, while two other Bovary girls, dressed, like me, in very short shorts and revealing red-and-white-striped low V-necked T-shirts, gave an exercise demonstration at poolside, usually right after lunch. The women didn't want to watch our fitness program and stayed away, but their husbands were very interested in three long-legged beauties in scanty outfits. So men were the only ones who came to see us, and they didn't buy the products. Once a week, we went to the Maplewood and to Pinewood at Mount Washington, to make our pitch on the lawns there, also to all-male audiences. Nobody ever took our exercise course or bought our beauty products, although I did give a few free facials. So, with no appointments on the books, I had plenty of time to practice water skiing and do water ski shows with the Bruce Parker Water Ski School, even riding the top of a human pyramid.

Being a member of the staff gave me a keen insight into the backstage workings of a hotel. I learned lifelong lessons: If you are a bad tipper, the entire staff knows it immediately; big tippers do get better service, and everyone knows who they are. Ernie was also learning this on his own at the same time. But since he wrote a restaurant review column and got his dinners free, he had to be an even bigger tipper. Together we became the last of the big tippers. Even after room service closed, we could usually get a full-course, elegantly served dinner in the middle of the night anywhere in the world.

Sunday night was staff night, so in glamorous gowns that I had made myself I sang with the hotel orchestra. Even there I just looked around at what other people were wearing and copied it. I also wrote out the chords in the girl's key for the piano, bass, lead reed, and lead trumpet. I began to meet some real show business people, such as Don Wolf, a Tin Pan Alley composer ("Azurte"). He couldn't believe that I didn't know any popular music. Don got me started on show tunes and learning obscure verses to pop songs. That summer I also met Gunther Seifer, a German Jew who had narrowly escaped Auschwitz and become a wealthy New York furrier. He was to become my best friend for several years. At the time I was only into best friend relationships. Gunther reluctantly went along.

Don, who was from a wealthy family, also became another of my best friends, introducing me to New York's world of popular music and café society. Thanks to my dates with Don and Gunther, I now went to the posh "in" places: Spivey's Roof, the Little Club, the Drake Room, Toots Shor's, Number One Fifth Avenue, El Morocco, Bertolotti's, Le Veau d'or, even Lindy's. Since I was always on a diet and didn't drink, we sometimes could take in three hot spots in one night.

Don took me to one of Elsa Maxwell's famous parties. Nan Burris, my housekeeper cook from 1958 to 1975, had worked for just about everybody in Hollywood from 1920 on, including Elsa Maxwell, who instructed Nan in the art of giving a successful party: Invite interesting people and have sensational food. It didn't matter if they sat on the floor. Tell the bartender to pour, for the first drink, a large double, then to watch and water the drinks down, as needed, the rest of the evening. That way the stimulating conversation would be the star of the party, and no one would pass out.

With my newfound glamour, nothing was impossible for me now. Here I was, at the center of New York café society. Pretty girls, I found, do get further and more easily. Don introduced me to his friends Mabel Mercer, Cy Coleman, and George Shearing. Also thanks to him, I entered the world of music publishing, the Brill Building circuit. I never actually bought sheet music again; I just called or stopped by the publishers to pick it up. They even allowed me to go into their archives of unpublished songs.

I was shoulder to shoulder with all the Runyonesque Broadway types. Even they could not crack my optimistic choirgirl demeanor. If I came across anything from the seamier side of life, in my mother's best Victorian style, I simply "lifted my skirts and walked through it as if it didn't exist."

In my fifth year at Juilliard, even with my classes more demanding than ever, I signed up for some more courses at Columbia, in radio. Some of the classes were held at Columbia; others, downtown at NBC Studio 3B. Needless to say, I chose the ones in Rockefeller Center; at least I was getting physically closer to New York show business. I breezed past the lines and guards at NBC as if I were working there and belonged at the studio. A few years later, when I was doing *The Tonight Show* with Jack Paar, the elevator operators and guards remembered me from my student days. One of my Juilliard classmates, Mark Michtom, had written a commercial for Ideal Toys' newest product, Baby Coos. The doll not only cooed, it wet. My strident soprano voice on the commercial was really bad, but Mark's father owned Ideal Toys, so the agency went with it. I sang the commercial on a record that was played on the radio and at Macy's toy department.

Because I was going to fancier places, I was making all my own fancier clothes. Now I bought the best-quality remnants I could find and afford. I could go into El Morocco, spot a model wearing a high-fashion sample dress, which would not be in the stores for eight months, go home, and copy it that night, and in two nights I could walk into El Morocco in the same dress. I was extremely well dressed for a girl who still took the No. 84 bus back to Tenafly after all those ritzy places I frequented. I couldn't ask these guys to drive me home to the suburbs, so they'd drop me at the 168th Street bus station. The No. 84 stopped fifty feet from my parents' house. I got to know the last bus time by heart.

In spite of my "sophisticated" busy life in New York, I was still active in the Tenafly Junior Woman's Club, singing solos and arranging concerts. I also sang not only in the Presbyterian church in Tenafly but also in churches in nearby towns, such as Hackensack and Englewood. I have always been happiest doing seventeen things at once.

At Juilliard I was one of the first women to be interviewed for the Kinsey Report on female sexuality. The boys used to clock how long any of us girls stayed inside the closed doors to be questioned, the longest-staying presumed to be the sexiest. The average interview was about fifteen minutes, but I was questioned for one hour, so they all figured that I was hot stuff. What they didn't know and would never believe was that most of my questioning was about feelings, about what turned me on that was sexual, not the act itself. I must have taken the cake as the most bottled up and repressed in the whole report. Of all the girls I knew, I was the one in there the longest—without ever having done "it." Good girls like me in those days simply did not "go all the way," even among the artistes in the practice room. You can take the girl out of Pennsylvania . . .

Despite my forays into New York night life and the world of show business, at Juilliard I was strictly an opera student up until my last year. My new voice teacher, Dusolina Giannini, changed all that. She had been a bel canto opera star, RCA Victor's first Aida, and commanded stages and rooms as if she were twelve feet tall, although she was barely five feet. Her brother, Vittorio Giannini, was the famous com-

72

poser. She had the vitality of a true performer and wore dramatic clothes and big rings. Her black hair was pulled straight back into a severe bun. When she looked directly at you, all you could see were her flashing eyes. I loved her low bow and never saw anyone else like her. In my first private lesson with her, she startled me by physically pulling my jaw down to my chest as I was singing. "You sound like an English soprano; open your mouth, allow the tone to come out," she said. Her methods were extreme for Juilliard, but her results were sensational; in a few weeks I was singing high notes I'd never dreamed of. Her unorthodox methods together with her disagreement with Juilliard's more traditional approach led her and the school to part company after one year, thank God, my last year. Later I found out that the loose lower jaw peculiar to most bel canto opera singers was called the "idiot expression." If your jaw is relaxed, you will have to support the tone competely from the diaphragm, with no tightness in the jaw at all, allowing complete ease and freedom of tone.

Dusolina also taught me an important lesson in acting control: I was singing a Puccini aria with a high sustained pianissimo B♭ ending for her. While singing, I was so caught up in the drama that a tear appeared in my eye just before the final note. Instead of the B♭ out came a cracked sob. Again, Dusolina walked over to me and, in a loud voice, said, "When-a you sing in-a opera, you don't cry in an aria. First-a you singa da B flat; *then* you cry!" What she meant was that you couldn't cry and keep a loose idiot jaw at the same time. Sing the technically perfect high, soft tone, the most difficult for a soprano to do; then cry all you want when you take those low-to-the-ground dramatic bows. I could just see tears streaming from those flashing eyes as audiences bravaed. The principle even applies in straight dramatic theater. If you're reduced to actual tears onstage, the audience is not moved, and no one can understand you. If, however, you never cry and hold to the verge of tears, by the end of the scene the audience will be crying.

One day Dusolina took the unusual step of inviting all seventeen of her lady singers to the hotel suite in which she was living. We did not know what to expect. She lined us up, then told fifteen of us to "go back-a to Kansas and-a make-a babies.'' Dusolina then encouraged the other remaining girl to go into the concert field. To me, she said, "You, with that-a face-a, go straight into musical comedy.'' I was crushed but ended up doing as she said. The next day she went back to her native Italy, closing forever the last classical door behind me.

FOUR

WITH DON WOLF'S HELP, Bea Walker, at the Brill Building, became my pop music coach. Her idea of how to sell a pop song was to move her quivering lips outrageously. She said, "It doesn't matter if you sing on key or off, just move your mouth, pause, and give one low, breathy sigh before your last note—aaah. Here's how you sell a song, kid." She proceeded to move her shoulders and arms forward in such a way that it looked, to me, like a spastic Australian crawl. It struck me so funny that I couldn't sing and do it at the same time. I'd burst out laughing. Since I had now gone "commercial," it became my party bit for my Juilliard friends. I would sing Schubert lieder while moving my lips, swimming my arms, and bumping my hips in Bea's inimitable ditzy-blonde manner. I was always a big hit. Later I saw a movie called *All About Eve*, where a new Hollywood starlet, Marilyn Monroe, was doing my funny party bit for real.

Richard Rodgers auditioned me for the road company of his hit show *South Pacific*. After I had sung for him, instead of the usual "thank you" he called me out into the darkened theater, talked to me for about an hour, and said I could have the job of understudy to the girl playing Nellie Forbush. The next season I would tour as the star of the show, and the season following that I could come to Broadway as the star of Rodgers and Hammerstein's next show, as yet unwritten. In two years I would be his Broadway leading lady. I never dreamed that, in reality, I would be a Broadway leading lady on my own in two years. But I did have enough guts to pause briefly, then say, "I'm terribly sorry, Mr. Rodgers, I don't want to be an understudy," and leave. My mother's lifelong silent message of doing something special (I still didn't know what) had been well received. I was going to be someone special.

During my last year at school I got a job working part-time for the Barbizon School of Modeling. I started out helping the students with their runway walks or how to pose and sit gracefully. I also taught makeup and hair and gave many of them their first fashion haircuts. Nobody had ever taught me to cut hair, but after one disastrous trip to the beauty parlor for a high school prom, where I got a terrible hairdo, I taught myself to cut my own hair. Each piece was parted to be cut from the ear to the middle of the back of my head. I would carefully pull each piece to my nose and snip. As I worked my way around my head to the back, each piece got progressively longer, giving me a perfect curved pageboy hairdo. All those years of cutting my clothes patterns had not been in vain. Later, on our trips to Europe, when Ernie was away from his regular barber, I would cut his hair for him. He was very fussy about his hair, and he wouldn't let anybody in another country touch it. His mustache he always did himself. On a haircut it was always easier for me to follow an existing cut than to create one.

That year the Italian cut, spiked and close to the head, was very big, influenced by all the movies made in Rome. Gina Lollobrigida and Audrey Hepburn had it. It became my specialty, the only one I could do. I remained a hair stylist at Barbizon until the day that the ex-model who narrated the fashion show for the weekly graduation suddenly did not appear. In true show business fashion I was called out of a haircutting session at the eleventh hour to "go on" for her. Apparently I was a success because from then on I narrated the big fashion show that accompied our graduations. At every opportunity I jumped in; I was fearless.

I was also asked to substitute doing career day lectures at all the suburban high schools in New York, New Jersey, and

show. The midwestern viewers proved not to be the twelve-year-old bumpkins that the advertising agencies thought they were.

Jepson was also living in New Jersey, in one of the towns north of Tenafly. It was closer for me to go her house than to Carnegie Hall. Besides, having also made movies, she understood that it was important to move your face and eyes while you sang and to relax and express yourself, even doing opera. I had sought her out because she was a teacher who had herself performed, in two media. She was glamorous, had beautifully coiffed blond hair, and after her stay in Hollywood looked more as if she belonged there than on the Met stage. Most of the opera teachers of that day looked like Shirley MacLaine in *Madame Sousatzka*.

Since time was closing in on me, I entered every contest I could find. As a lyric coloratura I won, usually with my biggie, "Love Is Where You Find It." I killed them with that last high A, which I held forever. I never won any money, mind you, but I did win lots of toasters and steam irons.

I also auditioned for everything, legit theater, nightclubs, anything. An audition card from my reading for the ingenue part in the play *The Late George Apley* said my movements were "awkward" and I "looked uncomfortable." Since I had never lived as an ingenue, I surely didn't know how to play one. What I thought were coltish teenage movements turned out to be a really bad imitation. After all, as my review said, I had played Noel Coward "with coloring and movement that were indeed ghostlike."

Inside, I was still an old soul and would always remain so. George Abbott later told me, when I became his Eileen in *Wonderful Town*, "You are not an ingenue, you never will be, but I will make you one for this part." And he did, but only on the Winter Garden stage. He mastered what I couldn't.

I tried out for Phil Spitalny's All-Girl Orchestra. I went to his apartment at the Park Sheraton for a private audition with Phil himself, only to be greeted at his door by jealous Evelyn and Her Magic Violin. Phil was nowhere in sight, and Evelyn, after looking me up and down, decided that the job had already been filled. On stage she played the kind of banal violin solos that I years later incorporated into a hilarious nightclub routine. I had "Evelyn" come out in long white gloves, with her violin under one arm and the bow in the other hand, with which she conducted the orchestra, badly. The orchestra played faster and faster, racing her to the end of her phrases so that she never actually got to play one phrase. I got even with her. Her biggie was "Golden Earrings," trite even then. It was directly lifted from a Hungarian peasant gypsy song called "Choca-Kishlan."

My first professional nightclub job was at the Riviera cocktail lounge, a semiposh bar in midtown Manhattan. I was given a one-week contract for sixty dollars after winning, guess what, a contest. It was an American Guild of Variety Artists (AGVA) contract, so I had to join the first of the ten dues-paying unions to which I eventually belonged. I had to be fingerprinted in order to get my cabaret card. I opened on August 11, 1949, singing my terrible audition songs, "I Didn't Slip, I Wasn't Pushed, I Fell—in Love" and "Pin a Flower to Your Clothes, Give a Treat to Your Nose, You're in Style If You Wear a Boutonniere." I hired a piano accompanist from the posh Number One Fifth Avenue club. With a spotlight on my myopic eyes for the first time, I didn't really notice the audience; what was important was that I was being paid for my first singing job ever.

Only after I'd finished my set and the houselights came up a little could I see that the audience was made up entirely of men. The club seemed to attract a nice clientele, who really enjoyed my show. They were polite and enthusiastic and congratulated me profusely. I couldn't help noticing that one of the young men, while admiring my long feather boa, picked up the end and draped it over his arm. It wasn't until he said, "But, my dear, it is more me than you," that I realized I was in a gay bar. Then gay bars were virtually unheard of. This, one of the few, was thriving and full every night. I was thrilled. The clientele were so friendly and nice, surely not hassling me, as they would have anywhere else. I had a terrific time, and by the end of the week I was everybody's buddy. It was the best entrance into show business that there ever could have been for me. By the time my brother came in on my last night and said, "Jesus Christ, what is this, a goddamn fag joint?" in his own inimitable style, I didn't even care. They liked me, and I liked them. Gay audiences have remained loyal fans throughout my career.

When my parents finally had enough money to take their first vacation alone, I stayed with my brother, who was now married and living in New York City. I entered a contest at WPIX-TV and became Miss New York Television. In this one I had first to wear a bathing suit and then to put on a gown to sing my aria. I bought an inexpensive version of a Grecian gown and some remnants of extra white chiffon material; I redraped the dress so that it was fuller in the bust and ended with a flowing scarf in the back. I tried to make it look like a prom queen's dress, not too haute couture. After all, this was only a beauty contest. In the photographs the gown looks a lot more expensive than the eighteen dollars I spent on it.

The next week, having won the local contest, I went on to Chicago, as far as the network cable went in those days, to compete for the first Miss U.S. Television title. This was my first big airplane trip, and the press and photographers had come to see me off at Newark Airport. Helen Jepson, a big star, had also come to the airport, and she is in some of the photographs, but on the sidelines. I was the center of attention, and I still didn't have a friend in the business but her. My mother and father were at the airport, but they seemed out of focus and in the background.

I won the title of Miss U.S. Television. My prizes consisted of yet more toasters and steam irons, a trip for two to the Saxony Hotel in Miami, some fake pearls, and a squirrel cape. I gave away or sold the necklace and cape before I left Chicago (if I couldn't wear the best furs, I'd wear a cloth coat, which I could make). I did get a lot of publicity. Jess Stearn, later a novelist and my good friend, was then a reporter for the *Daily News* in New York; he came out to Tenafly to interview the local girl who had made good. The best national break was a photograph that went all over the wires. Something had gone wrong with the wire service machine, so I appeared in the inevitable swimsuit with my head cut off and reproduced as though it had slid two feet away. The picture ran in *Life*.

Now that I had national publicity, I began to subscribe to a clipping service. My mother made the wires herself with the headline PUT THOSE CLOTHES BACK ON, having suggested that I would never again be photographed in a bathing suit. Needless to say, it had a reverse effect, and in every town in America the quote was *always* accompanied by a picture of me in a bathing suit.

The one good prize I had as Miss U.S. Television was a week's engagement at a large men's fashion show in Minneapolis with Mr. Television, Milton Berle. I was ecstatic. Not only did I get to meet my Tuesday night idol, but I also had a full orchestra with which to sing. I got to wear one of the prizes, my first dress by Ceil Chapman, Marilyn Monroe's designer. Milton never showed up for rehearsal, but his brother told me what to say when Milton introduced me onstage. He gave me only my cues for every one of Milton's jokes, which were old even then—known to everyone in the audience but completely foreign to me.

I met Milton for the first time onstage. He would give me my cue: "Don't I take you to the most expensive restaurants?" Then I would say my punch line, "Oh, yes, but you always drop your tray." The audience would laugh, and two seconds after they would stop, I would get the joke, then laugh out loud myself, because I had never heard it before.

Milton knew a good thing when he had it: me, the original dumb blonde. What was to have been a two-line joke "intro" to my song turned out to be a solid twenty-minute comedic routine, with the ever-popular comic and the ersatz Gracie Allen telling new old jokes. When he put his hand on my arm and squeezed, I was to stop talking and hold still. Milton was either timing or waiting for a laugh to die down. I ended up with a black-and-blue arm, but also my first lesson in comic timing.

In May of the following year I auditioned for, and got, the job of girl singer with the Artie Arturo's Trio, to play ten days each in Toronto and Montreal. For the date I bought a pink lace Nettie Rosenstein gown and a many-layered Grecian aqua chiffon by Traina-Norell, on sale, charging them to my parents' account at Lord & Taylor. When we opened at the One-

Two Club in Toronto, *Variety* gave me my first trade review
in its New Acts section:

> A well-trained operatic soprano, who hits her top notes
> with ease, Miss Adams has a standout style and verve,
> plus plenty of visual attributes. Though this is her first
> venture into the night club metier, the young singer,
> when caught on opening night, showed entire lack of
> nervousness and received a terrific reception. A stand-
> out blond looker, notable for lady like demeanor and
> deportment, plus a pink lace evening gown with wide
> flaring skirt, Miss Adams exhibited individual person-
> ality and complete assurance. She does her own song
> arrangements and scored with the opening night au-
> dience. . . . On training and lack of self consciousness,
> plus charm, chanteuse and her style is [sic] set for any
> media. . . .

Lou Chesler, the owner of the club, looked like the MGM
mogul and appeared to own all of Toronto. He always had
me sit at his table. Once, when I got up to do my set, he said,
"Sit down, kid, I own the joint. You'll go on when I say so."
Good girl that I was, I told him, "I'm sorry, but my union
states that you are paying me to do three sets a night, and
that's what I intend to do." As I left for the stage, I heard him
say, "She's a dumb broad." Maybe that's why he never
stopped chasing me. One of the other characters who sat at
Lou's table taught me to handicap horses: "Bet the paddock;
go to the window, hold off on your bet until a minute before
the race, and watch which odds drop the fastest. Put all your
money on that one." "Bet the paddock" meant that the horse
trainers, handlers, jockeys, everyone who knew which horse
had a sore foot or which jockey was hung over that day bet
three minutes before the race. If you could wait until one
minute before, you would be able to bet where the action
was. I'm not much of a racetrack bettor, but every time I go,
to this day, I win. George Solitaire, a renowned sports columnist, was a friend of Ernie's. One day the three of us went
to the track. After every race I was the only one counting my

money. George, in awe, asked, "How do you do that?" I said, "I bet the paddock like my friend in Toronto taught me to."

On the flight back to New York from Montreal, the American Airlines pilot, Mike Wardell, came into the cabin and started to talk to me. When he found out I was a singer, he suggested that I try the *Arthur Godfrey's Talent Scouts* show; he would be my sponsor. The photographer Bruno did my first professional pictures for the occasion, charging me three dollars for six shots. This was to be my last contest. I really had to get to work. On Thursday, June 14, Archie Bleyer, Godfrey's orchestra leader, after hearing me audition with my perennial war-horse with the high A, "Love Is Where You Find It," said, "That's great. If you want to win, sing that song, but if you want to work in show business, you must sing a popular song."

I did want to work in show business, but I still didn't know any pop songs, so I went to the Colony Records shop on Broadway, which is still there. I asked what the number-one song that week was. I was told Patti Page's "Would I Love You (Love You, Love You)." I bought the record and three copies of the sheet music and transposed the chords into my key for the piano, bass, and brass. Then I played the record over and over, until I'd memorized it. Then I sang it on the show *exactly* as Patti Page sang it, tempo, style, phrasing, diction, everything—and lost!

However, I had seven firm paying job offers. One was from Joe Behar, director of a new network show that was going to originate in Philadelphia and be hosted by a new funny fellow named Ernie "Kobax," as I wrote it in my appointment book. Behar called me in Tenafly about coming to Philly to audition. I had had the presence of mind to list my parents' phone in my new show business name: Edythe Adams.

*F*IVE

I SETTLED MYSELF on the train going to Philadelphia and in my new purse-size diary carefully wrote down my expenses for the day: subway to Penn Station—five cents, one-way trip New York to Philly, eighty-seven cents plus thirteen cents tax—and put the receipts in a separate envelope. My father had just started to take over as my "manager." He had driven me to the subway station for this important occasion. He had just started to drill into me the importance of what I was going to have to do, keeping records for my income tax, now that I was a national contest winner and on my way to becoming a big "star." Even Mother was softening and began to read *Variety* reviews of other potential "stars." This was an important audition. If I got it, I would be seen daily on the full network—clear to Chicago. I just had to get it. I tried to vocalize, humming scales under my breath, trying to keep the sound under that of the noisy train as I looked out of the window at nothing.

As I got out of the cab at WPTZ at 1619 Walnut, I was more concerned about my appearance, my voice, and writing the cab fare in my new expense book than I was about what was waiting for me.

When Joe Behar first introduced me to Ernie Kofax (did I hear him right?), he was much taller than I'd expected. I'd seen pictures of him, and he looked short. Even with his slouch and my three-inch heels, I could see that he was at least six feet two inches, maybe taller. He had on a rumpled brown suit and a wrinkled shirt with the neck button opened and the tie pulled down. He had on glasses and a hat with the brim turned up (he looked like a sketch rendition of an overworked reporter from *The Front Page*. All he needed was a bent card saying "Press" stuck in his hatband). He had a fuller-than-leading-man mustache and was smoking the biggest cigar I'd ever seen. When he took off his hat as we met, I saw a full head of tousled dark brown hair. He had tired, soft brown eyes topped by thick, shaggy eyebrows. He had big, warm hands and a smooth olive skin. When he smiled, an enigmatic half-smile, his eyes twinkled like those of a child who's just gotten his first puppy. In fact, he looked like a big, overgrown puppy you wanted to pat, coddle, and snuggle down to bed with.

In my whole life I had never before met anyone who affected me like this. While we were still shaking hands and saying our initial how-do-you-dos, I was completely nonplussed. I had these tiny electric shock feelings traveling up and down inside. I'd felt that delicious feeling only when I'd waken from those unexplained dreams and try desperately to go back to sleep again so that I could experience some more of whatever that strange feeling was that was running from my brain to my toes. For the rest of the day just being in his presence, without even touching, brought on this cold sweat, producing feelings from somewhere buried deep beneath a whole lifetime of trying to bury my true feelings. If this was what I was missing by trying to stuff my true feelings down deep, I wasn't going to do that anymore. Here was a living, breathing way out. From that moment on Ernie could get me with a look, a word, or even just his presence. He simply became the most important thing in life, even though I subsequently tried to talk myself out of him. From then on, as long as he lived, he was it. Here he was, tall, dark, mustached, with a hat, cigar, and a foreign name. He was separated, not divorced. He looked dangerous but spoke softly. Who could have resisted?

The show was to be Ernie's first in prime time on a network. *Ernie in Kovacsland* was to be a summer replacement for Burr Tillstrom's *Kukla, Fran & Ollie* puppet show on NBC, Monday through Friday evenings from seven to seven-thirty eastern time.

I sang the ony two pop songs I knew well. I was asked what other songs I could sing since I would have to do a rhythm song and a ballad each half hour we were on the air. I lied and said, "Oh, I can sing anything." So I was called back the following Tuesday, June 26, to sing two more songs, which I had to learn fast the night before. Ernie hired me on the spot to do the summer program, on each segment of which I would sing the two songs and do sketches with him. My first live show was the next Monday, July 2. On that program I sang "If I Were a Bell" from *Guys and Dolls* as my up-tempo song and "Don't Take Your Love from Me" as my ballad.

That finished the songs I knew. Because I was nearsighted and refused to wear the outsize whole-eye contact lenses that were popular then, I was always desperately trying to memorize new music and lyrics. After all, this was live and on the full network. Ernie said the first thing he remembered about me was my standing behind a set, frantically trying to learn the day's lyrics.

To my parents, and to most people, Ernie would seem too foreign. Everybody in show business then changed their ethnic names to Davis, Thomas, or other white-bread-sounding names. Nobody much wore a mustache then, except the bad guys in movies. Nobody smoked a cigar except gangsters, but Ernie wore his handkerchief in his sleeve so that he wouldn't crush the cigars in his breast pocket. He didn't give a "hoot in hell" what anyone thought of that. For me, Ernie was the "Mephisto Waltz," a Lorelei siren, the wolf call of the wild —irresistible. Everything about him seemed to fill some deep psychological lack in me. What I wasn't, he was. What he wasn't, I was. He fitted the odd-shaped pegs in my personality to a T. In 1989 Norman Knight, our former boss at the Dumont Network, said that when he first met the two of us, he'd never met anyone quite as naive as I, or anyone quite so street-smart as Ernie. Norman said we were "a colorful couple."

At first I didn't understand Ernie at all. I studied him, never having met anybody like him in my sheltered Presbyterian life. Though he seemed everything dangerous, he was always funny. He expressed himself colorfully. His language was so bad that it sounded all right to me. Sometimes, when he got mad, he would yell at the top of his voice, but always at things, never at people; if there was too much starch in the collar or the store forgot to deliver something, he swore in two languages. Like my father, Ernie never raised his voice to me. When I started to use some of the words in his vocabulary, particularly the current "army expressions," he had to explain them to me. (I thought "p.o.'d" meant "put out" and started to use it freely until Ernie said, "What are you saying?") They turned out to be even more colorful than I had thought. I didn't understand his French cunt green beans joke at all, but I laughed as though I did, so he thought I was sophisticated.

I moved into the Bellrich Apartments, a safe haven for young ladies from good families, at 301 South Fifteenth Street. He lived in Joe Behar's old bachelor pad on Sansom Street, behind the station and later moved to his own lavish apartment on Philadelphia's posh Rittenhouse Square. Coming from my frugal family, I couldn't understand his extravagance. Yet we connected right away. I never thought of him as a "date"; he was always special, because of his unique physical effect on me, even just standing close together. We started going out immediately and never stopped. After our first evening together, Ernie and I went back to his apartment to play George Shearing's recording of "The Nearness of You." We held hands, and I saw tears come out of his closed eyes. Despite his obvious larger-than-life appearance, Ernie had a soft core that not only was apparent to me, one-on-one in my living room, but came over on TV in everybody's living room. Chevy Chase remembers watching Ernie on television, fascinated by his imposing personality but knowing, "even as a kid, he wasn't ever going to hurt you."

For our first big dinner, outside at a fancy restaurant on the Delaware River, he showed up in a low-slung white convertible Cad-Allard sports car. He had just bought it with his life savings of thirty-five hundred dollars, "so you won't have to take a cab." I knew he wasn't making that much money and had a mother and two children to support, so I was terribly impressed that he would go out and spend his last dollar to live it up, especially for me. The word "extravagance" hadn't existed in my vocabulary until I met Ernie. In my family we used to have a board meeting just to cross the street on a yellow light. We had to account for every penny. As a child I split a percentage of my meager allowance into Sunday school envelopes; it was five cents for the church fund here, two cents for missionaries overseas. No wonder I just used to follow Ernie around. I was utterly taken with his live-for-today attitude; it unlocked another long-forbidden psychological door for me. From him I learned to spend money whenever I had it and sometimes when I didn't. He filled in all my blank checks.

In August 1951, while we were still doing the daily network show, I opened in the Celebrity Room, a mob-owned club down the street from the station. The owner told Ernie that I had "a great leg." Ernie wanted to know, "What's wrong with the other one?" During the week I worked there, Ernie did stand-up mob takeoffs. He could get away with it because one of his best friends from Trenton was Charlie Costello, a cousin to Frank Costello. Charlie, who raised Doberman attack dogs, took us to a fabulous Italian restaraunt in Trenton, Chick and Nello's, commonly known as the Homestead Inn, where we ate in the kitchen. Ernie stayed friends with Charlie, who was one of the first people to call me after Ernie's death, asking, "Is there anything you need? If anybody gives you any trouble, just call me." Ernie always told me, "You do favors for the boys, but never let them do favors for you."

While we were visiting Charlie in Trenton, Ernie took me to his house at 61 Vincent Avenue, to meet his infamous mother, Mary, who was living there with his two daughters, Betty and Kippie, who were then four and two.

With Ernie, for the first time in my life I was able to be a kid. He taught me how to play. He was a big kid and proud of it. He talked outrageous baby talk; I loved it. For a long time I couldn't tell anybody because it wasn't done then. (Our matched wedding rings are engraved "Swees [sweethearts] forever.") He was not afraid to cry and met life straight on with humor. For once I could talk to someone about my deepest feelings. He was bright, witty, intelligent, funny, and sophisticated. Ever since *Blithe Spirit* during my drama stint at Columbia University, I had yearned to be urbane, Noel Cowardy, and all of the above. Ernie wasn't all those things then, but I thought he was. At a restaurant he could order all the things I'd never had and the proper wines to go with them. I'd always been taught that such excess was sinful, but that's the way he lived. I couldn't wait to learn how he got that way.

Ernie Kovacs was born in Trenton, New Jersey, on January 19, 1919. His father, Andrew, had been born in a village outside Budapest, on May 1, 1890. Andrew's mother died when he was five, and he lived with his father and uncles, who were all priests, next door to the Catholic church. Andrew was an altar boy because he had to be, but he had a wild streak and no maternal supervision. The uncles were constantly admonishing him, so one day, instead of lighting the candles as an altar boy, he just blew them out and "ran like hell." At age fourteen, in 1904, Andrew arrived in New York with a name tag sending him to Trenton to visit relatives. At age seventeen Andrew married Helen Tomko. They had two children, who died, along with their mother, in the flu epidemic of 1917, and a son, Tom, born in 1911, who survived.

In 1918 Andrew married Mary Cherbonic, a professional Hungarian with piercing dark eyes and high Mongol cheekbones, who laughed a lot. Tommy, by then seven, lived with them. Mary was a seamstress and a pistol; Mama Rose in *Gypsy* was an hors d'oeuvre compared to her. She tried to run everything and even then terrorized everyone she was around. She loved a fight. Andrew "Pop" Kovacs had worked at the Roebling steel mill but was a cop when Ernie was born.

During Prohibition, in the 1920's, Andrew got into the "beverage business"—making bootleg liquor in his own still, hidden away in the woods outside Trenton. He used to say, in his thick accent, of the television program *The Untouchables*, "This is sissy stuff. I go to still, cops say, 'Put hands up,' I put hands up, grab ice pick I have over door shade. I go boom on hand, they yell and scream, and I drive off."

Pop also owned a waterfront dive in South Trenton, the Union Street Bar. Tom Kovacs quit school at age fourteen to tend the bar for his father and do the heavy work. If any of the guys in the bar were rowdy, Andrew would get two heads and clunk them together, then throw the guys out. One time he hit one of the boisterous drunks and hung him by his collar on a coat hook, leaving him dangling for some time as a lesson to other potential troublemakers.

Andrew branched out from making booze for his own place and suddenly made lots of money. In 1928 the family went from near poverty to a twenty-room mansion, on Parkway Avenue in Trenton. They even had horse stables and dog kennels. They held lavish parties and bought a velvet suit and pony for Ernie, who was by then nine. As Ernie said, "I had to be tough dressed like that." His retreat was to go into his room and read all the Tom Swift books, on which he later did takeoffs. It was the beginning of his self-education. From then on, wherever he lived, Ernie always had a desk, and his main occupation was reading and writing, even as a kid. For someone with only a high school education, he was one of the most well-read people I'd ever met. He'd read the classics just because he wanted to, not because he had to take a course.

One guest at a Kovacs dinner party during this affluent period remembered Mary's buffet table decorated in the colors of the Hungarian flag, red and green: all new green twenty-dollar bills under the red paprikas and stuffed cabbage.

By 1935 Andrew had advanced to owning a posh three-story restaurant, the Palms, on North Broad Street. A dumbwaiter took the food from the kitchen in the basement up to the third floor, by which time it was always cold.

In high school Ernie acted in plays, in part to escape from his family situation, like somebody else I knew. Eddie Hatrack, Ernie's high school friend who later did our music in New York, recalled their days together at Trenton High. "My first experience was when I shook hands with him and he had one of those hand buzzers on. He was always putting matches in the soles of people's shoes and lighting them, things like that. In those days Ernie and I were involved in anything and everything musical, particularly the shows. In

93

Pirates of Penzance Ernie played the Pirate King; I remember our dramatics teacher, Mr. Van Kirk, a wonderful guy, reprimanding Ernie and laughing at the same time when he took too many liberties with the lines. It was a constant joke with Ernie. Everything he said, it seemed, was funny. He just turned everything into being funny." Ernie always said that it had been his high school teacher and director Harold Van Kirk "who started the whole thing."

In 1936, the same year that Ernie's brother, Tom, got married to Mabel, Ernie's grammar school classmate, the Kovacses bought a Packard town car. All seemed to be going well. However, in 1937 Andrew's business, the Palms, went bankrupt, and he lost everything, $750,000. The year Ernie graduated from high school, 1938, his mother and father divorced. Ernie went to live with his mother, having testified in court on her behalf. Mary always maintained that Ernie and his father weren't speaking for several years afterward, but I have lovely letters from Ernie to Andrew during this period. They were very close and definitely cut from the same cloth.

After the divorce Pop inherited a bar that was losing money in the basement of the Hungarian Catholic church. The church asked Andy to turn it into a moneymaking proposition. He added live music, a cimbalom and a balalaika, and soon the church elders were asking him to suspend bar service at least until the first mass on Sunday was over. The bar flourished.

For a while after his high school graduation, Ernie taught drama in a girls' high school in Trenton, while taking postgraduate courses. He ad-libbed his own transformation in the second act of *Dr. Jekyll and Mr. Hyde* depending on the size of the audience. One day he planned an elaborate second act change, with an added scene and dry ice for smoke to give the audience a real show. The curtain opened, and there were three old ladies out there.

"Van" took Ernie off to a summer stock season at the John Drew Theatre in East Hampton, Long Island, where Van Kirk was directing. Ernie played a cowboy in *Green Grow the Lilacs*, the play that became the musical *Oklahoma!* A critic wrote of Ernie's performance as the major in Shaw's *Arms*

and the Man, "He had great vitality but overacted badly."
Van Kirk, in a newspaper interview years later, said, "He
didn't . . . Ernie never overacted, but his personality was so
that he simply overpowered everybody, even in a small part.
He couldn't have played it down. It wouldn't have been
Ernie."

Van Kirk's assistants in East Hampton included Martin
Manulis and Henry Levin, both later successful producers in
Hollywood. The three men believed in Ernie enough to help
him get a scholarship to the New York School of the Theatre.

Away from Trenton, Ernie found out what poverty was
really like. He was the typical small-town kid, subsisting on
hopes and dreams and little more. In New York he lived in
a run-down four-dollar-a-week rooming house on West Sev-
enty-fourth Street. He was still naive enough to be pleasantly
surprised when the police raided his house one day and ar-
rested his landlady and several of her attractive "daughters"
who had been operating their own rental business in the
basement. He ate at the Automat for less than a dollar a week,
on seven-cent cups of coffee, ten-cent plates of baked beans,
and homemade gruel. On Saturdays he lived it up with a beef
pie—a Horn & Hardart fifteen-cent special.

Ernie told me a funny but pathetic story of his hunger
driving him to the brink of desperation. One day, as he was
eating his daily ration of beans, a woman sat down at his
table with her tray. He looked longingly at her roast beef
dinner with candied sweet potatoes and other goodies. The
woman had barely touched her food when she suddenly leapt
up and left the Automat. Ernie watched to be sure that she
had left, then started to take her plate—only to be beaten to
it by the eager hands of a busboy. Ernie said it was the closest
he had ever come to committing mayhem. I think his tremendous drive, his capacity for work, and his hunger for
success and money can be traced to this period of his life.

During one vacation from drama school, Ernie went to
work in another summer theater, in Brattleboro, Vermont,
where Fred Clark was one of the actors and Robert Whitehead
was an apprentice. Ernie and his troupe would work on the
sets all day, act in the play that night, take their bows, say,
"Whose deal?"—then gamble into the wee hours. Gambling

was an obsession he had picked up in school, playing cards with the kids on his block, shooting craps in the street, and betting on just about anything.

In his second year of drama school Ernie collapsed from pleural pneumonia, a near-fatal disease in 1940. Instead of returning to either half of his broken home in Trenton, Ernie spent the next eighteen months shuttling from hospital to hospital as a charity patient. His first stay was at what had formerly been a prison, on Welfare Island. Roaches infested the wards, and mental patients were mixed in with the physically ill. Needing his sense of humor to survive, Ernie used the doctors for straight men and played all kinds of practical jokes. He wrote a daily newspaper, the *Lavabo Tribune*, satirizing medicine, doctors, and illness. He also ran a card game in the men's lavatory after lights out.

Once a week he had a date for fluoroscopy, a "living X ray" that permits observation of infected lungs. This provided great sport for Ernie, who prepared for these sessions by taping tinfoil letters on his chest. When he was called in for his exam, he'd remove his pajama top in the dark and step in front of the machine, flashing such messages as "Cut here," "Stop it," "Out to lunch," or "What's up, doc?" Then he'd wait for the doctors to groan.

With the help of Van Kirk, Martin Manulis, and Henry Levin, Ernie transferred to a somewhat nicer tuberculosis hospital, at Browns Mills, New Jersey, on April 25, 1940. But there the beds were always warm from the fast turnover. If people didn't eat, they died, so Ernie talked his roommate into ordering second helpings. "He looked so thin," Van Kirk remembered, "and there were holes in his shoes. I know he hadn't had enough to eat, but he never complained. We'd go to the hospital to cheer him up, but he'd cheer us up. Not only us, but all the other patients, too. Those poor, tired, sick old people, they never laughed so much in their lives. Entertain them? He convulsed them."

While at Browns Mills, Ernie, who was then a hunter, talked his father into disassembling a shotgun and bringing it to the hospital in a small package. Ernie succeeded in slipping out of the hospital with his package several times a week. He'd reassemble the gun in the woods and have his fill of shooting tin cans. This went on for several weeks. One day, after a thorough examination, a doctor told him, "You're coming along fine. If you continue this progress, you'll be able to sit out on the lawn for a few minutes a day."

"Thanks, doc, I sure could use some air," Ernie said.

Nonetheless, his illness was serious, and at times he was near death. After his recovery he said, "When you've been as close to death as I have and you're given another chance, you realize that every moment's a gift."

In 1943 Ernie left this last sanitorium without being released and, true to form, moved back in with his mother in Trenton.

At first Ernie worked in a drugstore, to help support himself and his mother. He stole the most expensive cigars from the store but refused to eat there. He would walk over to the Hildebrecht Hotel and eat the way he wanted to eat, being served properly. What little money he had he spent on his lunches. He said, "I'll starve first," rather than eat at a counter. When we were married and I wanted to eat in a drugstore because I wasn't "dressed," he'd still say, "I'll starve first." Mary described Ernie's salad days a bit differently: "We had only three dollars and Ernie went out and bought three charlotte russes. For days afterward we starved, on crackers, catsup, and water from the Automat." She sounded more as if she were romanticizing her own youth with a man of her own age. This was something I was going to have to watch.

Then Van Kirk directed Ernie to a job as a staff announcer at a local radio station, WTTM. Ernie's job was on a fifteen-minute daily program, where he began to create his unique comedy, writing and delivering "commercials" for such imaginary sponsors as Basher's Imported Sheep Dip, interviewing anyone, including night workers at local factories, and producing such spots as reacting like a rabbit during rabbit hunting season (with bullets whizzing past his radio microphone).

Ernie's kind of comedy, which he brought to full flower on live television, survives in Monty Python, *Rowan and Martin's Laugh-In*, *Saturday Night Live*, and, most noticeably, David Letterman. (Letterman's head writer, Steve O'Donnell, and his staff spent three months at the Museum of Broadcasting in New York, studying Kovacs kinescopes, so I know they're fans.) In 1981 I was flabbergasted when, as I guested on Letterman's show, his first question was to the effect, "Well, just what was it that Ernie Kovacs did? Could you perhaps explain his humor?" I was nonplussed, prepared for any question but that, knowing that much of the Letterman show's framework was pure Kovacs, including the broken-glass sound effects and the camera on the unknowing man-in-the-street. I tried to explain Ernie, as if to a ten-year-old. Imitation is the sincerest form of flattery, but ignorance is not. Aw, come on, David, lighten up.

In 1945 Ernie married a dancer named Bette Lee Wilcox on the spur of the moment. The famous Bluebelles, a dance troupe, were entertaining at the Hildebrecht Hotel, and Ernie had gone there for a date with a short blonde. The blonde didn't show up; but Bette said, "I'm here," and that's how they met. They married shortly thereafter, and both moved in with Mary. It was a disaster from the start, with Bette and Mary, two tough cookies, arguing constantly about money. Ernie's escape was to lose himself in work, as would often be the case later in his life.

He took on a newspaper restaurant reviewing column for the *Trentonian*, then also commuted by train to announce wrestling matches in Philadelphia, bringing along his own sound effects, such as a dog's crackle bone, which he used on mike as he described a crushing hold. This twenty-four hour workday turned out not to be the solution to his bad marriage. In 1949 Bette deserted Ernie and their infant daughters, Betty Lee and Kippie Raleigh. By this time Ernie had bought his own house in Trenton, so that his family wouldn't have to live with his mother. As soon as Bette left, Mary never missed a beat. She moved right into Ernie's house, ostensibly to help him take care of his little girls.

Ernie broke into television in 1950, when he was hired by WPTZ (later KYW), an NBC affiliate in Philadelphia. It was there that I auditioned for him. The unstructured, fly-by-the-seat-of-your-pants, this-is-your-first-and-only-take ambience of early live television was perfect for Ernie, who worked best under pressure and loved anything resembling a gamble. His crazy, hyperactive imagination enabled him to fill every second of air time he was given.

The first of his series that I was on, *Ernie in Kovacsland*, the NBC summer replacement for *Kukla, Fran & Ollie*, went off the air at the end of August 1951, but Ernie still had his TV talk show, *Three to Get Ready*, live on the local station from 7:30 to 9:00 A.M. Monday through Friday. In September an extra half hour was added from 7:00 to 7:30, and I joined *Three to Get Ready* in October. This was the first morning television show anywhere in the world; everything else available at that hour was radio, and Ernie was determined that this show would not have the look of a photographed radio show. If he played a record of a popular song, he would have drawn cartoons on a flip pad that usually had nothing to do with the song but were humorous additions to his interpretation of it. He called these "illustrated profuselys." If things were particularly dull, he'd throw eggs or other food at the drawings. All of us there were expected to come up with things to "kill three minutes" with only a fifteen-dollar weekly prop budget.

Andy McKay, our propman, had a hotel's dirty-linen cart full of items we could use. At first there were only three people in the studio crew: two on cameras and Andy McKay. When we had to move scenery, the cameraman had to get off the camera and move the set. When the newsman was on, we knew he'd be stationary for five minutes every half hour. The cameraman would lock the camera on the newsman, Norman Brooks. Then the cameraman was free to help Andy and me set up the next scene. There was only one man in the control booth, Joe Behar, and if he had to leave for any reason, one of us had to go in and cover for him.

If both cameramen were needed to move a set, I got to get on the camera, which was then manually controlled. I could put Ernie in and out of focus by changing the lenses with a lever on the side. The fisheye (wide-angle) lens was the most unflattering because it distorted features. Ernie would have the morning loosely planned, like a shopping list. It was up to us to create mischief for most of the two hours. From the beginning, I always felt more like part of the production team than the girl singer. I started by telling Welsh jokes, which were notable for their lack of humor, then graduated to Frau Braun's histrionic Schiller recitations. Since I didn't have a writer and wasn't writing my own stuff yet, I tried the classics: Zsa Zsa Gabor reading Shakespeare, "Out, out naughty spot." There was always room for my Juilliard party bit: Marilyn Monroe singing Schubert lieder, "Leise Flehen." It was a sure-fure laugh. Only steal from the best.

Garry Shandling's show's creator and producer, Alan Zweibel, a former writer on *Saturday Night Live*, said that all the writers on that show "had Kovacs at the core of everything we did; no matter what the bit, whenever there was a question, we said, 'What would Ernie have done?' It was Ernie Kovacs that we all idolized and wanted our show to be most like. We spoke to our generation; however, we prided ourselves on exploring the medium the way he did with electronics. He knew the conventional pictures but was more interested in the distortion of pictures and sound. He never spoke down to an audience."

When the large *Saturday Night Live* writing group won its first Emmy, in the midst of all the mayhem, Chevy Chase grabbed the mike and said a special thank-you to Ernie Kovacs. I'll never forget him for it.

When I did Garry's show in late 1989, it all came back to me, so much so that I felt the need to bring in mementos from the period to dress the set. I was playing the wife of an early TV nightclub comic, and I certainly knew the territory. I was amazed that those in Garry Shandling's group, aged about forty and under, are such cult admirers of Kovacs. I told them that although I'd been hired as the girl singer, my job was to see that the whole show, not just my part of it, was good. All of us had to keep an eye on the continuity because if Ernie was out of a job, we were, too. The sum total of the show was everybody's responsibility. For me, the object was not to be funny but to kill time. The only times I'd get outrageous was when something Ernie tried fell flat. We all had to be ready with a full-out save. That's the way I myself learned to perform comedy. On his show you played straight to him or you were full on center stage. Remember, it was two hours every day.

Sing a Pretty Song . . .

Doing the show with Garry Shandling recently was a real treat; it was the first time in thirty years I'd worked with anyone that open to any and all ad-lib suggestions. Garry's laid-back and underplayed style, especially when he breaks down the fourth wall and talks directly to the audience, warmed my heart and reminded me of the way Ernie used to work. Garry should always be on TV somewhere, regardless of "numbers."

We had our own group for musical numbers, the Tony De Simone Trio, who were always the first to arrive, straight from a late-night gig at a club. I had to get three copies of sheet music and write out the chords in my key. One day near Christmas they read my markings wrong and played "Silent Night" in the key of G, instead of C, and I had to sing it five notes above a coloratura. It was done in front of a church set, so I couldn't just stop and tell them to change keys.

One day Tony and the boys were late. Ernie wrote out Tony's home phone number on his large sketch pad, put it on camera, and told the listeners to call Tony at home and wake him up. We always figured nobody was watching anyway. This time the phone company called up and said please don't ever do that again. We had flooded the switchboard. Ernie was thrilled; at least we knew people were watching.

I began several notebooks, labeled "Birthdays," "Household Hints," "Hymn Requests" (I sang one every day), "Quickies" (things I pulled out of the newspapers), "Funny Bits" (which required props), "Songs," and "Quartets" (with the newscaster, Norman Brooks).

Since this was the first TV show anywhere at this time of day, and it was only local—an experiment—we were very casual about our work habits. With the earlier starting time, 7:00 A.M., we all had trouble getting to the studio on time, especially Ernie. Sometimes the other regulars and I would sit around for as long as twenty minutes chatting on the air while awaiting our star. He would say, "I was shaving, and I heard the theme song, so I thought I'd better hurry up."

Other times I would come to the studio with my hair still in curlers, planning to fix myself up after I got there. The cameramen or Ernie would spot me and shout out of a back window and down a deserted hall, or they'd chase me all over the place with their lenses aimed. Eventually I learned to hide behind our church backdrop, figuring that they wouldn't dare get funny with that. Ernie loved to get me with my hair up, no makeup, and my glasses on. We did a lot of talking to the dead camera, lining up possible funny bits with the control room. Sometimes Joe would punch up the dead camera and show me making faces or setting up a gag.

With only black and white and manually operated cameras we were in the silent movie era of television. In my lectures to college students today, I refer to myself as the Mary Pickford of early TV. It was both more creative and more personal. There was a nice intimacy in Philadelphia; you knew that relatively few people had television sets, and those who were watching weren't expecting perfection. As an audience they were making mistakes right along with us. We could say or do whatever we wanted to. Ernie personalized everyone in the studio. We knew Tom was on camera one and Sam was on camera two; they became part of the family. Andy McKay, who started as our propman, became part of every sketch. He did the longest spiral faint and death scene in history. It took him so long to die one day that Ernie said he wasn't going to write Andy any more death scenes.

One time, with a frozen orange juice can, a child's kaleidoscope, and a flashlight taped to the front of the camera, Ernie moved the patterns and designs to the beat of the music. This thirty-nine-cent special effect is now done electronically and costs thousands of dollars.

During this period I got to know Ernie's real family. I always loved Ernie's father, Andrew. He was a great, fantastic bull of a man, who stood even taller than Ernie, although he was about two inches shorter. He reminded me of Oscar Homulka, the film actor, brusque on the outside with lots of raw edges, but always charming. He must have been a great ladies' man in his youth. Pop was proud and tough, and he danced a mean czardas. In restaurants he would request that the violinist play sad Hungarian peasant songs, and he would sing along. As the tempo picked up, Andrew would get up and dance frenetically with deep bent knees, pausing only to blow over his shoulder. As the music got faster and the dancing got wilder, Pop did more over-the-shoulder puffing. I asked him what he was doing. He said that was "to blow devil off shoulders."

Pop loved the strolling Hungarian violins and would cry freely while he sang along, blowing his nose at the end of each phrase. Ernie, on the other hand, would say, at the approach of a gypsy musician, "Shit, here he comes, hold my hand." Then he would say, softly, "We want to be alone," and give me a soulful look. He would slip five dollars into the violinist's hand as he backed away, smiling.

Andrew used to say of Mary, "She's a devil. She smile at you—look out! She seem mad, you okay. She laugh today, you cry tomorrow." Mary hated Ernie's first wife so much that when I showed up, agreeable to anything and everything she said, she adored me. She thought that I was like putty. All I did was agree with her; if she said, "That's green," I'd say, "Yep, that's green," and if she then said, "That's blue," I'd say, "That's right, it's greenish blue." I treated her, too, like a patient. Mary was later to mistake my acquiescence for weakness. It was the easiest way to avoid conflict, much as I had done when my own mother was difficult at home.

Mary was truly a unique person. When Ernie and I first started going together in 1951, I was singing at the Sun and Star Roof at the Senator Hotel in Atlantic City. The hotel had given me free rooms, which I turned over to Ernie, Kippie, Betty, and Mama Kovacs. God forbid I should even stay in the same hotel as Ernie, so I stayed at the Seaside Hotel. This was so that my mother and father would never suspect that Ernie and I might be alone together in a hotel room. They called me from Tenafly daily, saying whenever they finally did reach me at the Seaside, "You're never in." They were right, but I didn't notice it or care because I loved Ernie.

In Atlantic City I was introduced to Mary's odd gypsy ways. I went over to visit her the first afternoon, and she had all their clothes hanging out all over the place—on the terrace, opened drawers, doors, chairs, lamps. I asked her why everything was spread out, and she said she was "airing out the clothes." So I assumed she would hang them in the closet that night. But they stayed strewn about for the entire two weeks of my engagement. The closets remained empty, and if she washed anything, it was flown proudly on the balcony, which was already full of wet bathing suits and towels. In my family drying anything on a balcony was on a par with a pink flamingo or an iron deer on the front lawn; it simply wasn't done. This was a painfully accurate introduction to Mary, showing me what I was to put up with for the rest of her life.

This engagement also provided my first introduction to Ernie's phenomenal largess when it came to room service and charging things. When I finished my two weeks, the hotel was to have paid me fifteen hundred dollars. However, Mary's room charges on my borrowed gratis suite came to two thousand dollars. She had discovered that could include much more than food: boat rides, Steel Pier, horseback rides, posh clothing, toys and other treats. The hotel offered Ernie a deal he couldn't refuse. They'd simply absorb the extra five hundred dollars as part of a promotional and not pay me. Not only did I still have to pay *my* hotel bill (by check) but it was Sunday and I only had two dollars in change in my purse. I had to ask Ernie for ten dollars pocket money. I was livid and mortified because I had never had to ask anyone for money before, not even my parents. I had never been without enough money. I had earned everything I needed by baby-sitting in the summers. My allowance had been planned on and given, but I had never had to ask anybody for anything. So I vividly remember this incident with Ernie. I made a pact with myself never, ever to let this happen again, where I would have to ask someone for money. Ernie, casually handing me the ten-dollar bill, was totally unaware of what was going on within me.

Money simply did not matter to Ernie. He always over-tipped. He had not stuck me with his hotel bill maliciously or chauvinistically but thoughtlessly. Conversely, later, if he had the money, he encouraged me to spend it as lavishly as he did. And I did.

That September I also played the Steel Pier in Atlantic City, and we made some records for an outfit called Top Tunes in Ocean City. The company had Tony De Simone record Ernie's "Oriental Blues" theme song instrumentally and Ernie sing "Hotcakes and Sausage" on the B side. It was really not very good, and we kidded him about it on the air. My record's

A side was called "Sailor Man." I liked the B side, "There May Be a Love," better. It was a pretty good melody and lyric and sung well, I realize now. But at the time I didn't have a sense of what would be a hit in popular music. I was and still am a singer who never had a record on the charts.

I began to see more of Ernie's family and began to get a closer look at their customs. He took me to his uncle's funeral in Trenton. Hungarians love to cry. They eat, they cry; they dance, they cry; they laugh, they cry, and when they cry, they really cry. They all must have been having a great time at the funeral because everyone was crying out loud. At one point the priest, who was wearing an elaborate black floor-length vestment with choir robe-like sleeves, interrupted the sermon to do what appeared to be (he was speaking in Hungarian) an elaborate commercial on Ernie, the new celebrity native son in the audience. He got so carried away that he raised both arms to the sky with his menacing sleeves fully spread. Mary, who had been moaning and wailing louder than anyone, stopped, looked up at the priest, burst right out laughing, paused, cut loose with a loud witch's cackle, turned to Ernie, and, in a voice audible to all, said, "My God, he looks just like Batman!," and went right back to wailing.

Ernie's stint on *Three to Get Ready* had evolved from his cooking show, *Deadline for Dinner* (dubbed *Dead lion for Dinner*) which also starred a housewife and a famous chef, around whom Ernie kibbitzed. Ernie was a good cook, but on the day both the housewife and the chef didn't show up, Ernie toasted himself with the cooking sherry and started throwing eggshells into the chocolate pot. After the next sherry, he threw spinach into the pot. Out of that came his "choco-spin" bit (chocolate-covered spinach for kids who hated it) and Mikos Molnar, the melancholy Magyar chef.

By the time I got there his remaining show had nothing to do with cooking, which was a good thing. He loved to kid me about my lack of ability in that area: "The kitchen, honey, is that yellow room that you never see; you might stop by there someday and look in," or, "You remember pies; they were round." The first time I ever attempted to cook for him was when he was sick with the flu (he always cooked when it was the two of us). He asked me to make some oatmeal. I

105

tried to explain that I didn't have the vaguest idea how. He said, "Surely you can make that. Read the label." I did the best I could and brought him a sick tray with a little flower on it and a dish full of this lumpy mess. When I came in, he was moaning from his temperature. After one bite of my inedible putty, he moaned even louder. "Don't ever try that again." I never did.

When Ernie moved into his fancy apartment on Rittenhouse Square, I helped him decorate it in the fifties moderne stuff that is now on L.A.'s trendy Melrose Avenue and at the Disney World theme park in Florida. He loved it, I hated it. I stayed on at the Bellrich but was definitely settling into Philly. My parents were not amused.

As we began to make more money, there were even more elaborate gifts and fancy dining. Ernie's mother and his kids spent increasing time at the Rittenhouse Square apartment, which was too small for Ernie, never mind Mary and her airing-out clothes. She was a houseful wherever she lived. Every time she moved or even visited, she went out and bought eight hundred dollars' worth of cooking pans. She did it in Philly and again in Englewood, New Jersey, New City, New York, Central Park West in Manhattan, and Bowmont Drive in Beverly Hills. After the holidays these pans would disappear, and we would have to buy more for the next holiday. One time in L.A. I saw some of them lined up across the lawn for the dogs to drink from, but otherwise I swear I don't know what she did with them. She may have thrown them out because she didn't want to clean them.

Mary would bother and embarrass Ernie by calling him up at the studio when he was on the air and all day long at the office. She would say such things as "I broke your father, and I can break you, too." She would send him desperate notes underlined on postcards, visible to all: "Ernie, they're turning off the gas, send more money . . . Ernie, I'm starving, how can you do this to me? . . . We're behind on the mortgage again." It got so that the switchboard or one of us would not put her through at all.

Just short of a two-year desertion period, after which Ernie would have been legally free, and right after his first network show, in 1951, Bette Lee Kovacs reappeared. She instigated a messy divorce and child custody case that took up most of Ernie's and my nonperforming time for about a year.

Bette, or Brx, as the girls called their mother (because she was always spelling things so they wouldn't understand), was even having me followed as the other woman in the custody case. My life was becoming a B movie, the kind I had never been allowed to see. Ernie's mother-in-law, Sally, and her questionable boyfriend went to Tenafly to my father's real estate office, Boddecker's, for money, or so my father thought. Now he was really unhappy about my involvement with Ernie. I began to notice that Ernie and I were now being followed everywhere, by a seedy man on a twenty-four-hour detail. You just feel it when you're being followed. When the private detective, if that's who he was, followed both of us, I told Ernie, "You go one way. I'll go another." The man followed me.

The court awarded Ernie custody of the children on the ground that Bette had deserted them, granting her visitation privileges to see the girls two weekends each month. I never met her or was in the courtroom, but I was brought up at the trial as the "other woman." I was only upset when someone at the court proceedings said that I "looked like a Sunday school teacher." That really got me angry, I guess because I did.

For the father to be awarded custody in Pennsylvania was so unprecedented then that Judge Emanuel Belloff, who made the ruling, used it in lectures on family law for years afterward. Belloff was considered a tough family judge, and he also ruled that Betty and Kippie were to be "removed from the care and influence of the paternal grandmother," Mary. She ignored the order, as usual, and moved into Ernie's houses from then on wherever they were.

In January 1952 the NBC network bosses in New York decided that they had something with us, but they didn't know what it was. They wanted us in the big time and foisted on us, without any consultation, network writers, performing guest stars, and a live studio audience. The only thing they asked Ernie about was what comic he admired. He said, "Oh, Fred Allen, 'Allen's Alley,' " so the New York creative types set up a show borrowed loosely from that concept, *Kovacs on the Korner*, where Kovacs indeed stood on a street corner and met up daily with a cop, a barber, and a man in a bad dog suit playing a talking dog. Neither one of us understood what we were doing in this scripted nothing. The show emanated from Philadelphia, from eleven-thirty to noon daily. Because he'd already had a radio show called *Koffee with Kovacs*, Ernie railed against the K in "Korner," so the C was quietly restored.

NBC did insist on hiring an entire new troupe to replace his regular *Three to Get Ready* family. I was kept on as "the singer." Ernie was forced to have on such guests as the road company "last of the red-hot mamas," who sang with Ernie standing onstage next to her, his mouth open in disbelief through the whole song. I never saw him in such pain again in all the years I worked with him. NBC also fired our beloved Tony De Simone and sent down the jazzier Dave Apple Trio from New York to glitz Ernie up.

The network also insisted on a staff of two writers, both of whom Ernie ignored and rewrote on the air. He described *Kovacs on the Corner* as "some of the worst moments in television history, setting back the variety format about thirty years." On the last show Ernie nailed one of the writers he least appreciated inside a trunk. She was slightly claustrophobic and, needless to say, furious.

Ernie now had to be funny for almost thirteen hours a week, plus do his own typing, weather charts, contests, and selection of musical numbers. So everything and everyone who came along became part of the humor. Some woman sent in a six-foot rag doll called Gertrude. Ernie would dance with her. If he was late, we'd aim the cameras out the window and throw Gertrude down for him to catch. She took a lot of wear and tear. When we played Johnnie Ray's "Cry," there were towels and tears all over the place. Ernie played records of pop tunes of the day in Polish. We were responsible for our own sets. I found that the cheapest one for me was to cut out my own cuculoris, a pattern set in front of a light and projected on a scrim behind me. That way I could create my own scenery, such as an umbrella or a palm tree, and have it projected behind me on the blank wall. Or we stole sets from a soap opera that was broadcast from our studio in Philadelphia, starring Susan Peters, until their staff found us out. From then on we had to disguise their sets by throwing a drape over a chair or by pulling a picket fence off the soap's set and then putting it back before they missed it.

We never thought about overexposure in early live television; we were there to kill time. The heavy work load and virtual total creative control allowed Ernie to develop camera techniques and comedy concepts that he had begun in live radio and later refined on his network shows in New York and Hollywood.

Some things on his shows didn't work, but it was all fun in the trying, including the half-hourly newscasts. Standing on a ladder out of camera range, Ernie dropped water on either the head or the script of newscaster Norman Brooks. The viewers somehow always knew who was doing it.

The most lasting legacy of *Three to Get Ready* was Ernie's trademark phrase "It's been real," which quickly became as famous as his mustache and cigar. The slogan, which evolved mysteriously, was used on every program, usually at the end. The Early Eyeball Fraternal and Marching Society, EEFMS, was another running bit, with its own membership cards. "Dorf" was another non sequitur good-bye that Ernie used later, in New York.

During the early months of Ernie's divorce and child custody proceedings, the legal aspects became most bitter and public. WPTZ employees enjoyed sending Bette's process servers in search of him up blind alleys at the station. One day, to avoid being served, Ernie just didn't show up for work. We had someone behind the screening smoking a cigar to stand in for Ernie when we needed him.

Once Ernie and I were on a Philly–New York train that jolted to a sudden stop. Everybody fell down, including us. The railroad made an appointment to have an insurance inspector come see us. We set the appointment for when we were on the air, pure gold as a time killer. The man didn't know he was to be on television. I was wheeled out in a wheelchair, all bandaged up, nearly giving the inspector a heart attack. Ernie grilled the man on air for a few minutes. The inspector nervously sputtered self-consciously. After watching him suffer for what I thought was long enough, I jumped up and said, "Nothing's wrong except that I ripped a pair of stockings; buy me a new pair." Very happily, he bought me a few pairs.

Early in 1952 the Dave Garroway *Today* show had premiered on the NBC network from New York, Monday through Friday 7:00 to 9:00 A.M., the same time that we were already on in Philadelphia in *Three to Get Ready*. The network understandably wanted all its affiliates to carry this expensive project. In most cities there was nothing on at that hour, so only WPTZ in Philadelphia objected. At first the station insisted that *Today* would never be taken on in place of its most popular local show. But as NBC kept pressuring WPTZ for its lucrative market for network commercials, the station caved in. The last *Three to Get Ready* show aired on March 28, 1952. The program was uncharacteristically tearful and sentimental, including appearances by Ernie's mother and daughters.

Kovacs on the Corner mercifully was also about to be canceled, with less regret. The best way to describe Ernie's and my reaction to that show was disbelief. Ernie had offers from the other two Philadelphia television stations, but we were more than ready to move on. Dan Gallagher, a producer who worked at WCBS in New York, offered Ernie his own local show in the daily 12:45 to 1:30 P.M. time that had been formerly occupied by Steve Allen on the network. Some of the *Three to Get Ready* cast were also hired on, myself included. Peter Hanley (who was to inspire the creation of the Nairobi Trio) came along as the boy singer, as did Trygve Lund, to do sketches. Angel McGrath, who had finally been hired as Ernie's secretary, and Andy McKay, our propman turned slow dier, also moved to New York with us. Tony De Simone and his trio did not go with us; Eddie Hatrack, Ernie's high school friend, became our musical director in New York.

Before we left Philadelphia, our dear friend Merrill Panitt, who covered radio and television for the *Inquirer*, told us about "this new little magazine" that had offered him a job. "I don't know," he said, "I've got such a good job at the paper." Ernie said, "Take it." The magazine was *TV Guide*, and Merrill eventually became its editor in chief.

Ernie was ready for his own new challenge; he clichéd, "I'm not afraid of you, New York." On April 21, 1952, *Kovacs Unlimited* made its debut on WCBS. The format was more of the same as in Philly, but this was New York City, the big time! *My* town!

DURING OUR FIRST TWO YEARS in New York Ernie and I continued doing live daytime television, on CBS. We now had production offices at Liederkranz Hall, on Fifty-seventh Street
near the Hudson River. We fondly called it the cow barn, but
we had a suite of offices right next to Garry Moore's, so we
had arrived.

I was still having to memorize three new songs a day. As
a result, I know thousands of songs and most of their verses
(because that killed time), such as early Rodgers and Hart,
operetta, some in German, all musical theater composers, and
novelty songs nobody else sang. I sang "I'm Looking for a
Guy Who Plays Alto and Baritone and Doubles on a Clarinet
and Wears a Size 37 Suit," done by Harriet Hilliard and Ozzie
Nelson. For a prop, I knew I could always find a size thirty-
seven suit. Since Juilliard had not taught me pop style, I had
the good sense to stay away from standards. I knew that Ella
Fitzgerald could do them all better than I, and she did.

Briefly I went back to live with my parents in Tenafly.
One night there I got a call from a male voice I didn't recognize: "Hello, you Edie Adams? We have an offer for you
from Harry's Club in Cleveland." He named a plausible price
range and said he just wanted to make sure that I was available
between June 12 and 17. I said that I was terribly sorry but

113

that I was not available. He hemmed and hawed and upped the price; the more I said I couldn't do it, the more he added: salary, musicians, traveling expenses, a suite. This went on for half an hour until it got to be three times what I was currently making. At that point I cracked and said, "Well, when would I have to leave?" When he said, "Aha, aha, I knew it," I realized that it was Ernie, but before that, even with my great ear for accents, I didn't have an inkling. I'd never known anyone before or since who could fool you that fantastically with a complete character change, including stuttering and mannerisms, on the telephone. It was much more than a voice change.

I had never met anyone like Ernie; he was special. He always talked about getting married; I never wanted to. I was going to be a star. As he made more and more money in New York, he bought me more and more expensive gifts. George Unger, a diamond peddler from Forty-seventh Street, used to make house calls backstage at all the TV shows. In each pocket he had a different selection of watches and diamonds. Ernie started by buying little gold charms to commemorate the anniversary of anything—like our knowing each other for two months. Then came a diamond pendant, a gold watch. Something in my background was warning me not to accept expensive gifts; however, I loved them. One weekend he showed up with what looked suspiciously like a velvet engagement ring box. After a very romantic candlelit dinner at the Four Seasons—Dom Pérignon with flambéed everything (main course, dessert, even flaming salad)—he got down on one knee and in a semicomic routine did a takeoff on a swain and asked for my hand in marriage. Without missing a beat, I asked, "What's wrong with the rest of me?"

I promised to think about it, but he said, "Wear the ring while you're thinking. This is a bulky box. It's crushing my cigars." Then he threw the box away and held the marquise-cut solitaire expectantly near my third finger left hand. There was nothing for me to do but put the ring on my correct finger, something Ernie had obviously counted on. We were to drive down to Trenton that weekend. He said, "I have to stop at the hotel to pick up some things." When we did, out came the bellman with two birdcages, two dolls, many large stuffed animals, beach balls, Saks dress, hat, and shoe boxes, F. A. O. Schwarz mechanical toys and games, and gift baskets loaded with champagne, exotic cheeses and fruits, a large cake, and a pound of caviar. There was barely room for us to fit in the car. We couldn't close the windows for the Pogo sticks. When Ernie got engaged, everybody got engaged. We drove up to the Vincent Avenue house, honking the horn. Out came Mary and the two kids, surprised. As Santa happily gave out his sleighful of presents, saying, "Ho-ho-ho, kids, we're engaged," I was still just a passenger on his train.

I thought it all odd at the time because an engagement in my mind was a very private time. However, Ernie was Ernie, and he was an unusual man. Looking back, I think it probably was to soften the blow to his mother of his getting engaged to anybody. It was a big party, and we all had a great time. Everybody there learned how to eat the best gray beluga caviar with a spoon.

While Ernie and I were doing the local CBS show *Kovacs Unlimited*, its producer, Dan Gallagher, suggested that since I wasn't getting any younger (I was in my early twenties) and had a trained voice, I should try out for Broadway musicals. He recommended that I start with Leonard Bernstein's upcoming musical version of *My Sister Eileen*, the popular play and movie about two sisters from Ohio who come to New York to make it as a writer and an actress. The cast of authors was almost as long as the cast of characters. Jerome Chodorov and Joseph Fields, who had written the play, were also doing the libretto for the new show, called *Wonderful Town*. Betty Comden and Adolph Green, who had also done *On the Town* with Bernstein, were writing the lyrics. The musical director was to be Lehman Engel, who along with Bernstein had been one of my heroes at Juilliard. Both men had visited the school often while I was there. Lehman Engel's book on Baroque music was one of my textbooks, and he often lectured at the school. When I first saw Leonard Bernstein come in to conduct wearing a loden green coat with a hood when everybody else was in ties, I thought I was meeting God. Lehman stayed my friend until he died.

George Abbott, another god, was directing, and Donald Saddler was doing the choreography. Jerome Robbins was to join the cast of authors on the road, as a show doctor and unbilled choreographer. Rosalind Russell had already been signed to play big sister Ruth. This was as good as it ever got on Broadway, before or since, and I couldn't think of a better introduction to musical theater.

I was now studying pop style with one of the top voice coaches in New York, Kay Holley, and working on my voice with one of the best vocal teachers, Mrs. Clytie Mundy, Meg Mundy's mother. So, along with every other soprano ingenue in New York, about 350 of them, I went to audition for the role of Eileen. When I arrived at the producers' office, the very Irish dark-haired and blue-eyed receptionist told me not to bother auditioning. Chodorov and Fields had told her that Eileen should look just like her. My blond hair and hazel eyes knocked me right off her list. She said, "I'm sorry, you're not the type." I was crushed and left the office.

But after the producers had auditioned everybody else, George Abbott was still desperate to find his Eileen. He called Richard Rodgers for suggestions. Rodgers asked his assistant, John Fernley, who said, "What about that crazy Adams girl, the one who refused to be an understudy for *South Pacific*?" They called me about auditioning for *Wonderful Town*, but I told them I'd already been turned away. They insisted on setting me up for a reading with Mr. Abbott. Getting the girl who had said she didn't want to be an understudy and the only soprano in town who hadn't auditioned for Eileen got to be a big thing. Alphabetically I was again at top of the list with *A*. I was told to bring shorts and silk stockings. I thought it odd but brought them anyway.

Since my mistake in dressing too sophisticatedly for the *Junior Miss* audition, whenever a part came up that I wanted, I dressed myself for it. So for the *Wonderful Town* audition, I went into my tiny back closet (I had one even then) and found a skirt that I had made and worn back in high school. I topped it off by sewing a puritanical Peter Pan collar and cuffs onto a blouse, and I pinned a cameo discreetly in the center of the neck. Since I was costuming myself for a specific purpose, I overlooked nothing: a different hairdo, tiny pristine jewelry (only a watch and one ring), petticoats, and plain closed pumps. I was my father's idea of perfection: simple, tailored, and young. I was Eileen.

After I had sung my audition song, in a mixed classical and theater voice, I was told, "Change into your shorts and silk stockings." I said, "Why?" They said, "Well, there's a scene in which the two sisters change stockings." I went up to change, came down, and read the leg scene. Somebody said, "Thank you," which usually means the end of any audition. I was furious. I stomped upstairs to the dressing room, packed up my things, and went down the fire escape and out of the theater. I didn't like shorts, Broadway, George Abbott, or auditioning for anything. I just wanted to go home. So I went home.

Mr. Abbott and his minions waited nearly fifteen minutes, assuming that I was changing into my street clothes. I mean *George Abbott*, God himself, waited for me. Hal Prince, the second assistant stage manager (the one who was later to say, "Five minutes, Miss Adams" before every act for the entire run), finally called me at home, demanding to know what I was doing and how I had the nerve to keep Mr. Abbott waiting. I told Hal that I had thought "thank you" meant "goodbye." Hal went and told George Abbott that I had left after "thank you" because I didn't think there was any point in waiting. He said, "Well, that's our Eileen, all right."

We started rehearsing *Wonderful Town* on December 22, 1952, and opened in New Haven on January 19, 1953. (During rehearsal I continued on *Kovacs Unlimited*.) There were many opinions about how I should play Eileen; I had four sets of directors. After George Abbott had shown me what to do, Chodorov and Fields told me how their Eileen had acted in the straight play—"Pause here, turn, then you'll get the laugh"—then Comden and Green came over with perhaps another way to sing a song. Donald Saddler had his thoughts, too. It was my first show, and I was confused. In TV you have to do it all yourself, with no rehearsal. At least the sometimes complicated music was relatively easy for me. Lehman Engel was surprised and pleased that I was a Juilliard girl. I was more than pleased to have the conductor who had authored my Baroque textbook.

Roz Russell, who was less secure about the music, had hired her old friend Lou Kessler as her pianist; he was fine as a revue-type pianist but not up to the difficult Bernstein harmonies. It was Kessler who warned me, "As a friend I have to tell you, don't give up your day job." I asked him to explain, but he wouldn't say any more that day. I was puzzled. I already had made a public announcement on TV about leaving Ernie's show and had a big sendoff party. One day, after a particularly strenuous rehearsal, I found out that other girls were being auditioned for my part. This was devastating, my first failure—up to now. Everything I had ever wanted to do in my life I had done. Now I was being replaced because I didn't know how to rehearse.

I thought about it for a long time, then finally called George Abbott at home and told him about my four sets of authors and directions. I was confused about which direction to follow. He said, "Don't you worry about it. Nobody will ever bother you again. I'll see you tomorrow morning at ten o'clock." At that rehearsal he made an announcement to all that from now on I'd be listening only to his direction, and would everyone stop giving notes to anyone. The auditions stopped, and everyone did leave me alone.

Three days later we did our first run-through for the Broadway gypsies. With a live audience I knew exactly what to do; the laughs were all there, and immediately producer Robert Fryer had a long-term contract ready for me to sign, at $175 a week. (The chorus members each got $125 a week.) Roz got $12,500 a week and a percentage of the concessions and programs. Abbott was always special in his direction with me. For example, when I was having problems getting laughs in the second act at the jail with all the policemen, he said one night after rehearsal, "About the jail scene, remember one thing: You are mistress of the mansion; they are your humble servants." From then on we got every laugh. It was brilliant comedic direction. If somebody doesn't give me that overview before I get to the live audience, I have to make it up.

While Abbott, Bernstein, and Engel were my idols, I had also worshiped Rosalind Russell, a real movie star, since I was a kid in Pennsylvania. Her picture was pasted on the slanted roof at Lily Lake. I never dreamed that I would meet her, much less be on the same stage with her for eight shows a week, playing her younger sister. Now that I was, I remained completely fascinated by her. One day, when she admired a black hat I had made myself, from an unblocked velour I had bought from the millinery district, woven like a basket and very chic for the day, I went right home and made her an identical one. Here she was wearing Galanos and Mainbocher gowns and *my* dollar unblocked velour hat. I would have done anything for her, even thrown my coat down on the mud so that she wouldn't have to step in it.

Roz, of course, wasn't a singer, but she surprised me in her ability to hold on to the more difficult harmony parts in our duet "Ohio." She had an unusual voice. One of the critics described it as "the Ambrose Lighthouse calling to its young." Flush with all my years of formal musical training, I gently tried to tell Roz in early rehearsals that she was singing one of her big numbers, "One Hundred Easy Ways (to Lose a Man)," incorrectly; she was growling on her vocal cords in the chorus. As a singer you could do this maybe once for a record, but not eight times a week in live performance. Many times I timidly tried, in many ways, to explain to her that her voice would not last. But Roz was the star, and she had no reason to listen to me. Sure enough, she lost her voice and was out of the show after the first night in New Haven. Her understudy, Patty Wilkes, went on the second night but didn't yet know her lines.

For seven performances in New Haven the ingenue they had tried to replace only a week before suddenly had to carry the show by not only doing her own part but also feeding the understudy most of her lines. Roz crept out of her sickbed one night and saw the show. By the time she was back in the show and we opened in Boston, January 25, she was more than willing to listen to me when it came to singing.

I don't think anything can describe the feeling that you get at the first orchestra read-through out of town. For months you rehearse with only a piano, usually out of tune, in a dingy rehearsal hall. The first orchestra read-through of *Wonderful Town* in New Haven, had Leonard Bernstein himself conducting. It was a thrill I can still remember. I wept openly as he played that score for us for the first time. I had never heard a bass saxophone before. It didn't just play; it snarled, and you felt its vibrations up through your toes. I particularly loved the dissonant ballet music, which was cut out of town. It could stand a second look; perhaps *Jerome Robbins' Broadway II?*.

At our first read-through Roz had trouble hitting her opening note in our duet "Ohio." Bernstein tried just about every instrument in the orchestra to cue her, but none of them worked. Suddenly I hummed her note for her, and she got it. From then on and throughout the run, Lehman cued me the way he would a saxophone solo. Roz was so insecure about that opening note that I had to hum it quietly for her every night from then on. It got so that she actually hummed it correctly before I did. I'd say to her, "You've got it, Roz." But she would always clasp my hands and say, "Oh, no, no, I don't, give me the note; *you* give me the note." Whenever I got a cold, she sent her limousine with special cough medicine for me. I adored her.

On opening night out of town she returned the favor when she overheard me asking, "Where's the makeup man?" In New York television I was used to having someone fix my face for me before I went on. She was the only one who realized that I wasn't kidding and didn't know there was no makeup man in the theater. So she came into my tiny dressing room and helped me with my first stage makeup. She had her Hollywood makeup man's face chart with her, custom-done for her, but carefully took the time to show me how to apply the makeup—on what was *her* big opening night, too.

After three weeks in Boston and two in Philadelphia, *Wonderful Town* opened in New York on February 26, 1953. The Joshua Logans hosted our opening-night party at their apartment in River House. Everyone who was anyone in New York—social, political, and theatrical—was there. Marlene Dietrich was our paper boy, going out to fetch our reviews, all of which were sensational. Brooks Atkinson of *The New York Times* wrote that my Eileen was "absolutely perfect" and that Roz "should run for president." Since this party was also my introduction to New York theater and café society, George Abbott acted as my "elbow man," whispering to me who all the famous people were: Judy Holliday, Katharine Cornell, Margaret Sullavan, Joseph Cotten, Henry Fonda, Hermione Gingold, Deborah Kerr, and Geraldine Page.

I was in absolute heaven, but Ernie was not amused. He seemed out of his element here, and he knew it. Chodorov and Fields used to say, when they saw us together in Sardi's, that Ernie looked like a garment center salesman. He was in his black Beau Brummel period and wore a Mississippi gambler string tie and, as usual, his handkerchief up the sleeve. Mike Marmor, a writer on our show in 1956, said that Ernie was the only one who could wear black and be loud.

My doing theater was a big, big threat to Ernie and nothing like his style of show business, where he had complete creative control. He found some of the commercial Broadway hits of the day "pretentious, time-wasting, and silly." With me, he didn't have to worry about another guy; the theater was his biggest rival. I was suddenly very happy in another world of which he was not a part.

Ernie was further removed from my evening life by having to move to the suburbs. Judge Belloff reminded Ernie that he could not leave his daughters with Mary, either at Rittenhouse Square or in Trenton; they should be with him in New York. He had been staying in free (for on-air plugs) hotel suites, first at the Hotel Edison, later at the posh Savoy Plaza on Fifth Avenue. Judge Belloff, who kept checking on us out of concern, suggested a more normal life in the near suburbs rather than in the city itself. Ernie picked Englewood because he knew the way there and the shops, at least the liquor store and the pet shop. He rented a house in Englewood and hired a live-in housekeeper. Now Ernie was where he didn't want to be and was not able to see me after the theater every night.

Ernie was particularly annoyed about George Abbott's taking me out to teach me to ballroom dance after the show some evenings. Abbott was a wonderful dancer, who specialized in Latin American rhythms, such as the mambo and samba. He taught me how to follow—not to put my weight with my right hand on his left hand, but to put my full weight on his right shoulder with my left hand. That way we danced as one body, and he could lead me any way he wanted to without my needing to know what was coming next. In one half hour I was an instant follower. Later George Burns told me that I was one of the best followers he'd ever danced with.

Ernie never danced unless he'd had a few drinks, and then only rarely. On those rare occasions he did only the Charleston, no matter what the band was playing. Waltz, fox-trot, twist, Ernie did the Charleston. Once he got on a dancing kick, he would stay on the floor for four or five dances in a row. I wasn't allowed to sit down once during a marathon of Charlestons. If the orchestra played a waltz, I would try to get him to dance it correctly, telling him I'd squeeze his shoulder when he was supposed to move. This would work for four bars, but then, sure enough, Ernie would go right back into the Charleston. It was the same routine no matter what music was playing.

If a woman asked him to dance, Ernie would get very embarrassed and say, "I'm sorry. I can't dance." She'd assume he was joking, and he'd have to plead that he really couldn't dance. Once he did actually go out on the floor and proved it by falling on his fanny. Nobody was there to squeeze his shoulder. It wasn't only that Ernie couldn't dance; he really didn't want to learn. At least if he danced with me, we could always somehow fake a big ending. It wasn't something he did for relaxation; when he danced, it was clearly for show.

I loved playing Eileen in *Wonderful Town* and the excitement of being Broadway's newest "ingenue." In two years of eight shows a week, I never got tired of singing those wonderful Bernstein songs, especially "A Little Bit in Love" and "It's Love." When you do the same show, night after night, after about three months it becomes difficult to concentrate onstage and not let your mind wander. George Abbott, looking in on the show six months later, said I was "the only one who has kept her performance consistent." Everyone else was bigger or tired, but Miss Perfect scored again.

There was one song I was happy not to be singing, "Let It Come Down," which we cut on the road. This was a sophisticated, throbby dirge that sweet Eileen was supposed to sing in Speedy Valenti's dive. If she could hold that paying job, the sisters could stay in their Greenwich Village neighborhood and not have to go back to Ohio. Even as a newcomer

I realized that this bluesy minor-key number wasn't going to work seven minutes from the end of the show. We cut it in Boston. Lenny pulled an old song out of his trunk, and Roz and I closed the show with another duet, the upbeat "Wrong Note Rag." For this one she didn't need the opening note.

Winning two Donaldson Awards for my work in *Wonderful Town* helped me forget that I was making a mere $175 a week, whereas on television I had been earning $1,500. I had always wanted to be in the theater, and finally I had a chance to use my "legit" soprano voice. By now I was calling Mr. Bernstein Lenny and he was so impressed with my conservatory-trained voice that he added a florid coloratura obbligato for me in the "Conversation Piece" number. This was a scene where Chris Alexander as the drugstore owner, George Gaynes as the newspaper editor, and assorted other mismatched characters tried to find common ground for discussion. I also met some new friends: Richard Rodgers's daughter, Mary, and Stephen Sondheim, before *West Side Story*. In those days Steve was very young and looked even younger. Hal Prince, Steve, and I would go off to Connecticut for the weekend to visit Mary. Ernie never came with us; he didn't want to have anything to do with my liaison with young theater folk.

He did, however, like the amiable veteran stage manager Bobby Griffith. One summer weekend Ernie and I went out to Bobby's house on the water in Connecticut. I decided to swim back to the house from a long walk on the peninsula with Ernie. He reluctantly agreed and soon lagged far behind, doing a kind of adult doggy paddle. He wasn't a strong swimmer, a fact I hadn't known before. Having grown up swimming, I assumed everyone else had, too. I ended up using my Red Cross lifesaving training, cross-chest carrying Ernie back to shore.

The first thing I did when *Wonderful Town* was assured of being a hit was to buy an MG-TD convertible, black with red wheels and red leather upholstery. I paid for it on time, throughout our long run, but Ernie later, for California, had the chrome all gold-plated—windshield, mirrors, bumpers, grille, taillights, everything. I loved that car so much that when we moved to California, it was shipped in a Bekins moving truck; I wouldn't let anyone drive my little pet across the country. It was to remain my eastern pride and joy in the neon world of California, gold chrome and all.

With my new steady job I rented a posh apartment at 60 Sutton Place South. Ernie played tennis regularly with Mike Wallace on Rip's Tennis Court down below and would shout up at me when he won. I was living it up in New York, while he was in Englewood with the kids and the housekeeper. He was not thrilled with this arrangement since he had to get up early and do his TV show, *Kovacs Unlimited*. In *TV Guide* I was a "chirper," and he was "zany, wacky, unpredictable Ernie."

From January to March 1953 Ernie's show aired at 8:00 P.M. on CBS Tuesday nights, opposite Milton Berle. Since I was working in *Wonderful Town*, I couldn't be on it. Like Bishop Sheen and everybody else who'd been up against Berle, Ernie fell by the wayside.

As a "chirper," I took on a hot new agent, Barron Polan, who booked all the female singers in the hotel cabarets, such as the Persian Room at the Plaza. My agent for television was apple-cheeked Marty Kummer, one of the new young lights at MCA. George Abbott and my other new theater mentors warned me not to return to television because current conventional wisdom had it that if you were on television daily, no one would pay the astronomical top ticket price of $5.80 to see you in the theater. The *Wonderful Town* salary of $175 a week wasn't going too far, considering my new life-style. I needed to make more money. Besides, I was never one to listen to conventional wisdom. Finally, I was allowed to do an *Ed Sullivan Show* one Sunday night. The next morning the lines for *Wonderful Town* were around the block, even longer than opening night. After that nobody in the theater troupe objected to my going back to television. In fact, they encouraged me.

We were an unqualified hit, the toast of the town, the hottest we could be. Despite my double duty on TV and stage, I never missed a performance. Florence Fosberg, my understudy, had been a classmate of mine at Juilliard. She was a beautiful, petite natural blonde with a fine well-trained voice and a pleasant upbeat but shy personality. I would often jokingly apologize to her that she'd never get to play my part. Little did I know how prophetic that was.

From the opening night on, one young man, a fan, waited for me outside every night, just to say a few words or walk me to the car. He was there so regularly that everyone knew him and greeted him nightly. On snowy nights, Al, the usually tough doorman, even let him wait inside the stage door—unheard of for Al. One night Florence went out with him after the show. The next day, Hal Prince called me at my music lesson, to tell me that Florence had gone out with him and was found stabbed to death in a nearby hotel. The man confessed. I always felt he was after me, only settling for my understudy because I was always with Ernie. Ever since that time I've been a bit wary of overly attentive fans.

On June 1, 1953, I got a $250 raise in *Wonderful Town*, to $425 a week. On the next New Year's Day I was to go to $525. Once the green light was on, and since I needed the money, in 1953 I somehow found the time to do television shows: telethons, *The Arthur Murray Party*, Eddie Fisher's live show twice, and Sherman Billingsley's *Stork Club*. In the midst of all this, I took jazz movement classes with the ballet-trained dancers from our show, taught by Peter Gennaro, who told me, "Edie, you don't need to loosen up; you need to go somewhere and tighten up."

I finally did go back to do *Kovacs Unlimited*, which was now on from 8:00 to 9:00 A.M. Monday through Friday. I had to get up early and be perky for the show. I couldn't face eating anything, so I devised a then health food energy drink. I'd mix blackstrap molasses, wheat germ, and a raw egg and have it with some black coffee. It got me through until about 11:00 A.M. After we did the show, I would rehearse the next day's show, we'd go out to breakfast, lunch, or brunch, I'd sleep for four hours, then get up and go to the theater. No wonder I was taking vitamin shots, which seemed to be the in thing that year (although my mother was photographed giving me a glass of milk). Roz was getting them, and so was I, although the B_{12} left a terrible taste in my mouth for a few hours.

One weekend in 1953, when Ernie had turned Betty and Kippie over to their mother from his house in Englewood for her scheduled weekend visitation, she disappeared with the kids. All that we guessed was that she had returned to her native Florida. Ernie was crushed because the girls had warned him this might happen and he had ignored them. Now, almost every weekend for months, Ernie, accompanied by his father and a series of private detectives, went anyplace there was a lead, including Texas and Illinois. Sometimes he'd be off the air during the week and we'd be on alone. We didn't tell the audience why Ernie was gone until August, when he decided to go public about his missing daughters.

Ernie sold his Trenton house and bought a three-acre place at 211 South Mountain Road, in New City, Rockland County, New York. The country house had been an 1850's post office. With his daughters gone, he gave up his rented house in Englewood for this one even farther out. He slept in his offices at the Savoy Plaza, in exchange for a plug on the air.

Mary, of course, moved into New City, this time legally since the girls weren't there. Every time his mother had visited Ernie at the hotel, she arrived for an overnight stay with eight empty suitcases and left the next morning with them so heavy that it took two bellmen and a rolling cart to get them in her car. She had to have spent the night raiding room service tables and housekeeping stations on each floor to have amassed the volume she did. I don't know where she stashed it in the meantime, but it all ended up in the New City house, which was bedded, tableclothed, toweled, silvered, and dished from the Hotel Edison. Even despite her efforts to camouflage her linens by dying them dark blue, the bright green Hotel Edison lettering always shone through.

In November I went on *The Jack Paar Show*, on Friday mornings from 10:00 to 10:30A.M. on CBS. Burt Shevelove was the stage manager, José Melis the music man, Larry Marx the writer, and Richard Hayes the male singer. Jack Paar was the most naive but honest man I ever met. Burt Shevelove and I at first thought that it couldn't be true, that Jack was acting. But Paar truly did discover things on the air, and when he cried, he really was crying. When he said he was going to walk off, he walked off the set. He was every mother's problem child, and mothers loved him like a son. He was at his funniest when something was wrong and he was angry, the pants came back from the cleaners too short. If everything was going smoothly, Jack was dull. So Peter Birch, the director, Burt, and I would devise things to make Paar angry, such as conspiring with the crew to drop something and make a loud noise. Then we'd have a brilliant show. We'd suggest odd pairings in the A.M., like Elsa Maxwell and Hermione Gingold, smoking a cigar.

Burt Shevelove became my lifelong friend. He not only knew the oddball early Rodgers and Hart, Cole Porter, and Gershwin verses and lyrics but also knew dirty lyrics to standard tunes. For instance, he got to wondering what would it would sound like if Larry Hart had written "Always" instead of Irving Berlin: "I'll be loving you, always, in a room of blue . . . or hallways." Paar thought Shevelove was really strange because he wore a jacket with a red silk lining and red socks. When Jack went on vacation I'd sing some far-out numbers, such as Leonard Bernstein's "I Hate Music." When we did that one, we thought that Jack was outside the program's viewing area; but he wasn't, and he called us, screaming, "What is that crazy song?" I also sang "Letter to Freddy," by Gertrude Stein and Paul Bowles. That one baffled him completely. The audience, however, wrote in to encourage us to do more of these songs that were different. The early owners of TV sets were the best audience, naturally curious, and the networks were already talking down to them. I've always tried never to talk down to an audience.

In those days you hadn't arrived until you owned a mink coat. With my increased earnings I bought my first mink, a good used one, at Maximilian's. Gunther told me which salesman to see for it. I was photographed wearing it in Town and Country with Alfred Vanderbilt. My parents suddenly thought that show business might be all right after all. All the Seventh Avenue fashion houses wanted me to wear their things on television, so I could get to try everything on for the show and, if I liked it, buy it wholesale.

For my Christmas present that year Ernie bought me a beautiful big black alligator purse from Mark Cross on Fifth Avenue. It must have cost $350. I loved it and carried it with me to the theater every night. Roz would say, "Oh, that bag. I just love that bag. You're wearing my bag again." So for

Roz's birthday I saved up and bought her the identical alligator bag.

Whenever she went on Ed Sullivan's television show, she asked me what to wear and was very impressed with my knowledge of lights, colors, and backgrounds. I even told her which light man to ask for at CBS. I've always been in a medium where I was responsible for myself. In opera you move your own chairs; in TV I was responsible for props, costumes, etc. The least of my work was the singing itself. Later, when I made movies, I found that all there was for me to do was lean on a slant board while everybody did everything for me. (In sketches I do a "wet nails lady," who can't pick up anything for herself because her fingers are extended, Sid Caesar's favorite character.) In nightclubs I could sew the curtain, write the music, and make the dress—but I could never go on without a hairdresser.

Before my audition for *Wonderful Town*, I'd had light brownish auburn hair, helped along with lemon juice and camomile tea. On the WCBS morning show in New York, *Kovacs Unlimited*, I played Cloudy Faire, YOUR Weather Girl, with a black wig. My Dietrich had a long ash blond fall sewed into the hat. "Shirley Temple" had her own sausage-curled wig. Since I was creating more characters, I was using more elaborate real-hair wigs, not just fright wigs from the prop box. My Marilyn Monroe wig was white blond and combed exactly like hers; I would put that on, and since I had full access to Seventh Avenue fashion houses, I could wear the same clothes that Ceil Chapman had sold to Marilyn. If she had something in white, I'd take it in pale blue. I'd wear it with a push-up bra, stuffed and low-cut; it was so obvious I thought it was the funniest outfit I'd ever worn. I called it my "clown suit." Now I was doing Marilyn singing a real song, instead of Schubert's serenade "Leise Flehen."

Everybody loved it and asked me why I didn't do my hair the same color as Marilyn's. For *Wonderful Town*, with Roz being dark, the producers said, "You really should lighten your hair." A hair colorist at Elizabeth Arden turned me into a "green blonde," the latest thing for 1952, not so obvious as platinum; the green was supposed to get the red out. There was lots of red in my hair, so I needed a lot of green. I hated it; it came out a drab gray blond. I was already in my drab stage makeup, wearing gray and light tan dresses for my big scenes. I felt that Eileen should be wearing pink and blue. Betty Comden asked me one day, "Where are the Eileen colors? These are not Eileen." But I had nothing to say about my costuming. Of my finale dress, gray satin, with darker gray ruffled sleeves, she said, "With those dead cabbages on your sleeve, birds could nest in there, and it looks like they already have." For her finale dress, Roz had talked the producers out of her true-to-the-period Mainbocher to wear her best Don Loper, a dazzling white beaded number on nude souffle, definitely not of the period but a showstopper nevertheless.

When Jerome Robbins, our unbilled show doctor called in on the road, saw my newly drab green-blond hair, he suggested that I cut bangs. I resisted, because it reminded me of my father's stepmother, the hated Aunt Mae. I did it, and he was right. I have them still. Robbins was the final authority on how everybody moved and looked. Even George Abbott said, "Jerry knows more about those things than I do." Yet another person was added to our creative cast of directors, choreographers, and authors.

When Rosalind left the show and Carol Channing was to come in as Ruth in a red wig, the producers decided that I should undergo yet another hair color change. "With that blond hair they'll think you're Channing." I didn't understand that because she'd be in a red wig, but they insisted that I go to their hairdresser, at Helena Rubinstein, who didn't know that my hair had already been double processed to make it that awful green.

She was another Hungarian and told me she was going to darken my hair and give me "streaks blond, dahling." She put the dark color on my already processed hair, and it came out bright auburn. I got a serious scalp burn with blisters the size of plums. So that night, when I made my usual entrance first, everybody thought I *was* Carol Channing and applauded wildly. When Carol, who was sporting the new bright auburn wig she felt she needed for the Ruth character, came on after me, to no applause, she asked, "What happened?" From then on I went back to my own hairdresser at Elizabeth Arden and slowly returned to being a "regular" blonde.

The only good thing that came out of the whole hair mess was that I got to perfect my Zsa Zsa Gabor accent, which is different from Ernie's father's dark peasant accent. His sounded more like a Russian accent, while hers is flavored with French. Carol and I were equally nearsighted; she wore only one contact lens, I don't know why. When we came down the stairs for the big "Wrong Note Rag" finale, we held on to each other tightly. It wasn't acting; neither one of us could see. We were two fast-moving bodies relying on her one contact lens. We became good friends. In talking to Carol, I found out that she'd had the same kind of mother I did. They even met once backstage.

Hal Prince and Bobby Griffith had optioned Richard Bissell's book *7½ Cents* for a musical. They were trying to raise money for the show, *The Pajama Game*, the first that Hal would produce. I invested five hundred dollars, which was all I could afford, but allowed Hal and Bobby to hold backers' auditions in my Sutton Place apartment. Since I couldn't be in the show, I became part of the creative team putting together this new musical, even including casting, something I loved doing. It was at those auditions that I first met Shirley MacLaine, Charlotte Rae, and Jean Stapleton, who first created the Edith Bunker–style character for *The Pajama Game*. I loved watching the minute details of a piece being put together; it was the sort of thing I'd done all my TV life. It was like the tiny building blocks in sewing, acting, singing, or writing. Again, you can't do the intricate handwork unless you have the whole piece in your mind.

Hal and I went to Harold Clurman's theater class after the Monday night performances of *Wonderful Town*. Even though Hal was producing at that early age, he told me he was only interested in directing, the same as George Abbott before him. Hal hired George, as I was now allowed to call him, to direct *The Pajama Game*. I happened to see the matinee performance of *The Pajama Game* shortly before which Carol Haney broke her ankle and Shirley MacLaine, her understudy, went on and won a movie contract with Hal Wallis.

Shirley arrived late, didn't even have time to warm up, but did brilliantly. Since she and Steve Parker, a producer and later her husband, had already been on our show, I knew her pretty well before this big moment.

On April 16, my birthday, Ernie's fresh new network, WABD Dumont, debuted his show from 11:15 P.M. to 12:15 A.M. daily. This was just after my 11:10 curtain in *Wonderful Town*. I'd take off my awful gray finale drag with the cabbage sleeves, get in a robe, grab the dress I was to wear on TV, and leave the theater before the audience came backstage. I changed in the taxi and arrived at the studio, sparkling with klieg lights, to find a live camera waiting to escort me from the cab, down the hall to the studio, where the show was already in progress. I sang two songs a night, live, did monologues and skits and my imitations, and found some new characters to play—business as usual.

One night Ernie and I met the French star Lilo, of *Can-Can*, another musical running on Broadway, and her husband, Guy de la Passardière. The next night Guy, who really was a marquis, sent his uniformed chauffeur to my dressing room with a big bouquet of red roses and monsieur's card. Standing five feet behind was the man himself. I knew that Guy had just recently married Lilo, and obviously, since I was wearing his ring, Ernie and I were a couple. It took me a long time to explain to this hand-kissing Frenchman that things didn't go that way in this country. We all soon became good friends.

Ernie created the Nairobi Trio in 1953 by listening to a record that Peter Hanley had brought to him. We were always bringing in records that might inspire Ernie. He was now staying at the Savoy Plaza during the week. Peter, Ernie, and I sat in the suite's living room, listening to the record. Ernie didn't say a word throughout, but the minute it was over he ordered me to sit at the piano and Pete to stand opposite while he sat on a nearby chair to conduct. As Ernie began to wave his hands, I piped up in my best "Choral Conducting 101" voice, "You're not conducting on the downbeat; for the downbeat your hand conducts straight down in front of you in the center, the second beat is on the left, the third beat is on the—"

131

"Oh, shut up," he snapped. "It's humor, not concert."

The three of us went through it three more times, but Ernie still wasn't satisfied.

Of course, Pete and I had no idea what was going on; we were just following Ernie's counting. He asked me just to look at him at the end of a phrase, as if it were a love scene between the conductor and the pianist. As he turned away from Pete to look back at me, it gave Pete a chance to hit him with the breakaway vase. We couldn't see Ernie's take to the camera with the ape mask on, so we never did know what was so funny until we were shown a kinescope months later. Pete and I did the counts exactly as Ernie told us. The idea evolved as Ernie played with it. He had envisioned it on first hearing the music and put it completely together in no more than a half hour.

When the Nairobi Trio debuted on the air, the crew fell down laughing. It is still hard to describe the piece: three people wearing ape suits, one playing the piano and one conducting, all moving like mechanical windup monkey dolls. Kovacs fans who hadn't seen it kept asking for it because they couldn't understand where the humor came from. It was all in the timing; if we missed the counts by even a fraction, the piece was ruined, the illusion destroyed. As usual, Ernie never explained the humor of the Nairobi Trio; perhaps he was saying that we're all wired windup apes going through our paces. (It later was to include Jack Lemmon, Frank Sinatra, and Milton Berle, at different times.)

During this same period that Ernie lived at the Savoy Plaza and created the Nairobi Trio he had a tiny live monkey that guested on our show. It was a pygmy marmoset, about as big as a fist, furnished by animal talent scout Lorraine D'Essen. The marmoset had the sweetest disposition. We just had to have him. We bought him from Lorraine, and Ernie named him Howard. He went everywhere with us. Coming from a tropical climate, Howard was fine indoors in the winter; in the 1950's apartments, hotels, and office buildings in New York were always overheated.

Outdoors in the winter Howard traveled in Ernie's inside jacket breast pocket. The only climatic problem Howard encountered was air conditioning in the summer; he couldn't stand the cold. At the hotel we usually left the radio hi-fi console on so that Howard could snooze comfortably curled around the tubes. We took Howard with us for a weekend at East Hampton, with Lilo and Guy de la Passardière. The Dune Deck Hotel didn't have air conditioning, but it also didn't have a hi-fi, so again Howard went everywhere with us. He liked the beach because the sand was his perfect tropical temperature. Howard didn't like restaurants that had air conditioning, so we tried to find ones that had outdoor dining areas. One night, as we were eating at a fancy French restaurant outdoors, Howard woke up and decided to stretch out of Ernie's jacket breast pocket. The captain was looking right at him, so I told Ernie to make Howard stay in the pocket. He protested, "But he wants to come out."

The next thing we knew Howard was out but still under the coat because the evening was chilly. With one eye Howard peeked out from behind Ernie's gray-and-white-striped tie. Talk about protective coloring, Howard had two white stripes up his tiny gray forehead. No one but I could see him yet. Ernie was seated with his back to a rather stodgy-looking elderly couple. I could see them over his shoulder, but he couldn't without turning around. Howard began to crawl under Ernie's arm and up his back to the right shoulder, all inside the jacket. Ernie slouched so that the coat would hang loose to give Howard breathing space and warmth during his exercise run. I noticed the woman at the table behind Ernie poke her husband and roll her eyes toward Ernie's back. Every time the husband looked over Howard stopped moving, so the man kept telling his wife just to eat her dinner. She kept insisting that the lump was moving. When he looked up again, it was gone, and the next time it showed up on Ernie's other shoulder.

During all this Ernie sat nonchalantly talking to me, looking quite casual. Now he was saying, "Don't crack, not even a smile. What's she doing now?" I reported on the woman's every move and her husband's every reaction. I continued to play it cool while Ernie somehow coaxed Howard down his jacket sleeve and into his hand. The waiter arrived at the old couple's table with their main course at the precise moment they got up to ask for their check and leave. Howard continued pulling on Ernie's tie until he got bored and crawled back into Ernie's breast pocket to sleep.

Howard died later that summer of 1952 at the Savoy Plaza of a chill. One of the hotel's maids had turned the hi-fi off in our absence. Howard left a lasting legacy, however; he had given Ernie some kind of skin condition, causing his eyebrows to fall out. They never did grow back quite right, but Ernie forgave Howard.

We even added an animal act to our show, a talking dog and deer act, the former live, the latter stuffed. A Boston terrier, my long-awaited replacement for Queenie, who had died in my arms when I was in high school, was carefully named Zoomar, after the close-up television camera lens. We had Zoomar in heavy discussions with a stuffed deer, Trevor. Ernie put peanut butter on the roof of Zoomar's mouth, so that when the dog licked it, his mouth moved like Mr. Ed's, giving out bon mots for the day, while on Trevor the crew had rigged a lower jaw and a spring, so it could move, too. He also gave out advice. Ernie rubbed hamburger on the deer's nose so that Zoomar would lick it. The deer would talk to the dog; then Zoomar would kiss Trevor on the nose.

One day, however, someone had newly sprayed the stuffed deer with a fireproofing solution. Zoomar got deathly ill after his ritual licking and was rushed to the veterinarian. Zoomar, retired from show business, moved in with my parents, Queenie's old digs, and lived to a ripe old age. The name Zoomar lived on, apart from the camera. Recently, when I was made a "TV Legend" at the opening of Disney World MGM theme park in Florida, I put my hand prints in cement and wrote the name Zoomar. As the Disney people were entering it in their guidebooks, they carefully noted that Zoomar was a camera lens that zoomed in for tight close-ups in the Golden Age of Television.

At the end of the year I decided it was time for me to go on a Christmas vacation. I made plans to go to Havana, where I'd never been, with Kay Holley, my vocal coach. Ernie would not be going with me because he had his nightly show to do. He wasn't too pleased that I was going to the land of the cigars without him, but I took his order. Kay and I went out every night and learned to dance the cha-cha, which hadn't yet hit the States. Ernie, who called me every night, wasn't too sure about the cha-cha; he thought it might be something more seductive than a dance.

SEVEN

VIRTUALLY ALL THE FIGHTS that Ernie and I had our first three years together centered on his wanting to get married and my not wanting to. I was an award-winning actress on Broadway, with a theater career apart from Ernie's. I was finally away from my parents, had my own apartment on Sutton Place and my own set of friends. I wanted to keep working. This had never been a problem with any other man; I'd simply gone out with men to have a good time and absorb all I could, and I told them all so. With Ernie it was different. While I had become completely my own person for the first time, I simply couldn't imagine my life without him. He'd added the one thing I'd never known: the joy of absolute, silly, spontaneous fun.

Ernie was equally smitten and didn't mind showing it. Although he was threatened by my theater career (it might take me away from him), he showed up at my dressing-room door every weekend of *Wonderful Town*, like some stage-door Johnny. Especially during this period of searching for his kidnapped daughters, I provided Ernie's only haven. I was the one person he could have fun with and be completely himself. I loved his spontaneous picnics, rides out into the country, and, most of all, going with him to Forty-second Street movie house second balconies, eating popcorn and laughing at terrible el cheapo space pictures that we later satirized on television.

I'd never sat in the second balcony of a movie theater before, much less gone to a drive-in. That was considered crass where I grew up. He drove me out to New Jersey, to my first drive-in. Even though he was sad without his children, he was teaching me how to have fun. It didn't have to be expensive fun, although we also went to the best restaurants. We drove out to the Grist Mill in Connecticut; on the way back we pulled into a cornfield and made love. I'd certainly never done anything like that before. He taught me how to laugh while making love. I'd come out of the john to see a sign painted on a paper bag with a cue-card pen that one of us always had with us. This was the first of the treasure hunt clues he would have around the room. At each clue there would be a treasure with an appropriately filthy saying. It ended up with clues painted on his body in mercurochrome. One said, "Faster, faster, or the bow won't stand up." Yet, wherever we went out of town, in those days, we always booked two rooms, using only one. My parents might call.

These times with Ernie were the best times I have ever had, before or since. Even the fights were funny. I'd say, "If you want a doormat, buy one!" He could always get me on the phone by using a different voice. Anytime I took anything seriously, he'd find great humor. We'd be in the middle of a fight, and he'd say, "Hey, baby, you've got great legs." I not only accepted him for what he was, but loved him deeply for it. I could be both as strong-willed and as silly as he was. For the first time in his life Ernie had found a woman he could trust—and have fun with—and I met a man I loved deeply.

There seemed to be so many reasons why I shouldn't marry. I sensed what might be coming with the package. I asked myself how I could possibly give Ernie, his children, and my career all that I should give each—100 percent of my time. While I always thrived on doing six jobs at once and thought I could do anything, this time I wasn't sure that there was enough of me to go around. For three solid years I told Ernie that I did not ever intend to be a hausfrau. I didn't want any part of domestic life but Ernie. And the last room I wanted to be in was the kitchen. (After five years of marriage he gave

me a gold pin in the shape of a faucet, with a teardrop diamond, a drop of water, coming out of the faucet; it was inscribed "Cinque years," meaning "five years" in Italian.
Another piece of jewelry, a charm for my bracelet, was in the
shape of a kitchen sink. The joke about them was that I'd be
able to recognize a kitchen sink just in case I ever saw one.)

Although we saw each other morning, noon, and night, I
tried to keep running from him. That was impossible. He was
as stubborn and determined as I. I was not prepared to cope
with those two unsettled children, who would obviously
need my total emotional support when they came back. Even
then I suspected that being a stepmother would be my least
appreciated role. There is no way you can anticipate the trouble that comes from trying to understudy a child's natural
parent. It simply does not work. At birth, sides are taken that
cannot be reversed, no matter how hard one tries.

Ernie's own moods understandably were up and down,
laughing one day, crying the next, then laughing through his
tears, predictably Hungarian. Not only was he, like all charming Hungarian men, not afraid to cry, but it was his God-given
right to cry. I also knew that dealing with Ernie's mother,
who was not going to disappear, court order or not, would
be a full package. I wasn't sure that I had the time or the
strength to deal with her, although I never quite said that to
him. Besides, I was still going to be a big star.

So I kept telling him, "I can't marry you or anyone else."
He carried on about it on the telephone, and I'd hang up.
Then I'd take the phone off the hook, and he'd come pound
on my door, yelling and screaming and carrying on. To shut
him up, I'd let him in; we'd make up and be right back where
we started. Whatever we seemed to be fighting about, the
bottom line was that I wouldn't marry him. Unfortunately
our fights on the subject weren't just between Ernie and me;
my parents were so unhappy about it that somehow their
attitudes got into columns, such as Dorothy Kilgallen's.

My mother and father would have been delighted by my
marriage—to almost anyone but Ernie Kovacs. He was brash,
offbeat, divorced and had these two children to raise. He was
also a Catholic and in his own way devout. Ernie prayed
daily. He knelt on the floor by his bed, not only at night when

he went to sleep but even when he was just lying down for a quick nap. He always prayed for his family, especially now to find his kids, and always crossed himself. I never asked him about his praying or his prayers; I felt it was too personal. You don't ask the person blowing out the candles on his birthday cake what he wished for.

Near the end of my contract, in the summer, things at *Wonderful Town* weren't going so well. In playing the part of Ruth, Carol Channing began to read Ruth's lines in her own inimitable style. The no-nonsense Ruth's orders to her younger sister now sounded as if they were coming from a wide-eyed Eileen. For dramatic contrast, the only thing for me to do now was to bark at Ruth, like a sergeant. It was clearly time for me to leave the show.

Despite my best intentions, Ernie persisted in pressing for marriage. The way he finally won me was carefully calculated. I had talked myself silly and said, "That is it, absolutely, finally, no, no way." After my closing, I planned on going alone to Europe on the *Liberté* to forget him. The day in July I sailed, my mother and father were to meet me on board to see me off. They went to my assigned cabin, with Ernie carefully pointing the way. He knew, and they didn't, that I was in an upgraded luxury stateroom on another deck. (Guy de la Passadière had interceded on my behalf.) They waited in the wrong cabin almost until the boat sailed. I never did see them before I left, and they were furious. All their worst fears had been realized. Ernie was everything they feared I wanted, and they were right.

When I got to my stateroom, there he was, with a horseshoe of flowers big enough for a derby winner, a bucket of Dom Pérignon, and a pound of pale gray beluga caviar, the best. I don't ever remember Ernie without a pound of caviar and two spoons on a special occasion. He was standing there smiling, as if nothing had happened, although the night before we had parted "forever." "Have a wonderful time," he said, "if you go to the flea market in Paris, pick me up some dueling pistols and armor of any kind." As I was writing it down, he was kissing me. Damn it, he'd done it again. I was back where I had been before our last-ever dramatic finale.

Sing a Pretty Song . . .

I have never been seasick before or since, but that time the ship wasn't past the Statue of Liberty when it hit me, with that awful buzzing, then the pulling behind the ears and queasy wrenching in the stomach. Farther out, as the boat pitched and rolled, the only place I had any relief was in the ship's pool because in there the water is doing the same thing as the seawater outside, so you have no balance problems. The few times I tried to make it to my table during the first three days, I had puckered hands and feet. Once recovered, I found that Guy had thought of everything. I sat at the captain's table nearly every night. Part of his deal with the *Liberté* was that I'd be visible to the ship's passengers. At the passenger show, I sang selections from *Wonderful Town* with the ship's orchestra.

Ernie called me nightly on the ship's phone and sent very funny long telegrams. During my first stay in Paris I certainly did go first class, again with Guy's connections. I stayed at the Plaza Athénée and went to all the best restaurants. I went sightseeing, and Guy even got me into a rare press showing of the Dior collection. I was given a card and a pencil to mark which styles I liked best. Instead, I carefully sketched in minuscule detail everything that went by. Two guards came to eject me, lifting me out of my chair by my arms when the head vendeuse came to my rescue, loudly whispering, "Non, non, actrice, actrice, américaine, américaine. C'est bien." Little did she know that I really was sketching, not for the American market but for me personally to whip up when I got home.

I was supposed to have been gone for a month, but after about ten days of lavishly being entertained by Guy's high-falutin' Paris friends, at the Opéra, Maxim's, and the Folies Bergère, I went to the flea market to find Ernie's pistols. I found a perfectly matched pair of eighteenth-century French dueling pistols in mint condition in an inscribed wooden box lined in maroon velvet. They were very expensive, but I had to have them; they were exactly what Ernie would want. I bought them for him but used up most of my money. I could have stayed on for the next weeks until the ship returned to New York because the hotel was paid and Guy's friends would entertain me. But the more I looked at those dueling pistols, the more I missed Ernie. I called him, told him exactly how I felt, and he said, "Fly home tomorrow."

I said, "I can't, I don't have enough money to fly. I have to wait for two weeks to use my return boat ticket."

Ernie said, "Pack, I'm wiring the money in five minutes."

He did, and the next night we had a tearful candlelight dinner together in New York. He said, "This is it; we've got to stop fooling around and do it now. You missed me, and I missed you. Let's go to Maryland and get married tonight."

That was too much for me, so I said, "Let's wait until after I do *Wonderful Town* in Dallas. We've got two weeks together here, to get our blood tests and whatever papers we need, before I have to leave."

Now he got caught up with the idea. "Isn't Texas near Mexico? Let's get married in Mexico." Neither one of us had been there, but we agreed that it would be exotic and special. It was to be a secret wedding; not even our parents would know.

I went to my doctor immediately, to get my blood test; Ernie forgot about his until the last minute before he had to leave. As he was riding in an elevator in the Squibb Building, picking up his plane tickets, he saw a sign for an M.D. and then remembered he hadn't gotten a blood test. Unannounced, he burst into the doctor's office and told the nurse he had to see the doctor right away because he was going to get married. She said, "Do you have an appointment?"

He said, "No, but I have to see the doctor right away because I'm leaving this evening. Do you understand, I have to see him right now. Get him out here."

She buzzed the doctor and said, "There's someone out here I think you should see."

Ernie went in, and the doctor said, "Sit down, calm down, everything will be fine. What's the problem? Just sit down and relax."

Ernie said, "I can't, I'm getting married. I'm leaving tonight."

"Is this a snap decision, or have you thought about it?"

Ernie replied, "No, I've been thinking about it for a long time. I need help right now."

Doctor: "How do you feel about women? Have you known this girl very long? Have you dreamed about this? Do you like girls?"

Ernie, who had been stuttering, "Yes, no, yes," was frustrated, until he finally looked up at the medical diploma on the wall. The doctor he was talking to was a psychiatrist. He got the blood test on another floor.

Imogene Coca and I had a wonderful time in Dallas, doing the show for two weeks at the Texas State Fair, beginning on August 23, 1954. At one performance Imogene dropped half a word. As Ruth she was supposed to come into the jail and say, "Well, it's cocktail time, already." This time she came in and said, "well, it's cock time, already." The audience started a rumble that became a roar, one of the biggest laughs I've ever heard in the theater. She is such a sweet lady; that is not her idea of humor. Although she'd been in the theater since childhood, she was blushing red on that one.

Neiman-Marcus gave its fashion award to a newcomer named James Galanos, for his first collection, while we were in Dallas. I got to meet him at the dinner and presentation and bought several of his designs for my trousseau. They were exquisite and so timeless that they are still in my fashion collection today. As I look at the fall previews in 1989, I could wear them tomorrow, like Mainbochers and Balenciagas.

I bought my wedding dress, a subdued Hattie Carnegie slate blue cocktail dress (Ernie had been married before, and I could not lie and wear virginal white), at a Neiman-Marcus fashion show. As soon as the show closed, I flew to Mexico City and waited for Ernie.

About a week before the wedding I had written a letter to Ernie describing my "tremendous anticipation, nervousness, happiness, desire to cry when I think of you. . . . I find myself doing foolish things, like trying on the wedding ring just to see how it will look to be a married woman. I guess it's the thing of no longer being an individual but two people as one. That gives you a sort of glow. . . . We've had quite a few rough spots and not only survived but love each other more for them somehow. . . . This all suddenly seems so right. . . . We both have moods, I know yours and you know mine. . . . What we don't know we have a lifetime to find out. . . . This is the first time I've felt peaceful and contented since I can remember. . . . I don't know how I can stand it until next week to see you and become Mrs. Kovacs. . . . Without you there isn't anything in the world." After Ernie's death I found this letter among a stack of others from me he had kept behind the socks in his dresser drawer.

Back on the East Coast, Hurricane Edna forced the cancellation of all flights, so Ernie was delayed for several days. I began to wonder if maybe somebody up there was trying to tell me something. Although I had never met him before, I found William O'Dwyer, the former mayor of New York and now ambassador to Mexico, to be very pleasant and charming company. He squired me to all the best places in Mexico City. The columnist Earl Wilson, who also knew everybody in Mexico City, had called O'Dwyer to say I was coming down and to take care of me. Thus I spent most of what was to have been my honeymoon with Bill O'Dwyer, in restaurants all over town. Bill and I became fast friends; he took an avuncular interest in me, asking, "Who is this Kovacs guy anyway? Are you sure you want to marry him?" By the time Ernie did arrive I had Montezuma's revenge from eating like a native in all those restaurants and was not in terrific shape.

When Ernie got off the plane, he said something obscene about the hurricane and the flight but calmed down quickly with the VIP diplomatic treatment O'Dwyer had arranged. Ernie was the first through customs. When he got to our hotel, if he noticed the heat and the lizards on the walls, he didn't say anything. I got out of my sickbed for the wedding on September 12 (although our matching rings had "9-11-54" engraved inside them). The ceremony, which was in Spanish, was in Bill's office. Neither Ernie nor I knew what was being said, so we had real trouble keeping straight faces. I didn't dare look at him because we already had a terrible history of breaking up whenever we were interviewed together on local radio shows. We also kept saying the wrong thing at the wrong time. I would say sí, and O'Dwyer would say, "No, I'll tell you when." He gave me away and drew up the legal documents. Acting like my dad, O'Dwyer also told Ernie, "You've got to take care of this little girl."

After the ceremony was over, Bill took us to a champagne

breakfast. Back at the hotel two smiling, bowing Mexican bellboys kept bringing bowls and bowls of heavenly-smelling gardenias, every hour on the hour. I kept saying, "How nice," until one of them who spoke English told me that in Mexico the gardenia is the symbol of fertility. From then on I shut the door in their faces. The flowers suddenly didn't smell so sweet. I kept saying to myself, "No more kids. I don't want any more kids, at least until I know what I'm going to face with his when they return."

When I said, "Good morning, husband," for the first time, he couldn't get over it, he was so pleased. He was in tears. I thought, My God, what you must have gone through with the other marriage. What I meant was "Boy, are you stuck with me now, for life." Once I had made the commitment, there was no turning back, ever. It took me a long time to agree to the status of married lady, given my Victorian background, where your personal needs came third, after your husband's and your children's. But when you make up your mind, all the fog clears. There was only one life for me: Ernie and his children came first. Grandpa Adams's domestic views had been well observed. Like the other women in my Welsh family, I was no longer the star in my own life but just a supporting player in Ernie's.

Ernie, not realizing the depth of my commitment, started to react in the opposite way, as if I were saying that everything between us was going to change, that the fun and the magic would soon be over, after the honeymoon. We were both silent and introspective for different reasons. Oddly, he ran around waiting on me, always asking if he could bring me this or that. He had done it before, but always with great humor, as if in a funny sketch. Now he meant it for real. It scared me, just as it always did when Ernie got serious. It took me a couple of days to get over it. My new seriousness also frightened Ernie, and it took him even longer to get over it.

Ernie and I, with a car and driver, went to Cuernavaca for lunch but never saw the town. We went to Xochimilco to see the floating flowers but were told that we couldn't pick them because the water was polluted. We were also warned not to let our lips touch the glass while drinking tequila, to lick the

145

salt on our fists and toss the tequila down our wide-open mouths instead. Since I had already had the *turistas*, I didn't want to get sick again and ate only safe foods. Ernie ate anything he pleased and got away with it until the end of our honeymoon. "Drink the wine of the country," Ernie always said. Of course, we bought everything for sale, such as a complete set of soft, heavy Taxco silver flatware (when you cut something with a fork, the tines bent together so that it looked like a spoon) and a lot of leather jackets that we'd never wear.

Returning to New York, we moved into my two-and-a-half-room apartment (living room, bedroom, kitchen) at 60 Sutton Place South, but that could never be enough room for Ernie. Shortly we moved to a two-bedroom apartment on East End Avenue so that we would have a bedroom for Ernie's daughters when they came back. The building was right on the East River, and for the first two nights we seemed to be on an equal level with the boat whistles. One blast could have me sitting straight up in bed, but after a few months we didn't even hear them.

I rejoined Jack Paar's CBS show, which was now on every morning, Monday through Friday, in March 1955. In April Ernie's late-night Dumont show was canceled, and in May he began doing radio again, on WABC, from 6:00 to 9:00 A.M. For the first time we were on in the same time period, opposite each other. He was off television until he replaced Steve Allen on the *Tonight* show in August, while Steve went on vacation.

About this time Toots Shor introduced Ernie to Jackie Gleason. When one saw the two together, the words "large" and "largesse" come to mind. Nothing was too much. Ernie sent Jackie a bale of day-old bread, and Jackie sent Ernie an eye-level wreath of dead flowers on a five-foot funeral stand. They liked each other.

One day Jackie asked Ernie and me to come to Shawnee on Delaware (Fred Waring and his Pennsylvanians' old haunt) the following Friday for a weekend of golf. When we protested that we didn't play golf, Jackie said, "So you'll learn. Come Friday and you'll leave Sunday. Honey doesn't play either. You'll be fine." (Honey was his current GF, a beautiful size-eight dancer.)

Ernie and I went out and bought golf clubs and golfing outfits and arrived at the Shawnee Inn just in time to hear Gleason shout across the lobby, "We meet for breakfast at seven and tee off at eight."

The next morning, sure enough, there Reggie van Gleason III was in his chicest golfing knickers, already at the table, ordering for everybody—sausage, eggs, pancakes, syrup, the works. Had to have a hearty breakfast, he said.

We played, or tried our best to play, until 10:00, when we saw a festive golf cart approaching. The man driving was clanging a dinner bell. "Oh, here's Al now," said Jackie. Al, Jackie's valet, had a full coffee break spread, complete with bagels, lox, cream cheese, sweet rolls, pound cake, and bear claws. Jackie said it would "tide us over" till about 1:00 P.M., when we got to the clubhouse where he had ordered a light lunch from the elegant chef. We started with vichyssoise, then came cheese soufflé, and a light radicchio salad, served with the best Meursault I'd ever tasted. "Just espresso, no dessert," Jackie said. "We've got to watch it."

Ernie had spilled a bit of vichyssoise on his shirt, so he went into the pro shop to buy a new one to wear. He was upset to find out that every T-shirt had a little alligator sewed on the left chest. As Ernie tried on the shirt, the clerk explained that it was the only brand the shop carried. Ernie asked for a razor blade and tried to shave off the alligator. When it wouldn't budge, he pulled the offensive cotton reptile out about three inches from his chest and asked the clerk for a pair of scissors. He snipped the shirt about halfway from his chest to his fingers, leaving a four-inch jagged hole in the new shirt and his bare chest proudly shining through. When Jackie asked him about it, Ernie said, "When you wrestle an alligator, first you have to grab him in the wallet."

We played all afternoon, until about 4:00 P.M., when again I heard the clanging of Al's bells. He had completely redecorated the cart for the cocktail hour. It was now a fully stocked bar, complete with blenders, mixers, and hot and cold hors d'oeuvres. He mixed Jackie's elaborate martini—which Jackie pronounced "Perfect!"—and did fancy individual cocktails for the rest of us. He followed us for about an hour.

At six, Jackie announced that it was time to go back to

the hotel to nap. We needed to rest up for the special dinner he himself was cooking for us later that evening. We both asked where, and Jackie said Al would pick us up at the hotel about eight.

At exactly eight Al pulled up in Jackie's limo and took us to a nearby town. When we pulled into a fancy driveway, I said, "Oh, whose house is this?"

Al said, "I don't know. Mr. Gleason rented it for the night. He needed a home kitchen to cook in."

Sure enough, he drove us around back to the kitchen, where Jackie, in a sketch-size chef's hat and an enormous tablecloth-size apron, was fixing his special Italian dinner for us: antipasto, scungilli (octopus), chicken cacciatore, linguine and clam sauce, Italian salad, garlic bread, and again espresso, no dessert! He didn't stop cooking until 2:00 A.M.

Ernie was a happy man. He said to Gleason, "I finally found someone who can actually eat more than I can, You're the champ!"

When Honey broke up with Jackie, she was a size eighteen.

Because of his early start on the radio show, Ernie engaged a regular cabdriver to pick him up at 4:00 A.M. Lou Pack, whom Ernie fondly called Pack the Hack, sat at the curb for the first few days until Ernie brought him coffee. One day Lou said, "You know, I could come up and start the coffee for you since I'm up anyway; it would be ready when you got up." Ernie said, "Sure, here's a key. Let's start tomorrow." The next day Ernie got up to a full breakfast of eggs and bacon. The day after that, Ernie got up extra early because he didn't like Lou's runny eggs. I told them they were like two old married people complaining about each other's cooking. The Associated Press ran a picture of the two of them cooking in the predawn hours.

One day the CBS brass called and asked me to appear at a Marine Corps function in Lexington, Kentucky. A military plane was to pick me up, fly to Washington for lunch at the White House, load on some other people, and proceed to the military ball in Lexington. Ernie, who hadn't yet developed his fear of flying, said that sounded good, he'd like to go along. We were to convene at a government airport on Long Island at 5:30 A.M. on a Saturday. No problem, that's when we got up anyway. We drove out in the dark and waited in the car for two hours, trying to figure what had gone wrong. We had the right day, place, and time.

When none of the marines showed up until 7:30 A.M., we should've realized how the rest of the weekend was going to go. (The organizers had given us a deliberately early call, figuring that irresponsible "show folks" would always be late. In fact, now that we were big-time network, the one thing we were never late for, no matter what our habits in the rest of our lives, was a show—especially in live TV; nobody waits for you there.) We got on the plane, which was not a cushy passenger job; it had no seats, only pull-down metal benches facing the center of the plane. We didn't fly very high because I could see outside. The doors didn't fit, and there were holes in the plane. Ernie's fountain pen leaked all over his shirt pocket because the cabin wasn't pressurized.

We finally took off at 10:00 A.M. and arrived in Washington at 2:00 P.M. A bus would have been faster. Of course, it was too late for lunch, so we just got back on with the Washington passengers and arrived in Lexington at 6:00 P.M. The affair had already started; so much for rehearsal. The band I was going to sing with was already playing cocktail music. I took my arrangements into a small rehearsal room with the leader and carefully went over every tune with him. He was to rehearse the band during its break while I changed into my performing gown and did my hair. While we were talking, he kept telling Ernie about this great bourbon they made nearby called Jack Daniel's and how he should get the black label, not the green. It was as "smooooth as the branch wahtah ya gotta drank with it."

Ernie quickly ordered the Jack Daniel's, pronounced it "terrific stuff," and I went off to the hotel to change. Since the show was set for 9:00 P.M., after dinner, I took my time dressing and vocalizing and arrived back at the ball at about 8:45. I heard the orchestra fanfare and the announcer say, "Here she is, Edie Adams." I went on to applause but didn't hear my walk-on music. I reached the microphone, and the applause died down to silence. I turned around to look at the band. The musicians were all looking at each other, shrugging

149

and leafing through music, doing a palms-up I-don't-know "take" to me. As I was nearsightedly looking for the leader, who was not even onstage, it dawned on me. He hadn't rehearsed or even passed out the music. He himself had passed out from Jack Daniel's.

I didn't know what else to do, so I asked the pianist if he knew "I've Got the World on a String" in A♭. I talked to the audience a little and sang the song. The orchestra's faking was not too good, so I decided that was going to be my only song. I talked some more, did some impersonations, thanked them nicely, and walked offstage toward one angry Hungarian. Ernie was swearing at the orchestra leader, who by now had come to. Ernie said that he wanted to leave Kentucky "right now—and not on that dinky military plane with holes in it but on a real commercial plane, with seats!"

The belligerent leader twanged, "But your waff only saing whon song," whereupon Ernie picked up my unopened music case with his left hand while I grabbed his swinging right hand and rushed him out. Ernie's moral to the story was: "Don't ever do anything for free; charge them the moon; ask for the impossible." You are treated exactly according to what you demand. If you work free or even cheap, that's how you are treated. If you ask for a Rolls limousine with a bar in the back and two suites stocked with your favorite champagne and caviar, that's what they figure you're worth. (At least, Ernie said, he discovered Jack Daniel's before Frank Sinatra did.)

I ordered new draperies for East End Avenue, but before they were even up, Ernie and I went to visit Imogene Coca in her enormous duplex penthouse, with terraces, at the El Dorado, 300 Central Park West. As soon as he saw Imogene's place on the building's south tower, he began to circle the matching north tower. He called downstairs in the building to inquire if by some happenstance the north tower might be empty. Strangely and unfortunately, it was immediately available. The next thing I knew we were moving in.

With my cutting eye, I saw that we could redo my unhung draperies, but since we had only three rooms of furniture and Ernie wouldn't wait for anything like the six weeks for delivery from a store, every Saturday we went to every auction in town and bought sofas, chairs, lamps, and statuary. This was a fast and cheap method since most people were leaving the larger New York apartments then and moving into smaller, more efficient ones. We were able to buy all these antiques at bargain prices and have them re-covered. That took only ten days. Instead of one sofa, with his office, his secretary's, the children's playroom, our bedroom suite, and servants' quarters, we needed at least six sofas, twelve side chairs, and "lots" of paintings. (I'd look at and bid on one, only to discover, upon delivery, that I'd bought one of a lot.) We even found some twelfth-century armor for the hall. Ernie did the furniture for that room, all Charlemagne chairs and heavy pieces of armor, chain mail, Saracen blades, shields, swords, and helmets. It was dark and ominous, the way Ernie liked. About 70 percent of our stuff for the apartment came from auctions.

Once, by accident, a lot of paintings that I had bought included a horrible seascape with a corner ripped out that I hadn't even noticed. Ernie patched it with two Band-Aids on the back and some blue house paint, touched up the front with a Q-Tip. We sent it back to the auction house and got more than we had paid for the entire lot it had been part of. It taught me to spend the week before the auction closely looking at, with my glasses on, everything we possibly might buy. We were buying so much that we had to split up on Saturdays to cover all the auctions. We'd reconnoiter in midtown to fill out two auction dance cards. We filled our $750-per-month apartment in about five weeks. (We got a bargain because nobody wanted to fill up that many square feet in New York then.)

I was delighted to see Imogene's expensive decorators at the auctions and watched carefully what they bought. When one of them bought twenty-eight feet of brass molding for about fifty dollars, I asked him what it was for. He said he would turn it upside down, cut it into eighteen-inch sections to form sconces, put a piece of marble on top, and charge the customers a thousand dollars a pair. Aha! The same thing goes on in decorating as in clothes designing, I discovered for the first time. I now looked at these auctions with my designer's eye and never used a decorator in my life.

Ernie's daughters were recovered from their mother in northern Florida in June 1955. The original police complaint against Bette had evolved into a grand jury indictment against her. After spending fifty thousand dollars for investigators and two years' worth of weekends, Ernie finally found his daughters living in a shack behind a restaurant where Bette worked as a waitress in Cassia, Florida, Southeast of Daytona Beach on Route 44, not on the way to anywhere. Clearly they had been neglected. I was waiting in our New York apartment with Norman Knight, our boss at the Dumont Network, who had financed the search. The girls kind of remembered me, and when I said, "I'd like you to meet our boss, Norman Knight," Betty, then nine, stuck her chin out, looked up into his face, and said, "F---you," and flounced out.

Their hair was chopped so short I couldn't comb it and had to curl it with a curling iron. The girls didn't know how to eat with a knife and fork and apparently had never brushed their teeth the whole time they were gone. They had thick southern accents, and every other word was a racial slur: "dirty nigger, dirty Jew." They *had* been taught how to hide. Later, when Ernie and I took the girls out on drives, they involuntarily ducked to the floor anytime a police car went by.

Betty and Kippie, who was seven, returned to Ernie just in time for our Edward R. Murrow *Person to Person* interview on June 24. Because of their appearance and language with Knight, I was understandably nervous about this *live* appearance. It went off without a hitch, but in viewing it recently, I saw that I looked petrified the whole time.

This kidnapping and its aftermath were dramatized in ABC's television movie *Ernie Kovacs: Between the Laughter* in 1983. Jeff Goldblum starred as Ernie and Melody Anderson as me. I played Mae West in a cameo role. An unrecognizable Cloris Leachman won an Emmy playing Ernie's offbeat mother, Mary. Although I was working, ironically in Florida, during most of the filming, ABC foisted the title of technical adviser on me. As with raising the children, I had all the responsibility and none of the authority—no creative control.

By telephone I was able to coach Cloris on Mary's loony speech and mannerisms and to have long talks with Melody. On matters of Ernie's character and the overall look of the picture, however, the producers ignored me. The dining-room scene at my mother's house was all wrong. I had even taken her dishes to the set, but they didn't use them. I had planned to re-create all the noise of that first dinner party, but the producers' idea of humor was to give my mother the line "Aren't you too warm with that mustache on?"

I had understood that the piece was to be about how Ernie managed to remain astoundingly funny in his work while all this tragedy was going on at home, but ABC took out several small, light, funny scenes that developed Ernie's character; they said the "comedy blackouts" did not contribute to their heavy drama. They took all the fun out of what I remembered as our life together. Because they were afraid of a lawsuit, they chose to use as working script the actual court proceedings from our lawyer's file exactly as the court reporter had taken them down. I found it only boring. The director, I later read in *TV Guide*, had known and disliked Ernie personally.

Jeff Goldblum can do no wrong. He captured Ernie's oddball, off-center sense of humor. Melody played me exactly as I was then—a terminally pleasant people pleaser. However, the writing made it look as if our lives were tragic. The most unforgivable thing was that Ernie came across as neurotic. He was a lot of things in his life, manic, zany, wacky, impulsive, extravagant, and unpredictable, but he was *never* neurotic. The movie depicted a life with him that I never lived. With all the stress of having his children gone, daily he came up with a funny show and still managed to be pleasant at home. I visited the set only once other than to do my Mae West scene. When I saw that Gertrude, the six-foot doll, was only four feet tall, I knew we were in trouble.

I had to hire a couple to take care of the kids and the enormous duplex (if we counted servants' quarters and odd bathrooms, it was twenty-eight rooms on two floors). We also needed a chauffeur to take the girls to school and their many other new activities and a secretary to keep track of all our

appointments. Here I was, in my middle twenties, not knowing how to clean or cook myself and never having had a
"staff." The only clue I had was my mother's copy of Mrs.
Beeton's Household Management, which was fine for dealing
with upstairs and downstairs maids in England at the turn
of the century but hardly related to New York penthouses in
the fast 1950's. As comfortable as I felt onstage or on live
television, that's how uncomfortable and inadequate I felt in
hiring and training a staff. It didn't help that Ernie's mother,
Mary, reappeared regularly on our kitchen doorstep. She ignored Judge Belloff's court order that the girls were to be kept
out of "the care and influence of the paternal grandmother."
Anytime I would find her in the kitchen, smiling, sitting, and
having coffee with the help, I knew they'd be gone in two
days. I should have listened to Grandpop Kovacs.

We had one Japanese couple called Lottie and Edward. I
asked Edward, one night before a dinner party, to light the
candles. I left the room and came back to a burning lamp-
shade. Ernie had put real candles in the antique candelabra
lamp. Edward had lighted the candles under the silk shade,
instead of the buffet candles. I didn't have to fire Edward and
Lottie, however, because Mary appeared and smiled at them
the next day, and they were gone.

Then we had a German couple. The man looked like Boris
Karloff; the woman cook looked tired and spent. His eyes had
a coldness I never forgot, and I began to see bruises on her
listless Nordic face. They cleaned very well, but there was
something lacking in her cooking. One day Ernie asked for a
a Spanish omelet for breakfast. She threw her hands up and
said, "Ach, Gott, das ist high kukery." Mary didn't even have
to smile at them. Ernie did the dirty deed.

When Ernie couldn't do it, I had a terrible time firing
anybody. One of our secretaries, Lillian De Gore, had the
patience of a saint and always said, "Everything's fine,"
when I called her up from work, even if all hell was breaking
loose. She could move mountains with her sweetness. Her
office was next to the girls' playroom, so she kept an eye on
them, too.

One of the chauffeurs purported to be an ex-priest, collar
and all. He turned out to be an ex-con who was driving us

all around with a Bible on the front set and a loaded gun under his black coat. Lillian was the only one who could sweetly do that firing.

I gave the girls a crash course in culture, sending them to ballet lessons and taking them to all the Broadway shows and ballets. They quickly became theater buffs. We registered them in day camp, Camp Hilliard, for the summer. They had a plastic blowup kiddy pool on the terrace, but ever-original Ernie and I seemed to get more use of out of it than they did on those torrid summer nights.

Despite their rough edges, Betty and Kippie had great personalities. Betty was brilliant, and Kippie was funny. Their outward appearances had to be fixed first. Their hair had been given bad permanents and was too short to do anything with. Whenever we went out or daily before school, their hair had to be curled with an iron. It broke my heart because they had always wanted long hair. They had such a need for a family-unit feeling that they wanted to dress alike. Luckily I knew the children's clothing design houses on Seventh Avenue and bought them a whole wardrobe of matching outfits.

I somehow wangled them a place at the exclusive Miss Hewitt's Classes for the fall. The distance from Cassia, Florida, where they had been found, to the top drawer of Miss Hewitt's was greater than I expected. Their first day they were taught never to say, when someone offered food of any kind, "I hate that." They were to say, "Thank you," and eat as much as they could. They were taught the private school curtsy and that when you meet someone, it was very important to look that person in the eye and always say, "Yes, ma'am" and "No, ma'am." Unfortunately, too late for Norman Knight.

Ernie was concerned constantly that his ex-wife, Bette, might snatch the kids again. They were always driven to school, at first by one of us in a cab, then by the newly hired chauffeur. The doormen in the building and the teacher who greeted them at school were warned about strangers asking for us.

After a few lessons in table manners the girls began to visit all the best restaurants with us. When they started to revert to eating with their fingers, they got a pinch on the knee under the table from Ernie or me. Both bright and fast studies, they soon were eating properly.

The one thing I couldn't get them to do was go to the dentist. I would make an appointment, time after time. When it came time to leave, Betty would hold on to her new four-poster bed, scream and kick and throw a tantrum, so we didn't go. I finally got them to the doctor by saying they needed an exam to be let into school, but they absolutely refused to go to the dentist. Ernie said, "Well, if it's that much of a problem, forget it for now. We'll do it later." I didn't believe it and tried to insist further but was outvoted. Later, in Beverly Hills, when the girls finally did go to the dentist out of sheer excruciating pain from cavities and rotting teeth, the dentists took me to task. As I was soon to find out, I would be outvoted four to one (Mary, Ernie, Betty, and Kippie) on all areas of discipline.

For the first two weeks the kids continued to speak in their deep southern drawl and talk about "dirty Jews" and "dirty niggers," without knowing what they were saying. Ernie joined me in severe measures to change their speech patterns and parroted prejudices. Ernie, whose delight was to take his Jewish friends to the steam room at the conservative New York Athletic Club, would not tolerate this. While he backed down on the teeth, he was first to take a firm stand on this issue. After a few weeks we never heard it again.

They needed a lot of work, and maybe nobody else in her right mind would have taken them on, but it never occurred to me not to. After all, I could do anything. Part of the problem was that I barely knew these children. I had seen them only briefly in Atlantic City and once or twice elsewhere and did not realize the extent of the damage already done to their psyches by their unsettled childhood. A psychiatrist who had examined them during the custody trial in Philadelphia asked to speak to me privately. He said, "You're going to marry Ernie. Do you know what you're taking on with these children, what they've been through with their mother and grandmother? You're in for a bumpy ride when they become teenagers."

After only a week with us the girls began to call me Mommy. I was surprised; it was the first time anybody had called me Mommy, and my instinct told me it was too soon. "Mother"—right or wrong—was a term I felt you earned, and the kids were desperately looking for any mother figure. Ernie was ecstatic; he said, "No. Listen to that; how about that? Leave it alone."

"Don't you think that we should have a long talk with them about this?" I asked. He didn't. Ernie was always against big talks.

We played hard at trying to be parents. I made Ernie dress down for our first parent-teachers' night at Miss Hewitt's, but the first person he saw was jazz musician Joey Bushkin, who made Ernie feel overdressed. I, again, had prepared carefully to dress for the occasion. I felt I had to look older. I went to Abercrombie & Fitch and bought a demure, severely tailored navy blue suit, pulled my hair back in a bun, and wore my glasses in public, a rare occurrence. Ernie said, "Who are you?" and laughed all the way over to the school.

I said, "Ernie, come on, be serious. This is not your show; it's your kids' school. You've got to straighten up."

"How long can it be, an hour? Then we'll all go to Sardi's."

I was recently going through pictures of elaborate children's parties, such as Randy Paar's birthday at the Stork Club second-floor party room, with live animals. Betty and Kippie quickly became part of the New York children's café society set. We gave at least one of these parties ourselves, at the Stork Club, complete with live music, magicians, and adult café society in attendance. Sherman Billingsley, the owner of the Stork Club, gave the girls a dog.

The court had ordered some sort of religious training for the girls. Ernie had been Catholic, but his first wife, Bette, had been a Baptist. He was now nondenominational, yet more deeply religious inside than anyone I ever knew. Ernie was not a joiner. I'd had enough church in my youth for all of us, but I felt it was important for the girls to go. At first Ernie wouldn't go with me, but I insisted. He finally went with us one time. Because I was a Presbyterian, I picked the Central Presbyterian Church, at Sixty-fourth Street. We started to go regularly, even Ernie. The girls, of course, went to choir practice. Ernie even liked the minister, Dr. John Fishback, who was a communicator. I liked his sermons.

One day I arrived home about five-thirty after a particularly difficult day. As I walked up the steps from the foyer to the living room, I could see Ernie through the open door of his den, standing with a big glass of Jack Daniel's on the rocks in his hand. I thought, Boy, would I like one of those.

Ernie shouted, "Hiya, baby, want some Jack Daniel's?"

I said, "Yeah, boy, have I had a day; you're not gonna believe this. Get me a drink." I walked in, and there sat Dr. Fishback. As Ernie told it later, when I saw the white clerical collar, I immediately put my Tenafly manner on, but it was too late, the boat had sailed. Ernie had set the stage and sucked me right into the scene. I was nonplussed until I saw that Dr. Fishback also had a glass of Jack Daniel's in his hand. It turns out he had been raised in Tennessee and knew Jack Daniel's before Ernie. I still felt uncomfortable. I had already reverted to my childhood days of stiff Presbyterian ministers coming to call. Everyone was very formal and polite, and we drank only tea. I didn't have an act for this one. Dr. Fishback and Ernie got along fabulously, the oddest couple I've ever known.

When the Cigar Institute of America named Ernie its Man of the Year in Atlantic City, Kippie, her father's daughter, learned to order her favorite food from room service: a pound of caviar and a spoon. Ernie had gotten through to her with his lecture on not doing personal appearances without certain "perks." Caviar and limousines were just the beginning. As at home, no expense was spared for Ernie's, the kids', or my slightest whim.

From March until December 1955 I did the Jack Paar early-morning show from Grand Central Studios. I replaced Betty Clooney, Rosemary's sister, during her vacation, but the producers decided to keep me on since I had been the girl singer on Paar's original Friday-only show. Paar denied that Clooney's firing had anything to do with her backstage romance with his bandleader, Pupi Campo. On December 12 Ernie started his own television show for NBC, from 10:30 to 11:00 A.M. Apologetically I asked Jack for my release from his show so that I could join Ernie's. He told me that he understood perfectly, that if his wife, Miriam, could sing, he would want her on his show.

Ernie's new characters included Uncle Gruesome, a kindly but misunderstood old gentleman who reads fairy tales designed for morbid children, and Matzoh Hepplewhite, a magician who lacks not only skill and dexterity but also enjoys the distinction of being the only conjurer ever to be pulled out of the hat by a rabbit. Howard, the world's strongest ant, and the Kapusta Kids in Outer Space also debuted in sketches. Percy Dovetonsils, the sentimental poet, surreptitiously sipped a martini as he read his own works, such as "Ode to Stanley's Pussycat" and "Thoughts While Falling Off the Empire State Building." My favorite was "Twas the Night Before Christmas . . . (on the East Side): "Twas the night before Christmas, and all through the duplex, just a valet was pressing (a glen plaid with few checks). . . ."

Now that I had been a hit on Broadway, my nightclub agents were happy and complacent and not too anxious to book me into nightclubs. They said I would never make it as nightclub performer; I wasn't the type. Now, I was hell-bent to do a club act. Reluctantly they said, "Put it together and we'll look at it." Whenever anybody says, "You can't do this," I take that as the gauntlet thrown down.

As I said previously, from the time that my aunt told my mother that I would never sing as well as she did, I had never been able to sing in front of a small group, in a living room or at a party. I had no problem singing for thirty-five thousand members of Rotary International at the Superdome in New Orleans, but with fewer than fifty in the audience I'm in trouble. Now here I was, singing for five of my own agents who didn't want to hear me. After I sang, Johnny Dugan, who was head of MCA's nightclub department, said, "Edie, you're just not a nightclub performer; you'll never make it in clubs." The other guys agreed with him and told me to go back to Broadway. Whenever anybody says, "That's as good as it gets," I look for seven ways to do it better. I kept rehearsing my act in spite of them. They, too, essentially had told me to "sing a pretty song and wear a pretty dress."

The Stork Club was one of the "in" places in New York in the 1950's. Sherman Billingsley, who owned the club, also did a chic television show from there, in which he, unfortunately, interviewed celebrities. He couldn't remember any-

159

body's name or what his guests were promoting. Ernie did a devastating satire on the CBS program, which got him barred from the Stork Club until I smoothed things over later. The "Kapusta Kids in Outer Space Puppet Show" did scathing takeoffs on Sherman's ineptness. When I was on Sherm's show, he mentioned that he was doing a live fashion show at the Stork Club on Sunday nights and that he would like me to narrate it. "Will the band be there?" I asked. He quoted a small fee, but I said I would do it for nothing if he would let me sing some songs and give me the band to rehearse with. He agreed. I wore little black cocktail dresses and gloves and fresh flowers. Sherman liked me; he didn't have to think when I was on. I finally softened Sherman up, and he and Ernie became the best of friends.

So, with the complete Stork Club orchestra, all the rehearsal time I needed, and a full audience of sophisticated live people, I launched my nightclub career. On Sunday nights it got to be the "in" New York thing to do, to come see Edie do her takeoffs of Shirley Temple, Jeanette Mac-Donald, Ruby Keeler, Marlene Dietrich, and Marilyn Monroe, all carefully wigged, costumed, and rehearsed from Ernie's morning show. As I worked up my routines, the fashion show was quietly phased out. We "videochirps" had no place to go to expand. I would do anything else I felt like doing, including coloratura arias. My lyrics to "Hey There" in fractured German, "Achtung, du mit die schnoz in die luft," were tried out at Sherman's Sunday soirees, in front of the chicest audience in town.

When I did an ANTA benefit, the great songwriting team of Hugh Martin and Timmy Gray wrote a piece of special material to link the impressions together, making it a solid fifteen-minute nightclub block. I bought the song and orchestration for a nominal amount because they had already been paid for by ANTA.

One night after *Wonderful Town* had closed, Ernie and I and the children were sitting eating dinner and otherwise minding our own business when my TV agent, Marty Kummer, called and said that the Plaza Hotel had telephoned. Polly Bergen, who was booked there, had called in sick;

would I like to go on in her place that very night, actually in one hour, at nine o'clock? I said sure. I gathered all my costumes and orchestrations and made it to the Plaza, just before show time. I gave the music to someone to distribute to the band, billed as "Mark Monte and His Continentals." Just as in old Hollywood movies, the newcomer replaced the ailing star and instantly became a star herself. As I thanked "Mark Monte and the Continentals," I turned and saw Ted Straeter, the Plaza's resident orchestra leader, take a bow.

The Plaza booked me for eight weeks on my own, an unheard-of engagement in those days. I don't know of any other singer or nightclub performer who began her or his career at the Plaza, the historical epitome of nightclub performing. This was the greatest of the supper club rooms. You had to have a certain style to command an international audience such as the Plaza's. All my Juilliard training had inadvertently prepared me for this. Edith Piaf was in her heyday. Before, I could use my Juilliard languages only comedically. I couldn't translate fast, but my French diction was better than anybody's, thanks to René Vaillant, my teacher who had taught me bergerettes, old French folk songs, and Gabriel Fauré, and Henri Duparc. Ted Straeter suggested I sing some of the songs in other languages seriously, without taking a pie. Could it be? At last! A chance to test before the paying public what I'd really learned in school.

Suddenly I was a big, "hot," highly paid nightclub performer. I had nothing glamorous enough for my own opening night. Remembering Roz's stunning wardrobe, I called Don Loper in Hollywood. I sent him my MM "clown dress" from Ceil Chapman. I said I wanted him to construct the same thing exactly, white-beaded, strapless, form-fitted, only I wanted a full flounce from the knee to the floor. The white one he sent was stunning and so inner constructed that it stood up on its own without a hanger. I loved it so much I asked for a second one in black, for the late show. It was like standing in one leg of a man's trousers. The dress was so tight at the knees that in order to make it up the two short steps to the piano, I had to put my two knees close up tight and stand pigeontoed, fanny out, with heels akimbo, and step up left, then right. Ted Straeter said I couldn't navigate without "ballin' the jack." Later it became the model for the original Barbie doll dress.

On my opening night there were flowers and telegrams from everyone, and the critics were wonderful to me. Straeter, a fixture who actually lived at the Plaza, and I did duets of Rodgers and Hart and Gershwin songs, all the choice oldies; it seemed to me that this *was* as good as it got. I had gone from rejection in my own agents' offices to the top of a different world in a few months. Like everything else I had tried so far in show business, it seemed ridiculously easy. When people ask me today, "How do I get into show business?" my answer is always the same: "If you want it badly enough, no one can keep you out."

My brother, Sheldon, and me, age
two

Me, age three

Mother, Aunt Gussie, and me. Three solemn people

Below, an average weekend at our Lily Lake cottage. Me—stage center

Mother and me. Grove City, age twelve

Below, my father and mother, Sheldon and Ada Adams Enke, when they came to see Frank Sinatra with me. They were devastated.

I wore this outfit to audition for *Junior Miss*—and left with the role in *Blithe Spirit*.

Below, first show: *Blithe Spirit* with Julia Meade and Harry Sayers. I'm on the right dressed in a sheet I improvised fifteen minutes before the pictures were taken.

Third show: Juilliard Vocal Recital—my "no sheet" dress

Pale yellow bathing suit that stopped the show at the first Juilliard
Musical Review, *Lose Your Tempo*

Columbia Fencing Team (I'm front row left)

COURTESY OF KEYSTONE PICTURES

Miss U.S. Television, 1950

Above, Parkway Grade School. Ernie is third from left in rear.

Ernie, age ten, on Sandy, 1929

Above, Ernie, second from left, organized a stock company that played in Morrisville, Pennsylvania, and Trenton and Bordentown, New Jersey, right after high school.

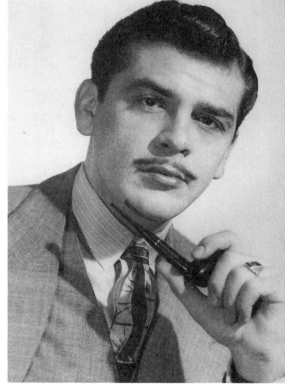

Ernie's New York School of the Theater glamour shot

John Drew Theatre, Long Island—
September 13, 1938—shortly before Ernie became ill

Ernie and me on *Ernie in Kovacsland* in August 1951 when I first met Ernie. (This was a 7:00 to 7:30 P.M. network show replacing *Kukla, Fran, and Ollie* for the summer.)

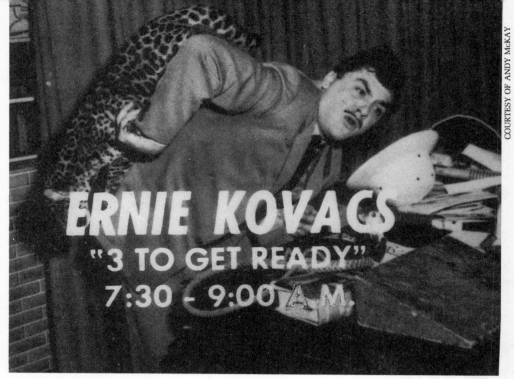

The first early-morning TV show—anywhere ever. I joined in September 1951 when it was expanded to two hours: 7:00 to 9:00 A.M.

Ernie waiting for an elevator at WPTZ, Philadelphia

My Don Loper "Barbie Doll" dress that stood up by itself. I could stand right up to it—"tit for tat"—or so it seemed. My Plaza night club debut, 1955

Here I am as Daisy Mae in *Li'l Abner*, 1956, with (left to right) Stubby Kaye, Joe E. Marks, and Bern Hoffman.

Julie Andrews (Cinderella) and me (Fairy Godmother), March 1957

Ernie and me on one of my quick trips to California to visit him on Sunday. Spring 1957, at the Beverly Hills pool

At the Tropicana in Las Vegas, 1957.
"Who *were* all those girls?"

When Ernie was on location and I
was pregnant with Mia. From left:
me, Kippie facing camera, Grandmothers Kovacs and Enke, Betty
with back to camera, 1959

COURTESY OF MICHAEL NAGRO

Above, Muriel commercial. I did these for nearly twenty years, 1960 to 1978.

Ernie and Mia in Las Vegas, 1961

Edie, Mia, Kippie, Ernie, and Betty.
This was the only picture Ernie had
in his wallet when he died.

Below, Merriman Smith (right),
JFK, and me. "I didn't—but it was
not because I wasn't asked."

My Nite Club Act

$\mathcal{E}$IGHT

NBC OFFERED ERNIE an exclusive one-million-dollar contract. The network's national program manager, Tom Loeb, had convinced its president, Sylvester "Pat" Weaver, that Ernie was too important a comedian not to tie up. Weaver was a Kovacs fan but felt that his comedy was an acquired taste. Right away Ernie was given his own daily show starting on December 12, 1955, from 10:30 to 11:00A.M. He was still warming up on ABC radio, from 6:00 to 9:00 A.M. with the Buddy Weed Trio live. On the NBC TV show he had fabulous staff musicians: Bobby Rosengarden on drums, Homer Mench on bass, Al Klink on clarinet, Archie Coty on piano, Gene Bianco on harp, Will Bradley on trombone, Dale McMickle on trumpet, and Mundel Lowe on guitar. They later formed the core of the famous *Tonight* show band. The floor manager was Joseph Papp, then trying desperately to piece together a summer of free Shakespeare in the park.

In July 1956 Ernie filled in as a summer replacement for Sid Caesar, from eight to nine on Saturday evenings, prime time with a big budget. Because it was such a large undertaking and he was still doing the radio show, Ernie had to hire three fine writers: Deke Hayward, Mike Marmor, and Rex Lardner. I especially liked Rex's stuff. Then Ernie got a full orchestra with Hildegarde's well-known conductor, Harry

Sosnick (at every show she said, "Some walking music, Harry"). We even had two rehearsal pianists, one for the dancers. As I was working with the pianist assigned to me, I heard glorious dissonances coming from the dancers' studio. I said, "I don't know who that is playing in there; but bring him in here to rehearse, and let the dancers have my pianist." It turned out to be Peter Matz, recently returned from Paris, having studied orchestrations with Mme. Andrée Honegger, wife of composer Arthur Honegger. He had come an odd route to being the dedicated musician he was.

He told me of his high school vocational test. To his disappointment, since music was his life, he was rated mechanical. He couldn't understand it, but he thought the school knew better than he did and went to engineering school for two years. He was so unhappy that he want back to his high school to double-check the records for a mistake. The school admitted that he had scored 99 percent in music, but the counselor said, "We knew you couldn't make a living in music, so we took the next thing down."

Our show was Peter's first job in his new profession, and he thought everybody in TV was crazy. Ernie's time was so limited that Peter could confer with him only while he was in the bathtub with a big cigar and a drink in his hand.

Peter was up for anything I wanted to try. While he was not billed as the orchestrator—Harry was—Peter actually did the arrangements. He and I had all the time in the world to work them out. Even Lily Pons wrote me a fan letter after I sang a vocalese based on the Gershwin Preludes Peter and I had done. The telegram I treasured most was from Ira Gershwin complimenting me on my "Gershwin without words."

Ernie guest-hosted *Tonight*, filling in during Steve Allen's vacation, for all of August. In the fall of 1956 he was alternating as regular host with Steve, appearing on Mondays and Tuesdays. We both were so busy, between my nightclubs and the NBC morning show and his three shows, that often we couldn't even listen to or watch each other work. Sometimes it was all we could do to show up for the show on time. As if that weren't enough, I started to rehearse another Broadway show.

Li'l Abner was a property that I had been tracking since

high school. At the Sadie Hawkins Dance I won a contest dressing myself up as Daisy Mae. I was a fan of Al Capp's comic strip, with its acerbic wit. His characters weren't just spouting platitudes; they were satirical symbols. Every time a producer optioned *Li'l Abner* as a play or a musical I let it be known that I wanted to play Daisy Mae. Lerner and Loewe and Richard Rodgers had it for a few years but never produced it. Another producer picked it up, but again, it didn't happen.

Finally, in early 1956, I read that it definitely was coming to Broadway. Norman Panama and Melvin Frank had written the libretto based on Capp's characters. Michael Kidd would direct and choreograph, and Panama, Frank, and Kidd were also the three producers. Johnny Mercer, one of my heroes in my newly discovered popular music, had written the lyrics for what was only his second Broadway musical (*St. Louis Woman* was the first). Gene de Paul, who had written a lot of pop hits, had written the music. I quickly had my agent contact all of the above, to alert them that I wanted to play Daisy Mae and to ask them please to watch me on *The Ed Sullivan Show*. I even called Ernie's friend and neighbor in New City the cartoonist Milton Caniff to ask him to be sure that Al Capp was watching, too. Milt had put me into one of his Steve Canyon cartoons as Poteet Kenyon.

On that Ed Sullivan show, with my real hair now really platinum blond like my former Marilyn wig, I sang a pop song and did my Monroe takeoff. The next week, at a meeting my agent had arranged to meet the creative team, I again carefully dressed myself as I imagined Marilyn would if she had wanted to play this part. Top-to-toe beige: hair, curvaceous sweater-dress, stockings, shorty gloves, bag, and shoes. They took one look, and the part was mine. I didn't even have to sing for them.

Around this time Leonard Bernstein called me at home from his retreat at Martha's Vineyard, where he was writing *Candide*. He told me excitedly, "I have written a funny part for you that you can't resist." It was the "Glitter and Be Gay" number where Cunegonde sits before a mirror and tries on her expensive jewelry. He said, "I'll send it to you; it's a takeoff on 'The Jewel Song.' You'll be wonderful." But since both shows were going to be done at the same time, now that

189

I'd finally been offered the role of Daisy Mae in *Li'l Abner*, I couldn't decide between the two parts.

I called up George Abbott for advice. In the craziest of businesses he was always like a levelheaded stockbroker. He said to me, "Edith, *Candide* is a wonderful show, but it will not be a commercial success. It will be played on college campuses throughout the country for many years to come. But your brief career as an ingenue is over. You need a sexy role in a commercial hit." My mind was made up. It was Daisy Mae for me.

The rest of the cast included Peter Palmer as Abner, Charlotte Rae as Mammy Yokum, Stubby Kaye as Marryin' Sam, some of the best and strongest dancers in New York, headed by Marc Breaux and Deedee Wood, some of the most gorgeous bodies in all of show business, such as Tina Louise and Julie Newmar and eight gorgeous weight-lifting guys who did very little other than walk across the stage and pose. *Li'l Abner's* songs were quite popular at the time. Stubby Kaye usually stopped the show with "Jubilation T. Cornpone." I got to sing "Namely You," "Love in a Home," "If I Had My Druthers," and "I Wish It Could Be Otherwise," a lovely song that was cut on the road because it was considered far too sophisticated for poor simpleminded Daisy Mae.

In the first few days of rehearsals I was puzzled about the style. What kind of comedy were we doing? Was it satire, sketches, a cartoon? Peter Palmer, although he had no experience, seemed to have his comedy built in. Michael Kidd, being about five-eight, had choreographed Abner as he would himself. He gave Peter "little guy" cartoon poses that really worked well on his six-foot-four frame. Daisy Mae was more of a problem. The role was written into the musical much the same as it was in the cartoon. Daisy was an ornament, hanging on Abner's arm in every scene, no matter what the action. In a possible acting range of ten, poor Daisy seemed to reach no more than three. She had nothing to say other than "I luvs ya, Abner, I luvs ya, Abner, I luvs ya, Abner." If I had been Abner, I would have batted this cloying imbecile off my back real fast. I was in every scene, two steps away from the action, center stage, posing through everything that was said, looking very much like Nancy Reagan turning her adoring gaze at her beloved Ronnie. I was so stuck in one place that the stagehands painted a tiny daisy on my spot two steps left and downstage of center. The rest of the cast bought me, they sold me, they married me, but they very seldom talked directly to me. Still, all I said was "I luvs ya, Abner." That was my whole act.

This show had more dancing than any other on Broadway in many years. We had more broken ankles among the swing dancers than any show before or since. Michael's choreography was tough on even the best dancers. The show also had live animals, such as ducks, two hound dogs, and Moonbeam McSwine's pig. Animals were always running around onstage, doing what animals always do. The Sadie Hawkins Day dance was particularly perilous. As we were running across the stage, we nearsighted folks had be told what places to avoid. They'd shout, "Upstage left, downstage right," so we altered our course and tried to avoid not only what was on the floor but other dancers coming at you. (During the run I tried my first pair of contact lenses, but seeing clearly, for the first time onstage distracted me. I'd notice specific things in the audience, such as someone without a jacket and tie or someone eating. Looking into the orchestra pit and seeing comic books on some of the music stands also ruined my concentration.) Running offstage in my bare feet from the lights into the darkness of the very short wings at the St. James, I never knew when to stop. Michael would always tell me to run faster, but I said I couldn't see. So finally they got two stagehands to catch me so I wouldn't exit timidly or crash into the wall. One of the stagehands, Tommy McDonald, was also part of our select stagehand group that Johnny Mercer and Gene de Paul took to visit jazz clubs after the show in every town on the road.

It was on the road, pre-Broadway, that I realized that this was the final script, with no improvements to come. *Li'l Abner* was going to open on Broadway without any of the great political satire I had hoped for. I had figured that Al Capp would be around to punch up the pleasant script. He finally did arrive, in Washington, D.C., but not only did he not fix the show, he made passes at all the gorgeous girls in the cast and at me, a very publicly married woman. He took me to dinner and made some adolescent and amateurish passes at me. I wasn't even upset, just disappointed. This show was going to be a lot of work for me. This seemingly simple role was to be one of the toughest I'd ever had to play in my life. To have a leading role and carry a show with no playable dialogue written for you was more than an acting challenge. I was costumed like Daisy Mae, but my head was still not there.

My parts were getting younger; as my duet with Stubby Kaye, "I'm Past My Prime," put it, ". . . seventeen last spring, still without a ring." I was dressed in a tight low-cut pink and purple polka-dot blouse and a short blue denim skirt, and I wore the blond hair and makeup of my Marilyn imitation. Since I played the role barefoot and in a skimpy costume, I spent more time making up my body, especially my feet, than I did my face. I bought Elizabeth Arden's sponge-on fake tan makeup, which was new, by the five-gallon pail. My mother had never allowed me to go barefoot in my life, so this was the first time anyone had ever seen my poor tenderfeet. The doctor told to apply tincture of benzoin to the soles of my feet to protect them. They were permanently stained brown. Every time I went for a pedicure the attendants were horrified by these brown feet and reached for the pumice stone to take it off. I had to stop them. The St. James was a very cold theater in the winter, so I had pink bunny slippers standing by backstage.

I packaged myself as Marilyn Monroe doing Daisy Mae, with the addition of a long blond hair fall, and seemed to be stuck with that image for most of my career, including nineteen years as the Muriel cigar spokeswoman. It has always bothered me that my professional success came not because of what I thought or how I sounded but because of how I looked. Done up as the Muriel girl or a slickly packaged Vegas nightclub singer, I have always felt like a drag queen on a gay cookout. When I apply my "on" makeup, the "full slap," as Juliet Prowse calls it, complete with jazzed-up hair, way overdone Cleopatra eye makeup, theatrical lashes, cheekbone shaders, lots and lots of lip gloss, I could easily sing Albin's lament from La Cages aux Folles as I "put a little more mascara on." That's exactly how this potential Sunday school teacher from Pennsylvania feels done up in this "clown suit."

Shirley MacLaine always told me that we performers had better treat our careers as a business, without a shred of ego. She would say, "We're all just a can of peas. It's up to you to get yourself done up as the most attractive can of peas and market it the best way you can. When you know that, you'll be all right. It's when you confuse your inner self with the product you're selling that you get into trouble." Shirley was the bravest soul I knew. She'd go into a costume fitting and stick her stomach out. Everyone said, "Are you gaining weight?" She'd say, "Yeah, I guess so." She had to tolerate all their insults so she could get a costume loose enough to dance in.

Li'l Abner taught me the greatest lesson in listening and acting concentration. It was the hardest work I ever did in my life. With so little to say and do onstage, it was a real stretch to make sure that I wasn't standing there thinking, Did I send my clothes to the cleaners? It was very hard to do the wide-eyed listening of the childlike Daisy in some scenes that didn't even concern me. I was there strictly to decorate the stage, to display, in as many poses as possible, my fortunately good legs. I'd arrive at the theater, and while I was applying my gallons of body makeup, I would begin to prepare myself for this specific acting problem by doing all the things Strasberg's Method could teach me to do. I would build a whole show for me in my head that didn't exist in the actual script. I would think, Golly, tonight I'm eighteen years old, and it's raining; there's a slight chill in the air. Every night I'd activate a complete set of sense memories and private moments for me that weren't written in the show the audience saw, and it worked. Lee Strasberg, borrowing from Stanislavsky, said it was the actor's job—even with a mediocre script—to bring color and shadings to a play and have a beginning, a middle, and an end in mind, even though they are not written down. In acting parlance this is called subtext.

Concentration with the intensity of a preschooler listening to a monster tale was the key to playing Daisy Mae; it was not simply a "look-at" part. If Daisy is bored and her concentration goes, so does the audience's. Playing her, I learned more than I had before or have since. When it came time to do *It's a Mad, Mad, Mad, Mad World*, I was more than pleased when Spencer Tracy said to me, "My God, you're the only one who's really listening in the whole crowd scene." According to most of the directors and film cutters I've worked with, if you can listen in the movies, you've got it made. It's a medium more of reacting than acting.

Ernie hated analysis of anything, including his humor. He would avoid any discussion of why he did something or what he was trying to say by doing it. The variety and sheer volume of ideas that poured out of him during this period (1955–57) astounded me. I'd never seen anyone that prolific. I asked him how he did it. He said, "No big deal. I just close my eyes, and whatever pops out of the back of my head comes out of my mouth or goes down on paper, and eventually gets on the screen. What I see in my head is what I want them to see on the screen."

I replied, "You sound like my Juilliard friends describing the nature of art: Is it art if it's on the shelf or only when performed?"

"I don't know about that. I just do it."

All life was a straight line for his kind of comedy. Anyone who took himself seriously was a setup. A plumber who came in and wanted to discuss his work earnestly—to Ernest— became the topic of the next day's sketch. Ernie would study him and try to joke with him. If the man refused, it made Ernie's day and the next day's show.

For instance, we went deep-sea fishing in Acapulco and caught a nine-foot swordfish, which Ernie left with the boat captain to have mounted. It didn't arrive for several weeks, so Ernie wrote a letter to the Mexican taxidermist, saying we'd paid for the swordfish, where was it? The man wrote a letter, saying, "Dear Señor, it is very difficult to mount a swordfish," getting dirtier and dirtier in his broken English. Of course, Ernie picked that right up and wrote back, saying that he didn't understand what was so difficult about mounting a swordfish; would he please explain in even greater detail? This went back and forth between Ernie and the taxidermist for months; every time a letter came in we'd alert friends and have a party to read the letter. As the letters got dirtier, the crowds got bigger. We all were very disappointed when the swordfish itself arrived. How different we felt about fur and stuffed animals then. If I caught that beautiful creature today, that fish would have an eight-by-ten glossy taken and go right back into the ocean.

If I read a book that analyzed anything, Ernie'd be furious. I'd have to put the jacket on backward so he couldn't see the title. Otherwise he'd say to the kids, "Well, here she comes now, Dr. Freud in person. Careful now. What's this? I can't smoke a cigar because it has a terrible meaning of some kind." It was a great act; I would laugh it off and keep reading. While I had a tendency to pull things apart to see how they worked, Ernie was completely spontaneous. I like to call it his "laughing in church" approach to humor. He believed what Oscar Wilde had said: "Life is too important to be taken seriously." I learned to believe it, too.

Just as Milton Berle had given me my first lessons in comic timing by grabbing my arm, Ernie gave me my Ph.D. He wiggled his upstage nostril when we were on live TV, to tell me to freeze: "I'm timing for the joke; stand still; don't blow it." Being nearsighted, I had to be pretty close to him to see if the nostril was flaring or not. When I was across the room, we had to have bigger signals for me to stop moving because he was going for a laugh. He changed the action and plot as he went along, so I had to watch carefully for his inserting comic takes that hadn't been planned. More often than not, there were more of them than there were of the planned bits or, later, the script.

I thought I'd been hired as the girl singer, but I became more and more involved in the planning and workings of the show. I told him, "I feel like the magician's assistant; I pose with my legs and go 'ta-da' whenever you pull off a big one." Later on live TV my shorthand for when I thought he'd done something extraordinary was a softly whispered "ta-da." In the early days an average rehearsal for Ernie was to say, "Bring a trench coat and a slouch hat in tomorrow; we're going to do a spy bit." That was it. I never knew what the sketches were going to be about until the cameraman went to a "tel-op" (title card) and he'd tell me what he'd planned for the next scene, how we were to fill time until the next card.

Ernie taught me to be one of the first to master the ten-second fill. That's when he had finished one bit and there were ten seconds until a commercial, not enough time to start a new topic. I would see that coming and run off and put on a weird hat or throw him a rubber chicken from the prop cart. He would say, "I don't know what's the matter with this crazy girl. Stay tuned, and we'll be right back and find out." He'd turn to me and say, "What are you doing, throwing a stupid . . ." We faded out and never did find out, of course. I've since read many cerebral articles about the heavy symbolism on Ernie's shows. Believe me, we were killing time with what-ever was available.

Kovacs's comedy didn't work as well on a nightclub stage, as we found later in Las Vegas and Lake Tahoe. It is difficult to make a slight raised eyebrow take without a tight close-up. Also, not having grown up in either vaudeville or night-clubs, he had no preconceived notions. He knew that tele-vision was a totally different medium, a magic box that entertained people in their own homes. He never forgot that we were in their private living rooms and bedrooms, across the rooms on small twelve-inch black-and-white screens. We had to do bolder strokes. He was the first to use cartoon frames, where the camera didn't move and he jumped in and out of the camera frame, much like a cartoon panel in the funny papers. He said, "The audience is closer, friendlier; you're a guest in their houses; each one thinks of you as their personal friend." He would try to include the viewers in every aspect of the show, by introducing the technical members of the staff on-screen, holding shameless contests, such as guess-ing how many beans in a jar—anything that would involve them and get them to write in. (In those days TV popularity was determined not by Nielsens but by the volume of mail that came in.) I thought this was a great idea until many ladies started writing to him with descriptive, graphic pictures of themselves, saying, "You've been in my bedroom daily. Wouldn't you like to come over in person?" Enclosed would be the name and address and the invitation: "Just knock on the door and ask for Sally."

Ernie never wanted a live studio audience who couldn't see the special effects because of the equipment; he said that with a studio audience you had "the worst of both possible worlds: The studio audience can't see the picture transmitted to the people at home, and the people at home are puzzled because we have to play to the audience they can't see." He was adamant about that. The crew was enough audience: "If I make them laugh, I'll make the audience at home laugh." I recently saw one of the shows from this period; I thought there *was* an audience because the crew was laughing so hard. Unlike musicians in a nightclub, where when the band laughs, you know you're not funny, the TV crew is a good yardstick. Ernie would have a live audience only when a network forced him to, but he never liked it. Ernie's special gift to his viewers was to enter their homes and interact with them.

I tried to compliment Ernie by saying he was making a great comment on the state of the world. He said, "Comment, schmomment. Get ready for the pie." He was totally apolitical. When Frank Sinatra was out campaigning for John Kennedy for President, Ernie, while thinking that JFK was the best man, said, "I stick to what I do." He thought that creators, writers, actors, musicians should stick to their respective crafts and stay out of politics. You saw only generic politicians on his shows; he never did a takeoff on a specific public figure. (Back in Philadelphia, on one of his early outdoor forays, he played a politician making a street-corner speech. The punch line was for Ernie to take custard pie in the face. However, the thrower neglected to take the pie out of its heavy metal piepan; he threw it diagonally and hit Ernie in the eye. We all thought it was part of the fun until Ernie didn't get up. He was out cold.)

When I went to the Actors Studio, Ernie ranted and raved. "They're going to destroy your natural timing," he maintained. "They've already got you thinking about it instead of just doing it." I protested, "But, Ernie, this comes naturally to you. I have to go and learn *why* I'm great some days and terrible on others. You know how to do things spontaneously; I'm desperately trying to learn; I need help." Oddly enough, when I asked Lee Strasberg about acting technique in class, he also said, "It doesn't apply to you; just do it." And he'd do hours of explaining technique to some actors.

Pinching his nose and gesturing, Ernie would do twenty minutes on the subject of the Actors Studio for anyone who would listen. He did it at parties, but not as a takeoff on me, just on Studio actors in general. He even did it on the show once. With a big sigh, he'd say, "Oooohhhh, you've got to feeeeel it." Or in a wheezy voice he'd do baby talk: "We doo-ing ah-tors 'tudio today." (He later met Lee Strasberg in California and played it straight and cordial, even liked him.)

Later, when I did the Marilyn Monroe bit on *Ed Sullivan*, Ernie carefully added to my monologue a takeoff on the Actors Studio. Lee Strasberg told me that Marilyn had seen it in Milton and Amy Greene's living room in Connecticut and laughed uproariously, loving it.

While I went to Strasberg's Actors Studio to get some insight into playing Daisy Mae, Marilyn Monroe showed up in my class on Tuesdays and Thursdays; she was auditing. She'd wear a kerchief and sunglasses and could be totally unrecognizable when she wanted to be, without makeup. She could be in the background as much as she could put her Marilyn persona center stage. It was up to her which she wanted to do. Since she didn't perform in class, many of the students didn't even know it was she. Later I had this weird feeling when I found out from costumers that Marilyn and I were exactly the same size, height, weight, measurements, even our unusually large head size (23½), glove and shoe sizes.

When I had first seen her on TV, I thought Marilyn was the funniest woman I'd ever seen in my life; everybody else thought she was a dumb blonde, a Jayne Mansfield type. But she had created the Marilyn character as carefully as Jean Stapleton did Edith Bunker. I really was a fan and kept doing Marilyn in my act until I got to know her in California. She always made me think of the actors' adage: "To succeed in show business, you have to have the hide of a rhinoceros and the soul of a butterfly." She had the soul but not the hide.

She was vulnerable; she couldn't take any kind of rejection. When Ernie was talking to her on the phone and said he had to hang up, she'd say, "Wait a minute, just a few minutes more." The more I knew her, the less funny my takeoff seemed to be. When she was on top, I could do the takeoff, and both she and I liked it; but when I knew how troubled she was, it was no longer funny to me, so I had to stop "doing" her, long before she died.

In my favorite five-minute live television bit, Ernie read the King Menelaus speech as a serious actor would do it. He came out in a Spartan helmet, breastplate, and sandals. At the sight of him in that getup, everybody started to giggle, of course. But as he read the speech and became more serious and dramatic, the audience settled down, still waiting for the laugh. A minute into it, you're still waiting for the laugh; two minutes in, and you start to think he's a pretty fair actor. Four minutes in, you think, Damn, he's terrific; just when you get to five minutes of this setup, he does a little time step and exits with a shuffle off to Buffalo.

By now we were no longer trying to kill time; the networks were getting more sophisticated, and advertisers had a lot more to say about programming. The networks would say, "The sponsor won't stand for that long a sketch. Nothing happens for the first four minutes; you have to cut that down, make it shorter." Ernie'd say, "No, you can't cut it down. That's the whole point; it takes that long to set it up right."

About another bit, they'd say, "Repetition, too much repetition." And he'd say, "You've gotta repeat to set it up. That box is across the room; it's small, so they don't see it like a full studio. You either have to keep repeating it or set up the cliff-hanger, because if you don't, they're going to go to the refrigerator or the bathroom."

Ernie truly loved his work. The studio was his playpen; the camera and the images he created were his toys. Even though he now had networks and, more important, sponsors to contend with, he would never be bound by conventional thinking and always looked for new creative frontiers to conquer. He demanded and got from his fellow workers the same dedication that he himself gave to producing a television show. They all were his playmates. Even the serious business

199

of dealing with the money and networks provided blocks for his toy building set.

In the studio Ernie treated his crew as surrogate family. He did extra little things to make sure that the people who made his kind of live TV comedy possible had a good time. On the early CBS show Russ Gaynor, our fabulous sound man, was given free rein. On one half hour the crew spent the whole time producing random sound effects, such as gunshots, drumrolls, and horse whinnies, in the background, to Ernie's obvious delight. To satisfy the censors, he had to put one particular sound in as "drainboard" on the script, but of course, what the audience heard was an unmistakable loud toilet flush. (The censors didn't usually tune into the programs, so we used it daily, until finally one of the censors did tune in, and we promised to cut it. In about two weeks the flush was on again with the same regularity.) Once he hit it big in New York, and for the rest of his life, whenever Ernie gave one of his frequent lavish parties, everyone from the show, including the pages, was invited.

Some of our CBS crew also worked on *The Late Late Show*. One of their favorite sports was to turn the master control sound switch down just a little bit after each commercial break. The viewers who were still there would have to get up and adjust their volumes accordingly; we didn't have clickers then. When the final movie segment came on, the crew put it back up to its full network standard volume, then ran like hell to watch all the city's lights go on as the people who had dozed off leaped up from their beds to turn down the sound. Even without him around, the crew was in tune with Kovacs. Nobody working television yet took it seriously. The unions were not that strong.

Ernie was always in complete control, in the driver's seat. If that was threatened or shaken in any way, that was no good. He said, "When it's right, it's right, whether you're painting it, dancing it, or violining it." There was only one creative voice. Once you worked with Ernie, you realized that it was his voice or no one's. If you didn't agree, he'd leave. Usually his just threatening to leave would do it. He was incapable of working any other way. Somebody had to have the overall picture, and right or wrong, everyone had to agree that his vision was it. What Ernie got from his crew was the best creative support possible. He never told the crew how to do it; he'd just say, "Here's what I want to do; you make it work the best way you can from your department." Bob Kemp and the other crew members from Ernie's ABC show have always told me it was the most rewarding work they'd done because they weren't told what to do or how to do it but were asked to participate with the best of their ability. Special effects, props, everybody contributed, but there was still one boss, one overall creative control.

Ernie once told me he went to a Milton Berle rehearsal. Milton was in a bathrobe and had a whistle. While he never dreamed of doing the same kind of comedy as Milton, Ernie was in awe of Milton's being absolutely right technically on anything comedic. Every time he stopped the rehearsal and whistled it was because something was wrong. Ernie said, "I could never do that, but I have tremendous respect for Milton's control and knowledge of comedy."

In November 1956, just as I was opening in *Li'l Abner* on Broadway, not only was Ernie for the first time not doing three shows at once, he wasn't even doing one. ABC had canceled the radio show, and both NBC shows went off. He was still under contract to NBC, and the network was looking for a new format for Ernie, which he did not want. He wanted airtime and to be left alone.

At a meeting at NBC, in a big boardroom, to determine the content of his next program, the network presented him with an appointed creative team. This strong producer, executive producer, and director, each of whom was adamant in his idea of what Ernie should do, tried to streamline "zany, wacky, unpredictable Ernie."

Each one presented, from the head of the table, his idea of what Kovacs was all about, while Ernie sat silently on the sidelines. As he told me, two or three times he tried politely to interrupt, to say that it wasn't going to work that way, but nobody paid any attention. The director was saying, "No, this is absolutely the way it's going to be done." As the director was continuing in his diatribe, Ernie raised his hand like a kid at school and said softly, "Excuse me, I have to go make a phone call," and tiptoed out of the room. Once outside, his

Hungarian temper must have boiled over because instead of going to the phone, he kept right on down the hall, down the elevator, and out the Sixth Avenue entrance. He walked home, north about forty blocks, to Ninetieth Street; although it was bitter cold, he didn't seem to notice. He had left his vicuña coat, muffler, hat, and alligator briefcase behind. He walked into the apartment, still in a fury, told me the story, and sat down at his typewriter. He stayed there for nearly two weeks, having only carbon paper, food, and an occasional drink delivered. He napped on the sofa in his den whenever he was tired. Otherwise he wrote straight through.

When he handed me *Zoomar*, a novel about a rising television executive in the middle of the network power structure, its fictional characters read very much like our life. The Miss Wipola sounded suspiciously like a certain Miss U.S. Television contest in which I had been very much involved. The couple had a nice country place up in New City, New York. Rereading the book recently brought back into sharp focus what day-by-day life was like in television and at home as we lived it in the 1950's, fake flip dialogue and all. After all, the leading lady was named Eileen.

The hero of *Zoomar*, Tom Moore, is an advertising account executive "at liberty" who suddenly finds himself a TV producer and an expert in a field about which he knows nothing—par for the course. As Ernie's alter ego he comes up against a host of characters who were thinly disguised real people we all knew. He even included in the novel an extramarital affair for the man, something I felt was totally unnecessary.

When the book came out, Pete Martin of the *Saturday Evening Post*, the best interviewer I ever met, asked Ernie how he could have written the book in thirteen days. Ernie told him:

> When you're writing about a subject you know, because it's all you've done for eight years, it's spontaneous writing. You don't even have to do research. . . . I wrote my book this way: I had no plot, I wrote the first line, then I wrote the second line, then I wrote the third line. I kept on that way. Some days I wrote 40 pages, some

days two. . . . I would never revise. The TV shows I
wrote went straight from my typewriter to the copy-
makers. I don't change a thing. I figure the first things
a man says are his spontaneous things. I know it sounds
ridiculous but I looked at *The Man in the Gray Flannel
Suit* and *Don't Go Near the Water* to see how long they
were. They are good books, so I'd make mine the same
number of pages. Then I had an even better idea, "I'll
make mine as long as *From Here to Eternity*." At that
point I had six hundred pages, then I got a hurry up
call to make a movie, so I made the book shorter, pages
lopped off—about a hundred. It was just as well, I
would have talked too much if it had run as long as I
had originally planned.

During our five years together in New York, 1952–57,
Ernie and I were on television somewhere in almost every
time slot—from early morning to late night—and on all four
networks, ABC, CBS, NBC, and Dumont. Ernie was an acquired taste, and networks didn't quite know what to do with
him. His fans were, and still are, loyal and followed us from
network to network, no matter what the time slot. If they
looked really hard, they always found us. Most TV personalities had a regular time slot: Sunday at 8:00 P.M. was Ed
Sullivan, Tuesday at 8:00 P.M. was Milton Berle, etc. While
we never had that luxury, we were always on some network
somewhere for nearly ten years, in Philly, New York, or Los
Angeles.

When I opened on Broadway as Daisy Mae, Ernie sent me
a tubful of daisies; they weren't in season on November 15
in New York, but that didn't bother him. He had them flown
in from Australia or from wherever they were in bloom. Ernie
always sent me flowers, for no reason. Sometimes he sent
them when it was raining; I didn't like the rain. (He loved
it.) Later, when I played Las Vegas alone, he had a red rose
delivered every day.

The public liked *Li'l Abner*; we were a big hit. But for me,
the show was a lot of hard work with no big payoff for Daisy
Mae. If I had had to face *Li'l Abner* for the one full year of
my contract without stimulating my mind, I'd have gone mad.

So I kept learning all I could. Consequently, in the dumbest part imaginable, I learned to act.

Lehman Engel, my buddy from *Wonderful Town*, also conducted the orchestra in *Li'l Abner*. At one point Abner sings a chorus of "If I Had My Druthers," followed by a dialogue scene. Then I wanted to start my chorus, in another key, cold, without a bell note. I told Lehman that I could remember the pitch from Abner's key and find my own entrance note. It worked every evening, until one day when I was vocalizing backstage, to Abner's chorus. It sounded odd to me; the pitch and tonality didn't feel right behind my ears. Then I figured it out: Abner had changed his key, but Lehman had warned everyone not to say anything to me. I walked on stage, did the dialogue, and looked down to Lehman's folded arms and pixie smile; he was not going to give me any bell note, even for a new key. When I came in on the new correct note, I could see him snapping his fingers and mouthing, "Damn, I didn't get her." But he beamed from ear to ear through the whole song.

When I left *Li'l Abner*, after a year's run I had lost twelve pounds and permanently gained a shoe size. I had to throw away a dozen pairs of imported Italian shoes because they were too small. Ernie said, "Many an actress has gotten a swelled head playing a starring role, but Edie's the first to get swelled feet." Although I had worked my way up to a thousand dollars a week in *Li'l Abner* (still much less than what I got for TV appearances), I found out that everybody in the show but me had a contractual provision for a two-week vacation. Ernie was even madder than I about it. Our show's doctor agreed that it was unfair for everyone else to have time off and not me. He conspired with me to tell the press I was tired. He "prescribed" a two-week vacation for me immediately. Ernie and I, with Betty and Kippie, went to Acapulco off-season. It was marvelous. We were the only ones there, so had all fifteen waiters to ourselves at dinner. They'd break their necks for us. One would go out to market in the morning, then find us and tell us he could get a beautiful goose for dinner; would we like that? Ernie got a particular bang out of that and would consult with the waiter on the preparation of the goose. Betty and Kippie quickly became even more expert in room service. They learned the Spanish word for ice cream, *helado.* Soon they could order ice cream in any language from room service in any country; they had inherited their father's passion for being waited on.

On Wednesdays and Saturdays, matinee days, we could not have our six o'clock dinner at home. Ernie and the kids would come down to the theater district for dinner at Sardi's. Then Betty, Kippie, and I would go right back next door to the St. James Theatre for tap lessons. One of the dancers in the show had his dinner early in order to give us lessons on the stage. The girls had always wanted to learn to tap-dance, and I needed the practice.

One day I told the kids to run their bath as I was preparing to go to the theater for the evening performance of *Li'l Abner.* I was just leaving the bedroom floor, twenty minutes later, when I saw a green river cascading down the hallway toward the elevator door. Betty and Kippie were watching TV and had forgotten all about the bath. Standing in ankle-deep water, I turned the faucets off. It was now 7:35 P.M. and I had to leave immediately to make my 8:00 "half hour." (In those days Broadway shows started at 8:30 P.M.) The last thing I saw as I left for the elevator was Ernie standing in the hall in shorts with a bucket, trying to throw the water back into the bathroom. The German butler and cook, otherwise still fully dressed in black for dinner service, but in socks and with pants and dress tied up to their knees, assisted. Ernie swore furiously: "You and your fucking theater; that's why we have all this trouble." The more he ranted in mock anger, the more the kids and I laughed. I smiled my best Daisy Mae smile and said, "Y'all have a good time," and ducked out the door in case the bucket was coming at me. No matter how bad the situation, it always ended in laughter.

Another night, as I was leaving for the theater, Betty and Kippie announced that they had to be dressed up in elaborate peasant costumes at school the next day. "Betty, I get home at midnight and you leave for school at seven A.M. I don't see how I can do it," I protested. Betty said, "But I thought you could sew; besides, Grandma always does it for us." So I did it, although it took most of the night. "Don't try this on me again; give some notice next time," I said. This was my first real decision about the girls, and looking back, I feel I made the wrong one by giving them the benefit of the doubt by staying up all night.

In looking back on my life with Ernie, it becomes evident that when I took my role as parent to the girls seriously, and did not—as Ernie seemed to want—become one of his three girls, I began to lose him as a playmate. Nothing specific comes to mind. I just feel that at this point I stopped being a "we" to Ernie and became one of "them." I feel, intuitively, that this was when the affair he described in *Zoomar* began.

Several times, after the Saturday night show, Ernie picked me up in a limo and announced that we going to the airport to take a flight to Havana for the weekend. I'd say, "Ernie, I'm dressed for a New York winter, with a wool dress and a fur coat." He'd say, "What the heck, we'll buy clothes to-morrow; the hotel shop will be open, buy anything you need," as he poured the Dom Pérignon and handed me a caviar spoon. I'd ask what we were going to do, and he'd say, "We'll look at the humidors." The cigar companies had been alerted to open the humidors on Sunday. I've never seen Ernie hap-pier than when walking through these humidors, selecting the best cigars. He was in heaven sniffing the sensuous aroma of top-grade cured Cuban tobacco.

If Ernie was in a room where someone was smoking a cheap cigar, he'd leave; if he was in a taxi where the driver was smoking a bad cigar, Ernie would change cabs. If there was a cold cigar in an ashtray, he'd throw it in the trash. If someone left a burning cigarette in an ashtray two rooms away, he could smell it. He'd get up from a nap and find the offending cigarette to put it out. He smoked cigarettes only in airplanes, which wouldn't allow cigars. He'd take one puff and half of the cigarette would disappear, he was so used to taking long drags on cigars. He used to try to find places on the sets of his shows to hide cigars, so he'd always have one at hand; people would steal them. Going to the Broadway theater, he'd do the same. He'd find a place outside the lobby to hide his cigar and would be the first one out after the act finished to retrieve it. Every once in a while he'd come upon a smiling bum with Ernie's expensive Cuban carefully clenched between his teeth.

NINE

IN EARLY 1957 Richard Rodgers and Oscar Hammerstein II wrote the first original musical comedy for television, *Cinderella*. Julie Andrews, still in *My Fair Lady*, was signed for the title role. Hammerstein, in writing the libretto, adhered pretty closely to the original fairy tale's plot, but added some depth of character and humor. I played the Godmother as a young salty-tongued woman who didn't think it was fair to rely on her magic wand. She used her powers with great reluctance, and her big song, a duet with Julie, "Impossible," was all about how you *couldn't* turn a plain ugly duckling into a princess. Nonetheless, the pumpkin did become a golden coach and gave Julie and me, riding off to the ball in it, a nifty first-act curtain scene plus a reprise, retitled "It's Possible."

The best known of Rodgers's nine songs for the ninety-minute production is "Do I Love You Because You're Beautiful?" The live and in color CBS show, which preempted *The Ed Sullivan Show* and *General Electric Theater* on Sunday night, March 31, 1957, had a then-astronomical budget of $385,000. Ralph Nelson was the director. Kaye Ballard and Alice Ghostley played the wicked stepsisters.

Rodgers and Hammerstein prepared the show as they would have done for Broadway, except that there was no understudy for Julie. We did the show in a cramped old converted studio that was two stories high. Because it was such a tiny studio, we couldn't shoot widths, we had to shoot depths; the stairs were always visible, and much of the action took place on them. Rodgers sat in the crowded control room throughout the rehearsals. They were as intensive as for any TV show up to that time, quite a contrast from working with Kovacs. William and Jean Eckart did the costumes, the first really glittering ones on a television spectacular. Both my baton and my eyelids sparkled.

Because Julie and I both were in Broadway shows, we began eating our evening meal together, a proper English tea in her dressing room at 4:00 P.M. After *Cinderella* Julie and her then-husband Tony Walton, the set and costume designer, came to Ernie's and my apartment for dinner often. (In 1964, when she moved to the West Coast to make the movie *Mary Poppins*, Tony, who had stayed behind to work in New York, called me often to say, "Please take care of her. Don't let her 'go Hollywood.' " Ernie's and my daughter, Mia, who was five when Julie was making the movie, was a devoted fan of the *Mary Poppins* book by P. L. Travers. I asked Julie one night to come home from the studio in costume and walk into Mia's room at bedtime. "Ooh, Mary Poppins." Mia squealed delightedly. It was a moment she remembered her whole life.)

Also in early 1957, while I was still in *Li'l Abner*, Ernie was sifting through the many offers that he had received after his *Eugene* silent show. From them he selected his first movie role, in *Operation Mad Ball*, starring Jack Lemmon, Kathryn Grant, and Mickey Rooney, produced by Jed Harris and directed by Richard Quine. Blake Edwards was among the writers of this comedy about soldiers conniving to hold a wild party off base. Ernie got second billing for the movie, the first under his four-year contract with Columbia's Harry Cohn, soon to become Ernie's new best friend. More important, Ernie and Dick Quine, who was to direct him in three more pictures, became good friends.

Quine and Kim Novak also became "good friends" and after work often came to our house and stayed overnight. They left for the studio together in the morning. This gave rise to the rumors that Kim and Ernie were an item; it wasn't so because I helped her with her hair when she got up in the morning.

The first time Ernie and Harry Cohn met was when Harry visited the set of *Operation Mad Ball* and yelled out to Ernie, "Hey, actor!" Ernie responded with "F---off," and it was the beginning of another big friendship. Harry later came to visit us often in Las Vegas and unerringly picked the least attractive girl in the chorus line as his companion.

Whenever they were in New York, Ernie brought his fellow Columbia contract players to our place on Central Park West: Kathryn Grant (later Mrs. Bing Crosby), Felicia Farr, and her boyfriend, Jack Lemmon. I really liked Felicia. She was funny, smart, and beautiful and had great cheekbones. She had a warm, infectious laugh. Everybody, then as now, loved Jack. Jack already admired Ernie from his TV work and would nail his Havana cigars to the tables on the set to attract Ernie's notice. Every time Ernie tried to pick up a cigar he'd get a handful of shredded tobacco. Nonetheless, Jack and Ernie also became immediate fast friends.

On March 24, 1957, on the plane to Los Angeles Ernie was full of optimism. He wrote me a continuing letter from the time he took off. It was full of gags, complaints that the flight attendants wouldn't let him smoke a cigar, and descriptions of sleeping passengers on whom he was threatening to paste airmail stickers. It also contained these thoughts about us: "Darling, I am the luckiest guy even though I am a sad one at the moment. I am lucky because I am sad. . . . It is so good to love the one right person in the world. It isn't really like being in love, it's more than that. It's like finding the one thing in the whole world that two people were born to have—the careers, money, everything, is a background part of what you and I were born for. . . . All I know for sure is that I love you, darling."

Reading this letter, I realized that I really had it all: I was starring on Broadway and television, had a beautiful apartment, two kids, the latest clothes, and a strong man who really loved me and wanted me to have it all. What more could I ask for? I had everything I ever wanted, plus what most people would consider the perfect life.

Although he would do it when he had to, Ernie really hated to fly, and the insurance company on the picture would not allow him to fly once the picture was shooting. So I had to. After the Saturday night show I would usually take the 12:30 A.M. red-eye from a corrugated World War II "temporary" building at Idlewild Airport (later JFK), arriving in Los Angeles at 7:00 A.M. I would get to the Beverly Hills Hotel by 7:30. Ernie and I would get reacquainted and then head for the swimming pool, where we would sit all day. During the week he would go to Jac's (of Jac's Slax) and pick out these great sports outfits for me. He would get me leather coats, gingham shirtwaist dresses, and Jax famous slacks in every color. I was surprised to learn that Jac's also cut their ladies' slacks in two pieces, as the navy had done with my brother's bell-bottoms. When I got back to New York, I made a pattern for all the girl dancers in *Li'l Abner*, so they, too, had the newest in California sportswear before anybody else in New York.

Ernie and I would go out for a nice dinner Sunday night and spend a glorious night at the hotel. I'd catch the early A.M. plane Monday back to New York, just about in time to be at the St. James for the 8:00 P.M. "half hour." My understudy, Joyce Gladmond, always had an interesting weekend, having to brush up on the part and wondering if I was going to make my tight connections. I always did, so she never got to play the role until I left the show.

One weekend I couldn't fly to L.A. at all. As usual, I was planning to go meet Ernie, but our friend Frank Farrell, who was a *World-Telegram* columnist, said, "I think it would be very wise if you would stay in town this weekend." I said, "No, I'm all set to go to the Coast, and Ernie's expecting me." He kept insisting that he and I should go to the Tony Awards. I said, "Frank, how am I going to win a Tony with a part like Daisy Mae? I'm going to Hollywood." Then he said, "I must insist that you stay." The tone of his voice told me that I had better stay in New York. So I did, and to my astonishment, I did get the Tony Award, for a part that I didn't even consider to be in the running. Apparently, my Broadway peers understood how difficult it was to have a leading role and be onstage most of the time with little or nothing to do. I look at the Tony every day and say, "Thank you fellow actors and Frank Farrell."

Ernie was having a meeting with someone at the Beverly Hills Hotel Polo Lounge when he was approached by Henry Rogers, of the public relations firm of Rogers, Cowan and Brenner, who launched into a sales pitch. "You need a big West Coast PR firm," Rogers told Ernie. "We'll get you national publicity like you've never had; we'll even get you a *Life* cover!" Ernie nonchalantly walked over to the front desk to get his mail. Right on top was an advance copy of the next week's *Life*. There was Ernie's face and massive cigar staring right at him on the cover. He showed the magazine to a flabbergasted Henry and said, "The cover of *what*?"

Although I didn't make my first trips to California until the spring of 1957, Ernie had made a brief trip there a year earlier to audition girl singers to replace me on his television show when I went into *Li'l Abner*. On that trip he hadn't known anybody, so he had spent most of his time trying out restaurants. But this extended solo trip for *Mad Ball* was different. Julie Andrews and Tony Walton had suggested that he look up Kay Kendall and some of their other friends. Besides staying at the Beverly Hills Hotel and getting to know his new buddies Jack Lemmon and Dick Quine, Ernie was in great demand socially. He was considered a single man in Hollywood. He went out every night, just as he'd done all his life, whether I was there or not.

He met Frank Sinatra, who was then single and lived in a one-bedroom bachelor pad near the top of Coldwater Canyon. It had a fabulous view and a separate screening room bigger than the main house. Ernie told me about many evenings up there, playing cards and drinking Jack Daniel's. He liked Frank's taste. Later Dean Martin told me that some of these poker games were garnished with hot and cold running naked ladies, but he added, "Don't worry, Edie, Ernie never looked up when the bedroom door opened and shut."

Dean recently told me that Ernie was one of the unforgettables, the only guy who could make him laugh while he was taking the entire poker pot. No one could ever forget Ernie.

Since he lived at the Beverly Hills Hotel and had already

memorized the menu, naturally Ernie had to eat out every
night. Kay Kendall was the first to take him to Dominick's,
the hot restaurant in Beverly Hills with an unlisted phone
number, the first such industry "club." Dom would take reservations only from people he wanted there; you walked in
through the kitchen, waving to Mrs. Dom, who was the chef.
Addie, her sister, was the only waitress; the three of them
did it all. They served only three things: broiled chicken,
steak, or pork chops. One night someone inadvertently came
in the front door and saw all empty tables. Dom said, "Sorry,
we're completely booked." Dom was a colorful character who
made the best martinis in town. He had an ancient, even then,
jukebox that played only early 1940's tunes, with which he
sang along. "Ol' Man Mose" was his favorite. Movie people
liked Dom's because you could come from your last shot of
the day, still in makeup with your ratty old jeans on. Nobody
cared, because everybody was dressed the same way. Billy
Wilder, Jack Lemmon, Edward G. Robinson, Jimmy Stewart,
Kim Novak, Warren Beatty, and Robert Wagner and Natalie
Wood were always at Dom's. Ernie often dined with Kay
Kendall. His other frequent dinner companions included Kim
Novak, Kathryn Grant, Mervyn Le Roy, and Shirley Mellner,
his last associate producer on New York TV, who had pre-
ceded him to Hollywood to take a job at Desilu.

Suddenly, with one half of my life on the West Coast, at
least for the time being, I found myself with some free time.
Besides Betty's and Kippie's classes and other activities to
supervise, I had my nightly stint in *Li'l Abner* and my own
classes at the Actors Studio, vocal coaching, singing and
dancing lessons. By this time I had my own dressmaker, even
though I was still designing my clothes. My sketching needed
improving, so as a perennial student, I attended the Traphagen School of Fashion Design.

Because Traphagen was on West Fifty-seventh Street and
my class ended at 8:00, I was allowed an unprecedented 8:05
P.M. as my "half hour" call. Theater pros were serious about
punctuality and discipline, and Equity had strict rules. However, I was serious about perfecting my costume design skills,
so they relented because I was always on time. I had never
signed in at any theater since *Blithe Spirit* because I was

always the first one there; the stage manager signed me in. Not signing in is a privilege you earn not through stardom but through years of punctuality.

Although I was missing Ernie, I was busy with the show, my classes, publicity, and attending to refining the kids. In those days there were Thursday matinees in Philadelphia for shows coming to Broadway, so I would take the kids out of school and on the train to see these special new shows, such as *West Side Story*, before they came to Broadway. I had seen the actors' run-through of *West Side Story* and thought it would be an important part of Betty and Kippie's education. To this day Kippie and Betty can indentify songs from Broadway musicals of that period; they can even say they saw them out of town. Larry Kasha, our stage manager on *Li'l Abner*, who then wanted to grow up to be Hal Prince, took me to after-theater lectures by Robert Lewis on acting, as Hal had taken me to Harold Clurman. Frank Farrell was always in the center of anything that was going on in New York and ready to squire me to any PR or other party I cared to go to. Panama and Frank and Peter Palmer and their wives took me out to dinner, and Johnny Mercer, whenever he was in town, would take me on a tour of Fifty-second Street jazz joints.

Because my feet kept changing sizes, I quickly accumulated a collection of 150 pairs of shoes. I also had acquired seven furs; little did we know then that thirty years later animal activists would make wearing animal skins as unpopular as smoking in airplanes. The full-length coats of chinchilla, mink, sable, and sheared beaver all had special pockets sewed into the inside lining so that Pamela, my new two-pound Yorkshire terrier, could be my constant but silent companion everywhere I went in New York, including Sardi's, El Morocco, and the Stork Club. (If Pamela could feel the warmth of my leg, she wouldn't bark, but if I left her in the checkroom, she would.)

Lorraine D'Essen, our TV animal agent, had found Pamela for Betty and Kippie, but Yorkies are a peculiar breed. They usually do not like children, and most of them do not like men. That left only Lillian, our secretary, or me. Pamela would go to the theater with me. When I came home at night, Ernie would ask if I'd walked Pamela. Of course, I hadn't, so he would walk this dog, the size of his foot, up and down Central Park West (I wasn't allowed to walk out alone at 1:00 A.M.). She'd do nothing on the walk, but the minute they came into the apartment she'd squat by his foot. Ernie and Pamela did not get along. But Lillian would put Pamela on her desk, where she sat contentedly, like a two-pound paperweight, all day. Lillian could lift her off the desk, pick up the papers under her, and put her back without the dog's even waking up. Pamela, later, in my nightclub act, played Zsa Zsa Gabor's Yorkie, in her own chinchilla coat. "Zsa Zsa" explained that it had been given to Pamela by a "veddy, veddy velsy Doberman pinscher from Texas."

On April 16, 1957, my birthday, Ernie, still in Hollywood, hired Mamma Leone's, the Italian restaurant, to send a party backstage, including a cake with his picture on it and champagne for everyone. For our third wedding anniversay, in September, he sent a mariachi band backstage, complete with margaritas and a tub of floating gardenias. This was standard operating procedure for Ernie, and by now I loved it and wallowed in it. Even Lily Lake was never like this.

The Tropicana Hotel in Las Vegas was under construction in May, when Ernie stopped by on his train trip from L.A. to New York to check out the unfinished hotel and showroom. Monte Proser, who wanted us in with our nightclub act in November, following Eddie Fisher's opening of the main room, was with him. At Monte's and Ernie's request, the hotel happily opened one crap table at the casino, so they could have a little game. Ernie, who made a point of never telling me about his wins and losses, was obviously having trouble telling me the exact amount at Sardi's over the *boccone dolce* on his arrival in New York. He kept struggling with it, and I kept at him, finally saying, "Honey, just tell me where the commas are." He laughed, but never did tell me.

Later I would learn not to press for amounts of his losses but to find out surreptitiously from other players a range, not exact amounts. Instead of questioning him, I'd then go buy something I didn't need for the same amount. I bought a 1780 ten-foot-long Venetian harpsichord from French and Company after learning of one evening's losses. When Ernie objected that we couldn't afford it, I said, "I'm just matching you, dear. If you want to me to stop spending, stop gambling."

One day in 1957, during *Li'l Abner*, in the midst of transcontinental commuting, I got a call from our business managers, Braunstein and Chernin, in New York. Chernin himself said, "It's very important that I come over to your apartment and talk to you personally as soon as possible. What are you doing right now?" I explained that I had to leave for the theater soon, but he persisted: "I'll be right over; it won't take a minute; wait for me." In a very few minutes the intercom buzzed from the lobby. I invited Chernin to come on up, but he said that I should come down to the lobby to talk to him. When I protested, he insisted.

Puzzled, I went down to the lobby as he requested and found Chernin in a very agitated state. He looked left and right, then motioned me to sit next to him on a straight-backed chair close to the center of our building's reception area. I demanded to know what this was all about "I want to be sure that this conversation isn't bugged," he said, looking over his shoulder. I was stunned. I'm sure it was the first time that I had ever heard the term "bugged." "You and Ernie are in big tax trouble," he said. I said that I hadn't known; Ernie had mentioned some tax problems, but I thought that they had been taken care of.

I never paid much attention to finances with Ernie. He'd say, "I've got it covered . . . don't worry . . . I've taken care of it . . . it's okay." I had heard that we were in a 91 percent tax bracket but didn't pay much attention since we both were working at least two jobs. Money was plentiful. For the first time in my life I was not only able to, but was encouraged to, indulge in every whim and extravagance I'd ever dreamed of. Whatever I liked I could buy in every color. I just enjoyed myself. I was shocked to hear from Chernin that our taxes for 1957 would be a certain amount. I may not remember the exact amount, but the incidents and proportions are correct. I'm going to say that Chernin said the taxes due were forty-five thousand dollars.

"However," Chernin said, looking around the lobby furtively, "the IRS man says that if you and Ernie give him ten thousand dollars in cash, he'll make your tax come to only fifteen thousand dollars, so the total you'll have to pay out this year will be only twenty-five thousand instead of the forty-five thousand. When you fly out to the Coast this weekend, talk it over with Ernie and bring the cash back." I asked him why he didn't call Ernie himself. "I can't talk about this on the phone," he said, indicating with his hands that the phone might be bugged. "Just talk to Ernie, he'll understand; everybody in show business does it." He mentioned one big name who did every year.

This was all outside anything I'd ever come across in my proper but limited WASP upbringing. I told Chernin that I didn't have to ask Ernie: "What you're suggesting is illegal, immoral, and I believe called bribery. I won't do it, I won't ask Ernie to do it, and I know he wouldn't do it if I did ask him." Chernin insisted that I talk to Ernie and call him when I got back.

I didn't even want to hear about money problems, taxes. Surely we earned enough for everything. I went directly to a bookstore and bought a large paperback book on income taxes. I spent the entire plane trip going back to California reading the book, underlining, and making notes for five hours. By the time I landed I understood fully that a 91 percent bracket meant that only 9 percent of what you earned really belonged to you. The rest belonged to Uncle Sam. Ernie's cavalier attitude had always been: "Screw them, I earned it, I'll spend it."

Unfortunately the IRS did not agree. I pointed out that we weren't even on the right pages. As a writer he could deduct the many periodicals we subscribed to and maybe even his trips to research his next book, a novel. I carefully rearranged my wardrobe into those dresses I could sit down in (personal dresses) and those I couldn't (costumes). Dinah Shore had forced the definitive IRS decision on this at about this time. I told Ernie that I didn't see how we could do this thing that Chernin was suggesting. We had enough to worry about without waking up in the middle of the night thinking someone was going to drag us off to prison. Ernie said, "I can't either; tell him no."

When I returned to New York on Monday, Lillian, our secretary, said that Chernin had called to say that unless he had the cash and the right answer by the next day Ernie and I both would be very sorry. We didn't, and true to his word, our tax for that year was forty-five thousand dollars.

Ernie's New York poker buddies had included Russel Crouse, Howard Lindsay, Hal Friedman, a producer married to Marie Torre, the columnist who went to jail rather than reveal her sources, and a good friend of mine, Barry Shear, and Herbie Sussan, producer of *Wide World of Sports*. We later, in Beverly Hills, had an NBC tie line to call New York for free. (Ernie was still under contract.) Herbie was supposed to be in India. NBC called him in India, and the crew there plugged it into our tie line in Beverly Hills, where Herbie was in the midst of a three-day poker game. Ernie and the others treated it with their usual irreverence. "NBC, big deal!" The network, like everything and everyone else, was there only for the amusement of the boys. I just went along.

I was learning too well all of Ernie's lessons that money didn't matter, that having fun was what was life was about. After all, we both were working full steam ahead at everything and making a lot of money (I never knew how much). We had charge acounts everywhere. Who kept track? I just sent my salary checks to the business manager. Lillian took care of the incidental expenses. I never signed outgoing checks, applied only occasionally for "mad money," and never thought about it further. It didn't look as if I had to. Ernie's largess was his way of life, bigger than anyone else's. Everything had to be larger, the latest, the best, and the biggest!

He was constantly upgrading electronic equipment. In 1958 we had the first telephone answering "device" in Hollywood (complete with an English secretary on the tape: "You have reached the residence of Mr. and Mrs. Ernest Kovacs. . . . Please leave a short message."). The messages were often very short: a groan, a crisp "f---you," and a click. We also had two car phones, one in the front seat and one in the back (in those days car phones were only on a ship-to-shore frequency, through a maritime operator); the equipment took up so much space that there was barely room to close the trunk, much less put any luggage in it. Ernie insisted on two car phones just so he could say, "There goes my other phone."

On my closing night in *Li'l Abner*, one year after we had opened, I took my final bow in best Sydney Chaplin style, raced to a waiting limousine for the airport, and flew to Las Vegas to join Ernie for rehearsals for our Hotel Tropicana opening. We were booked for four weeks. It was my first time in Las Vegas, but my nightclub act had been perfected by all those weeks at the Persian Room, right down to ten-second costume changes done over rhymed couplets. Ernie, however, had never done a club act; all of his humor was visual, honed on "that little box across the living room." We both were concerned that his material, however brilliant on TV, might be misunderstood by a drinking audience geared to broader strokes. Even though he disliked rehearsal, he wanted this to work. We rehearsed for two full weeks, something he'd never done before, and took in every show in town, including the lounge acts. Ernie particularly admired Shecky Greene, whose lounge show then was done six times nightly from 9:00 P.M. to 6:00 A.M., at the Tropicana. We heard from Groucho that Shecky was also his favorite comic. Every night we saw Shecky at least once and never saw the same show twice.

Ernie had always had a preconceived idea of nightclub comics. He considered them generic, with predictable jokes. Shecky was a man who used impulse and improvisation to create his own special brand of humor, much as Ernie did. Shecky was Ernie's favorite living comedian.

Our show opened with eight gorgeous, leggy show girls, walking and posing, looking like something I had seen only on the late movies or in my French costume books. (The large French shows, such as the Folies Bergère, had not yet been seen in Vegas.) Then Ernie came on with some "teasers," as he had done on television, his most famous being "The Coty Girl," a takeoff on a commercial then running on TV, in which a beautiful model in a large hat would raise her bowed head, pose sweetly, and say, "Hello, I'm the—" splat, as a cream pie dripped over those gorgeous cheekbones. I did the next teaser. After a long walk out to the mike in a form-fitting gown, I leveled my gaze at the audience and opened my mouth to sing. Louis Armstrong's voice came out. I lip-synched his version of "Cold, Cold Heart." Then Ernie came on and said, "Good evening." He did a rambling monologue before introducing me in my act based on Martin and Blaine's number for the ANTA benefit. I called it "The Late, Late Show."

I impersonated several movie queens, doing complete wig-to-floor changes to a rhymed couplet. These included Helen Kane, Jeanette MacDonald, June Allyson, Shirley Temple, and Marlene Dietrich and ended with Marilyn Monroe. As Helen Kane I came on in a flapper dress and cloche hat and sang "I Wanna Be Loved by You (Boop Boop-a-Doop)"; I rushed offstage and to Ernie's rhymed couplet changed into Jeanette's red wig and large pink hat and matching pink bouffant skirt and sang sixteen bars of the "Italian Street Song," throwing flowers and ending by putting my fist through the tambourine. "June Allyson" came out in navy blue with a Peter Pan collar, sniveling and singing a very tepid "Wild, Blue Yonder," with a very loud, rude nose blow at the end. "Dietrich" came on in a trench coat and hat and sang, in a low, wobbling baritone, a minor third away from the real key, usually sharp. I finished with my dynamite closer, nationally hailed from my appearances on *The Ed Sullivan Show*. "Marilyn" came out in her beaded Ceil Chapman dress and a new white fox stole to the floor. "She" first did a short talk on "Method acking" and, in my best Bea Walker glossed and moving mouth, sang "S'Wonderful," carefully punctuated with bumps by the tuned kettledrum. Baroom.

Ernie never had a problem with alcohol; he was always on a manic high, whether he drank or not. But one day he had a few drinks before the dinner show, not his usual habit (nobody drinks before a show). Not only did his monologue wander even more, but his ten-second introductions to my characters extended to two or three minutes each, longer than the takeoffs themselves. The front office needed every show to be exactly the same length (something that Kovacs had never done, even on live TV) to get the audience back to the gambling tables. The pit bosses got on to me about getting Ernie to tighten up the act and asked the stage manager to tape-record the entire show. I played it back for Ernie and said, "Just listen to your timing." He knew it was really off and fixed it for the next show.

After that longer show, as I stood next to him in the Tropicana lobby with a turban on my head (I didn't have time to do my hair between shows), a woman rushed up to him and said, "Ernie, Ernie, you were terrific. And all those beautiful girls, doing those impressions were sensational." Ernie, putting me on, said, "Oh, really, thank you, thank you," not offering to correct her. Then she said, "And how's Edie? Is she still working on Broadway?" Ernie played her like a violin, rolling his eyes and looking at me. "Oh, she stayed home this trip." The woman went on: "All those other girls were just wonderful, but she's great, too. Say hello to Edie." Ernie smiled and waved her off, laughing and assuring her that he would. He turned back to me, who was ready to kill.

Las Vegas was still a small town; this was long before Howard Hughes and other corporations took over the hotels and clubs. Mike Todd and Elizabeth Taylor arrived on their private railroad car from the East. On their stopover in Chicago, not only had they done the usual Pump Room pit stop, but Mike had bought out Marshall Field. He bought her jewelry, cashmere blankets and coats, perfume, and every luxury. She told me, "I told him I don't need it." He said, "Yes, you do," and kept buying. I had never met her before, and those violet eyes were extraordinary. I have never seen a woman happier or more in love than Elizabeth Taylor at that time. Mike waited on her hand and foot. It was the big love of his life, too.

Ernie and I had worked with Mike before, on one of his benefits. He didn't ask you, he told you he was sending a car, but of course, always decked out with Ernie's favorite cigars, champagne, and caviar. Mike was Ernie's kind of guy; they were the same person. I vividly remember Elizabeth sitting quietly at the table, just watching his every move. She followed him everywhere. He wasn't tall or handsome, but he had something.

The Tropicana paid Ernie in cash, twenty-five thousand dollars, for the two of us, from the cashier's booth in the back of the casino. Ernie by now, as a serious gambler, of course, couldn't walk out the front door of the hotel without going past all of those irresistible crap tables. I don't know how much he lost, but we sure had a lot of cash money to lose.

Monte Proser's "partner" in the big cabaret room of the Tropicana was Johnny Roselli, a nice, personable silver-haired man who smiled a lot but had the coldest pale blue eyes I'd ever seen, like ice. One night he got drunk and started to tell Ernie and me a funny story about a heist from a bank during which he was shooting the tommy gun while the driver was driving so badly that Johnny missed his targets and almost fell out of the car. He laughed, as if it were a joke, and said, "That Joe, he was some driver." I didn't know what he was talking about, but it clearly was something that Ernie and I should not be hearing. I just laughed and said, "Hey, come on, Johnny, I feel like dancing. Let's dance." I was afraid he'd wake up the next morning sober and in the cold light of day realize who he'd told his gangster tale to.

Johnny was very protective of both Ernie and me. One night the stage manager came to my dressing room in tears. I asked him, "What's the matter?" He told me this long, sad story: "I can't make the rent; my mother's sick; my wife just had a baby." "How much do you need?" I asked. "Five hundred dollars," he said. I gave it to him. After a while (it took me a little longer to put my hair together), I walked out to see the stage manager at one of the crap tables, rolling the dice and yelling, "Come on, baby, come on, hard eight." I mentioned to Johnny "that the stage manager seemed to be so sad and in so much trouble, but I had just seen him at the crap table, gambling, when his mother's sick and he has a new baby and he can't pay the rent." Johnny said, "Oh, no, how much did he get you for?" I told him, and he said, "Don't worry, you'll have your money back tomorrow night." And I did.

Roselli's "boys" were always more than polite to me, saying "yes, ma'am, no, ma'am." They always acted like gentlemen when I performed. Johnny sent me flowers, chocolates, and big, heavy gold charms.

Once after Ernie died, I went to a prizefight in Las Vegas. I went up to Johnny Roselli to say hello, but he quickly turned

EDIE ADAMS

away and said, "Cool it, kid." I didn't know what to think. After the fight he came into the club and said, "Hey, are you crazy or something? Those cameras were on you; that's national TV out there; you shouldn't be seen talking to me on national TV, what's the matter with you?"

One time, much later, in the mid-1960's, I closed in Las Vegas on a Saturday and was to open for the first time at the Copacabana in New York on Monday night. I was apprehensive because I'd heard all the stories the other performers told about the owner, Jules Podell. He was rough on entertainers; if he didn't like you, you knew it by Jules's scowl and the way the waiters acted. If he like you, you were taken on a tour of the kitchen; that was a surefire sign. I had a spot in the act where someone in the club was to come up and light my Muriel. I wanted to ask Jules to do it but was terrified because of his reputation with talent. As I got onto the airplane in Vegas I saw a limousine drive out on the runway to the airplane stairs. A man got out and sat down next to me. During the flight to New York Ed Kelly asked where I was going. When I told him about playing the Copa and my trepidation about working with Mr. Podell, he said, "I know Jules Podell, I don't think you'll have any trouble." He asked when the opening night was. I told him, and he said, "You can expect a lot of people there. Don't worry about a thing."

By Monday morning's rehearsal the monster Jules Podell had turned into a pussycat. I was immediately given a tour of the kitchen and assigned my own waiter: "Anything you want, kid." He not only lit the cigar but was enthusiastic about the opening and smiled throughout the engagement. He said, "I don't know whether you know it, but you've got a lot of friends here." I guess he didn't expect it, but the place was packed. One Saturday night I looked at the bookings for the next night. I said, "Jules, Jules, there's nobody down here." He said, "Don't worry, Sunday night is family night; they'll all be here—they just don't want their names on no reservation list. They don't want nobody to know where they're gonna be." He was right. Again the place was packed.

During late 1957, whenever he was in New York, Ernie continued to do television, as a guest on such shows as *What's My Line?* He told Pete Martin why he did that weekly panel show, pointing out that "it's only if I'm in town and I feel like it. The contract doesn't lash me down. The first three weeks I wasn't on the panel because I preferred to take Edie out to dinner. Since being on *What's My Line?* paid me $750 an appearance, those dinners were fairly expensive, about $775. . . . You get so little out of being alive. Then suddenly you wake up one day and say, 'I wish I enjoyed myself more.' Edie and I are enjoying ourselves now."

$\mathcal{T}$EN

ERNIE TOLD ME THAT he needed to live in Los Angeles while he made a second picture with Jack Lemmon and Richard Quine, *Bell, Book and Candle*. Kim Novak and Jimmy Stewart were also starring in this film adaptation of the hit John Van Druten play.

When we first had gone to Vegas, to play the Tropicana, we were told that MCA would send one of their local agents, Roy Gerber, to meet us. We deplaned, and I looked around for the traditional black suit and narrow black tie, New York MCA's standard uniform. All I saw were cowboys.

Out of the crowd came a strapping six-foot-two Vegas cowboy, complete with turquoise and silver trim on his boots, belt buckle, shirt collar, string tie, watch, ring, and kerchief holder. He took off his ten-gallon hat to reveal a completely bald Yul Brynner head. I expected "Howdy, y'all" and instead got in a thick, unmistakably Bronx accent, "So, where's the cards? Whose deal?" Ernie liked him immediately and always said that if he had a production company in L.A. he'd like Roy to be part of it. (Roy, who had once roomed with Danny Simon, Neil's brother, was the role model for Oscar in *The Odd Couple* and collected years of royalties for the character.)

Roy, who stayed in Vegas until 1962, had called ahead to ask Marvin Moss, Ernie's Los Angeles MCA agent, to arrange for a furnished house on Cañon Drive in Beverly Hills for a month, beginning December 1. This way, when the children's vacation from Miss Hewitt's came, we could bring them out to California and have Christmas together. Marvin even got Eleanor Quinlan at MCA to deck the halls for us, complete with an eight-foot Christmas tree. But the house cost eighteen hundred dollars a month, outrageous in 1957. Our publicity had preceded us: The big spenders were in town.

Lana Turner and her daughter, Cheryl Crane, had formerly lived there. It had the standard Olympic-size pool and a large backyard. Ernie immediately put in a trampoline, but Marvin said, "You can't let those neighbor kids use that; if they get hurt, you'll have a lawsuit bigger than any amount you've ever thought of." While the exterior of the house was fine, the interior had some problems. Downstairs the living room, dining room, hall, and kitchen were adequate. But the upstairs had three bedrooms and only one immense bathroom, something that would never do for the four of us, including two kids and me with my makeup.

Right away, I went to my first Hollywood party; Ernie, the socialite, had several months' lead on me. Edgar and Frances Bergen, who lived across the street, gave their annual Christmas bash. Edgar always made the glögg, and the food was spectacular. It was the first time I ever saw aquavit glasses without bases; you had to chugalug the whole thing at once. The only way to put the stemmed glasses down was to turn them over. I'd never had gravlax before; it was delicious, as were the many other Norwegian delicacies. Their beautiful adolescent daughter, then called Candy, had just returned from school in Switzerland. I had worn my best black Mainbocher and pearls and felt very out of place amid the garden patch of pastel colors. Everyone had on aqua, yellow, or coral. Anybody I'd ever read about or plastered on my slanted roof over my bed at Lily Lake was there.

This West Coast show business establishment had different rules from those I'd known in New York. "Casual" out here meant not a short black cocktail dress but the latest Italian designer palazzo pants and your "casual" diamonds. Very soon we were dining out every night in yet another elegant home, all of which looked like movie sets. When we went to the Billy Wilders, Audrey Wilder, the chicest woman I ever met in my life, said, "Oh, you're not *that* Edie Adams." (Eadie Ione Adams, then in her fifties, had been a bit player and an MGM Ziegfeld Girl. She later opened her own real estate office in Palm Springs, with a logo featuring her celebrity-style signature. Through twenty-five of my peak working years many of my friends have told me that they had wonderful service from "my" real estate agency in Palm Springs. When they checked to see if the office was owned by the actress Edie Adams, the agent would coyly reply, "Well, she used to be." The lady died in 1983. I've often wondered if they continued their ambiguous response and I've been dead since 1983.) Broadway theater news obviously did not travel west in those days.

Others who entertained us when we first arrived included: Jackie Cooper, Frank Sinatra, Mel Frank, Groucho Marx, Harry Cohn, Tony Curtis and Janet Leigh, the Daniel Tara-dashes, Debbie and Eddie, Dino and Jeannie Martin, Mervyn and Kitty Le Roy, Skip and Henry Hathaway, Norman Panama, Kleinchen and Lauritz Melchior. Our regular restaurants included Dominick's, Chasen's, Romanoff's, Perino's, the Escoffier, and La Rue's, whose maître d' would call us whenever the chef had his special rack of lamb, and we always went.

I was really looking forward to playing the Mocambo, a Hollywood nightclub famous throughout the world. I'd read about it in my movie magazines for years. So when MCA asked me to do New Year's Eve week, starting on December 27, 1957, I said yes. I was really in Hollywood. As the act opened, Ernie was discovered onstage in an easy chair, reading, with a floor lamp. I don't know what it had to do with anything; it was a non sequitur that did nothing but guarantee Ernie's presence at every show. All Hollywood did come. By the end of the engagement I'd met everyone I'd admired for years. One night an Arab sheik and his entourage arrived in several limousines and dark glasses. I talked to him at his table for a half hour, trying to make small talk. It wasn't until years later, when I started to date Bill Blatty, that he told me that he was that sheik. He and his friends had dressed up just to play a joke on Ernie and me.

The famous Mocambo had obviously fallen on hard times, which was made even clearer by contrast to our recent stint in glitzy Las Vegas. Here I was paid in cash, too, but in handfuls of small, dirty bills instead the crisp new C notes the boys gave Ernie in Vegas. When I saw the Mocambo's boss, Mary Morrison, who had inherited the club when her husband died, scraping up these wads of money to pay me, I felt so sorry for her I almost gave it back. I was the last act to play there.

After the girls went back to school at Miss Hewitt's in New York in January 1958, I appeared on Dean Martin's show, and Ernie said, "There's lots of work out here. Why don't you stay for a while?" He pointed out that the girls were more than amply looked after in New York, with the couple, the secretary, Lillian, and, of course, the Ghost of Christmas Past and Future, his ever-present mother. Besides, Ernie and I were going back to the Tropicana for two more months in the spring. He had been extending the monthly lease on Cañon Drive but started looking for a house, I thought to rent. By the time we left for Vegas, in March, we had found one.

The house was on Bowmont Drive, just down the hill from Frank Sinatra's bachelor pad. I had wanted our California house to be in "the flats" of Beverly Hills because it was easier to get around, it was close to the schools, and the living was more structured. You could get things delivered and walk the dog. We had passed the house many times on the way to Frank's, and every time we climbed that one-lane dirt road carved in the side of the mountain I was scared. Coming down was worse because there were no guardrails and I was on the passenger side, looking straight down. But Ernie liked the hills, with their Heathcliff-like morning fog until noon and the challenge of hillside living.

Ernie also made another classic impulsive Kovacs move at this time. He decided to get his teeth done by Dr. Goodley, who had done most movie smiles: Burt Lancaster, Kirk Douglas, Tony Curtis, Frank Sinatra, and Elizabeth Taylor, all the dazzlers. Ernie had had temporary snap-on caps made for his front four teeth in Philadelphia. There was a space between his real front teeth that he was more self-conscious about than he should have been. Now, in typical Kovacs style, he said, "Doc, if you can do the whole mouth, uppers and lowers in one weekend, I'll do it." Goodley had to think about it for a while, but he said, "Okay, we can give it a try." The weekend Ernie picked was the weekend we were moving into Bowmont, so he was completely unavailable to help, having all thirty-six teeth capped. Dr. Goodley made temporary caps, which Ernie wore in Las Vegas. While we were up there, Dr. Goodley made two "house calls." By the time we left Vegas, Ernie had perfect, evenly matched pearly whites. But he had trained himself, all his life, to smile never showing his teeth. Now he still didn't show them.

Ernie's teeth were responsible, at that point, for one of my many "Achilles" toothaches. Every time I was under stress my jaw would swell up and the dentist would say, "It looks like you need a root canal." On a TV show once I wore a rhinestone toothache kerchief and sang my ballad in profile with the swollen jaw on the upstage side. It would never occur to me not to appear on live TV.

Ernie paid $125,000 for our twenty-room ranch-style house on Bowmont Drive. Over the next three and a half years he spent another half million dollars making "small" improvements. As soon as we moved in, he decided it wasn't big enough. Instead of planning the additions—God forbid we should plan anything—we would redo a room here and a room there as the mood struck him. We wanted to keep the same feeling in the house, so we tried to use its original architect for remodeling, but he finally gave up on us.

There was a roller skating rink already there. We had a special treehouse built for the kids overlooking the rink. We put in a slide for the pool. When Ernie saw the attached, converted two-car garage he said, "Oh, great, I have a study." I thought it was a little small for him, but I had no idea what he had in mind. I saw him looking down the hill. Soon he had sketched out, for the architect, stairs down to a second level; he said, "Make it as big as you can, but remember that we have to be ten feet from the property line." As it continued down the hill, the study narrowed. He went as far as he could and put in a screened-in terrace with an awning. As they were pouring the cement, Ernie asked one of the workers if, in addition to the walls, he could put in a floor. The man said sure. *Voilà!* Ernie had an instant temperature-controlled wine cellar, on what was now the third floor down. Now I knew what he meant by a study.

Ernie's desk looked like a modern age jetliner flight deck. George Burns remembers Ernie trying to sell him a steam room. The original sauna he had ordered from Finland hadn't come fast enough, so Ernie had bought another one locally. When the Finnish one arrived, he had two walk-in steam rooms.

Once the shell was up, Ernie decorated the den himself, building in a desk and having the carpenter distress the heavy wood for record shelves. One rock wall extended from the fireplace upstairs down to his desk. While all the construction was going on, Ernie requested a fishpond in the floor of the study; using recycled water from the waterfall down the rock wall, Ernie could keep the tank clean. The water cascaded down the stone wall from an African water buffalo head. He said, "Besides, it sounds nice."

Ernie's study was his highest priority, was the *pièce de résistance.* He planned it very carefully, sitting up for nights on end, building a balsa-wood scale model of what it would become. He stole my perfume bottle caps to make circles for the fireplace fan. It was his dream study, something he had always wanted. His armor collection kept arriving, along with brass and copperware and irons and a grandfather clock. Then came the Indian stuffed tiger, a former Indian prime minister's toy. There were custom cabinets for his tape recorders and other gadgets, but in the midst of these lavish expenditures Ernie suddenly economized. He had one of the existing windows moved out to a new wall when his study was enlarged. He was very proud of that small saving; no wastrel, he.

I have no idea how much the study cost him; we never talked about it specifically. Like everything else to do with moving into and building onto this house, it was a lot of money. Ernie knew that we were having financial troubles, but he justified the den by saying that it would save him from having to rent an office. He built the study through a separate corporation, one of four that we had. There could be no liens on the study, and Ernie figured that even if we had to sell the house, he could drive up the driveway and get into his office. Once you got into the top room, it was self-contained, with a fireplace, bar, refrigerator, small stove, and bathroom.

Ernie's interior decorating problem concerned his wine cellar. Of course, he already had the bottles, the finest champagnes and wines money could buy. Yet he realized that something was missing: Being a new cellar, it was too clean. A propman friend of his at ABC came over and sprayed the bottles with a hot gun to create rubbery cobwebs. When you pulled a wine bottle out, the cobwebs snapped back into place. Ernie was the happiest kid you ever saw.

Up on the top level, his card table, which he specifically designed himself, was a massive wooden poker table, about five inches thick, supported by a single central pedestal, so no matter how many players sat around it, bumping into table legs would never get in the way of the game. The man who made it thought it was a mistake and had delivered it at cocktail height, fifteen inches off the floor. He didn't believe Ernie when Ernie said he wanted to raise it up to cardplaying level. He sat on a chair and said, "About here." The table maker had to take it back and redo it.

Hanging on the door of Ernie's den was a lighted white frosted glass sign on which he had painted NOT NOW; when that sign was lit, no one entered the room unless he or she was willing to risk pain of death. Ernie did his best work at night, and often I would go to sleep when the sign was on and awake the next morning to find it still lighted. If he had slept at all, it was a nap on his daybed, but more often than not he worked straight through. Once in a while, after a long isolation in his office, one of the kids called him on the intercom, just to make sure he was there.

His other luxury was his steam room, which was big enough to hold eight poker players. He went in there four to five times a day and then straight from the steam room to the pool to cool off. He always ran into the steam room before we went out for the evening. It relaxed him, but it drained me; I'd have to go right to bed after I had been in there. I'd crawl out even after just a few minutes, but he'd come out and say, "Boy, let's go." It invigorated him. Many times when we came home late at night, he headed for the steam room.

I came out and woke him up after fifteen minutes. The doctor said it was dangerous to the heart to stay in any longer.

One night we came home very late, and he said he was going to take a "short steam." I decided to stay awake, just in case, but somehow drifted off to sleep. The next thing I knew it was broad daylight and no Ernie in the bed. I went racing through the house, half crazed, in my nightgown and bare feet. I opened the door to his study to find a card game going on. I said, "Sorry, I thought you fell asleep in the steam room—I—excuse me." Ernie just smiled the smile that said, "I'm fine, what's the worry?" I said, "Excuse me," and left. One of the other players later told me that after the door shut, Ernie said to the other players, "Who *was* that?"—anything for a joke.

For the next three years Ernie was constantly adding to his domain. From his massive desk, into which would be built an oscilloscope, record turntable, two tape decks, film editing equipment, and a typewriter, Ernie could also monitor any room in the house, heat up his sauna, open the gate, or activate the driveway turntable, by pushing any one of his row of twenty-three buttons.

All told, the house had nine television sets, two electric pianos, four regular pianos, and a harpsichord.

We moved into Bowmont Drive right away, even though the refurbishing had already started. Somebody had just re-done the house in Bronx Renaissance: walls of faked antique mirrors and lots of aqua and coral, which both Ernie and I hated. He insisted on repainting the pool area black. I thought of it as just another house, in addition to New City and New York. But we began to buy furniture, and Ernie said, "Here, free rein, decorate it any way you want." I went along, think-ing we might rent the house while we were on the road work-ing; it might even be a good investment.

The girls came out to Los Angeles in mid-March for their Easter vacation from Miss Hewitt's. We had decided to drive to Las Vegas this time. Betty and Kippie, now nine and eleven, had been given two rabbits for Easter; they couldn't bear to leave them, so of course, the rabbits had to ride up to Vegas from L.A. in the car with us, on the girls' laps. With their toys that filled up the back seat. Dick Quine's wife, a last-minute window-side passenger in the front seat, was known to get carsick even without rabbits. I braced for a long trip in the middle of the front seat. We started off, a happy group, complete with a picnic basket because there was no really good restaurant and we didn't want to take the time to stop. We drove for a few hours, but I didn't recognize any land-marks from my one previous car trip. Ernie, who was not good with directions, finally stopped to ask. Someone with a sense of humor, who might have recognized Ernie or re-sented the big Lincoln we were driving, had sent us off to Las Vegas, New Mexico, some five hundred miles out of the way.

We were due to arrive in the Nevada Las Vegas in the early afternoon. When it began to get dark, the girls began to get cold. We stopped in a small-town general store and bought them blankets.

The rabbits began to smell, not having been walked like dogs. For Mrs. Quine we had to keep the window open, or she'd get sick. For the girls we had to keep the window shut, or they'd freeze. No one in the car on this extra-long trip was happy. We finally arrived at Las Vegas, Nevada, at dawn, having left L.A. at noon the previous day. The rabbits inside the blankets were smuggled into the girls' room in our suite, and all seven of us took up residence.

Next time I had to make a one-day trip to L.A. from Vegas, I did what all the other performers did on the Strip: hired an ambulance to pick me up right after the second show, so that I could sleep and be refreshed for an early-morning meeting in L.A. and sleep again on the way back. I arrived fresh to do two shows.

Once on the way down to do the nightclub act, I saw the room service waiter wheeling a table topped by a platter un-der a big dome. I stopped him and said, "What's that? We didn't order room service." He looked at his check, and said, "Oh, yes, it's a special order." I picked up the dome, and there, carefully cut up and spread out like a fresh deck of blackjack cards, was a week's supply of carrots, celery, radishes, zucchini, and cucumbers. Mounds of red cabbage, iceberg, and romaine lettuce completed the display. Now even the rabbits were ordering room service. I said, "Ernie, we can't do this; it's just not right." He said, "Oh, why? The rabbits have to eat, too; come on, we're gonna be late for the show."

Betty and Kippie were in heaven in Las Vegas. Anything they wanted was a phone call away. A hotel driver, provided by Johnny Roselli, would take them anywhere they wanted to go, roller skating, shopping, horseback riding. They were having a wonderful time.

I was busy doing two shows a night, seven nights a week, and decorating the Bowmont Drive house in absentia. Every day at the Tropicana pool I sat with my Scalamandré silk velvet samples, sketching on graph paper. I planned the draperies and upholstery in mostly Renaissance painting colors, such as bottle green and bittersweet red. Scalamandré himself was one of Ernie's New York poker buddies, but even at wholesale these were the most expensive fabrics available anywhere. Whenever I'm planning or designing something, I'm very happy, so everything seemed under control. I still have those beautiful draperies stored away; I've always intended to make myself a *Gone With the Wind* green velvet gown.

On Good Friday Ernie and the girls came to me at the pool. By their attitude, I could tell that some new plot was about to unfold. Ernie said, "The girls really like it here. I've checked out the schools, and Paradise Valley will accept them next Monday. All we [meaning me] have to do is call Miss Hewitt's and request a leave of absence." So, on the day after Easter, the girls did not go back to Miss Hewitt's but enrolled at Paradise Valley public school in Las Vegas. Of course, the school wasn't as demanding as Miss Hewitt's Classes, and the girls didn't have to wear the conservative city uniforms. There was no dress code in Vegas; anything went, even shorts. They had a lot more free time because school was so easy and some friends from their new school, the children of hotel employees who were in awe of the girls' suite life.

Betty and Kippie even went onstage with us closing night. By this time they knew my whole act, having done the imitations so often for us in the car. They alternated the imitations. I didn't think Kippie could go on that night because she had a fever. In true theater style she went on and the fever went down. She had the closing spot doing Marilyn and got tremendous laughs. When she came off, I said, "What did you do to get those laughs?" She said, "I just kept real still until they stopped laughing; if they laughed at the next pose, I'd do it again." Natural timing, from her father. We had seen Kippie in a Miss Hewitt's play where she had the role of the Friendly Giant. Ernie and I had been amazed even then to see how much talent she had. Betty was a natural dancer; she took to the ballet faster than any of us.

The Tropicana was still paying Ernie our salary in cash, twenty-five thousand dollars a week. "Funny money," as Ernie called it, was still just that to me. I never saw it. I didn't even know how much of it was getting to the business managers.

Back in L.A., at the Academy Awards in April, Ernie was presenting an Oscar. So he had his own set of tails made. Although they were beautifully cut, fit, and tailored, it wasn't Ernie. The outfit was just too somber for him, suggesting that something should be taken seriously. I never saw him take anything seriously. This getup didn't have anything to do with the Ernie I knew. Was he perhaps becoming more West Coast than I had thought possible? Every time he put them on I laughed. It didn't faze him. He just said, "Come on now, we're being dignified here."

At the ceremonies Joanne Woodward won as Best Actress, for *The Three Faces of Eve.* It was a brilliant performance, but I was even more impressed that she accepted the award in a dress she'd made herself. That was the year the show ran twenty minutes short, and right there on live television Jerry Lewis, the host, called all the winners back onstage and, in that inimitable voice of his, instructed, "Come on everybody, dance," while he conducted the orchestra.

In May two important people joined our topsy-turvy household. Nan and Leonard Burris came to us as a live-in couple, she to cook and he to drive and valet for Ernie. But their duties over the years extended over the edges of any job description. They were to baby-sit both Ernie's mother and mine, keep peace in the house, ride herd on the rest of the staff, and run the show when Ernie and I were gone. Nan became my friend and confidante, although she always referred to me as "the Mrs." They were with me until Leonard died in the 1970's, and Nan stayed on a little longer. She is always still by my side whenever I need her. Since my own mother died, Nan has been that to me. I still talk to her once a week. Nothing throws Nannie, or threw Leonard, who became Ernie's buddy, too. They were never just servants. They had to be very special people to put up with us. Apparently they had worked for everybody in Hollywood, including Howard Hughes, Marlene Dietrich, and Elsa Maxwell. But they stayed longest with us. Leonard liked the challenge; he said, "There's always something going on here."

Whatever they wanted they would have. Conversely, if Ernie wanted a big dinner party put together at the last minute, somehow they would do it—and happily. They would play the role of butler and cook beautifully, but I was still uncomfortable with servants and had a hard time thinking about them that way.

Nan's grandfather had been a slave in Louisiana. Her mother died when she was three. When Nan was about eight, she went to work for a wealthy southern family to take care of twin babies. The wife and mother of the family insisted on Nan's going everywhere with the two babies, even in the Deep South in the early part of the century. Nannie went wherever the family went, even to hotels and restaurants; "The woman spoiled me rotten," she said. When Nannie was about fourteen, she wanted a fox fur chubby coat; the woman bought it for her. With her coming from that background and my having had no racially difficult experiences, the race issue eluded us both the same way, for different reasons. In the 1960's we didn't know what all the fuss was. Nan's first job after the family and her chubby coat was at the Cotton Club in Culver City, in the 1930's, dancing with Lena Horne. (Louis Armstrong and others were trying to re-create the Harlem Cotton Club in L.A.) After that she began to work for some of the biggest names in Hollywood. Nan liked show biz and clothes almost as much as I did. She had my extensive wardrobe memorized and could lay out the whole outfit down to the shoes.

She didn't talk much about her previous employers, but she did say that Howard Hughes had kept three refrigerators: one for guests, one for employees, and one for himself, the only one of which he kept locked. Irvin S. Cobb, Anita Loos, Edmund Goulding, and Jennifer Jones and David O. Selznik were among her other employers. Nan knew that Sam Goldwyn liked to eat early, at 7:30 P.M., and which wines Denise Minnelli liked. You got to our wine cellar through a trapdoor in the den—in the narrow part where the two couches faced each other—covered by a coffee table, in the middle of the action. Nannie would say, "Don't go down into the wine cellar when the people are here; Mr. Goldwyn'll fall in." So we had to be sure to get all the wine out before the guests arrived.

Ernie and I returned to New York with the girls in late May so they could finish the term at Miss Hewitt's. I had to do Ed Sullivan's show June 1, but then return to the Coast later in June, to do *The Chevy Show*, while Ernie had to finish a show in New York. He and I both felt that the girls needed more individual attention. So I said, "Why don't I take Betty with me on the train to California. Why don't you and Kippie do the same thing next week?" Betty and I did and became as close as we ever would on that trip.

The house on Bowmont was still incomplete when we arrived, with open holes to the outside covered loosely with plastic. Neither Betty nor I could sleep much that night. The hills provided a whole new set of frightening sounds; we'd never heard coyotes howl twenty-five feet from our bedroom window.

When we looked in the master bedroom, we saw a gaping hole five inches from the floor and a workman holding a set of plans. I said, "No, that's for the television set; it's supposed to be five inches from the ceiling so you can watch in bed." He did a classic comic sketch routine and turned the plans upside down. "Oh, yeah, you're right, da *ceiling*."

We'd also heard that the Lauritz Melchiors, who lived nearby on Mulholland Drive, had been robbed recently, so we both were really scared. Betty and I slept fitfully together, that night, in the master suite, me with my glasses on and all the outdoor lights lit. Our dog, Pamela, finally came into her own; she shed her glamour image and went right back to her real instincts. In the morning, when we woke up, we saw Pamela standing proudly with one paw on a rat as big as she was that she'd killed during the night. (Yorkies are bred as "ratters" for the miners in the north of England.) That night she vindicated her Vegas silliness and became the heroine of the day. But we were still so frightened that we immediately moved to the Beverly Hills Hotel. I never let Ernie forget that Pamela had saved us.

On *The Chevy Show* I was one of three people replacing Dinah Shore for the summer. John Raitt and Janet Blair were the other two hosts. After all those daily shows with Ernie this wasn't a challenge. The crates and vans started to come from New York with my costumes that I wanted to use for the show. I couldn't get them unpacked fast enough, with the house in such chaos. Ray Aghayan, the show's costume designer, outfitted me with some beautiful clothes. Ray and I both were fans of Charles James, and even on this GM summer show, he was able to design me some James look-alikes, one in black wool and brown peau de soie. It certainly wasn't Chevy, but I loved it. Ray and I, along with fourteen others, formed what later became the Costume Designers Guild.

During *Li'l Abner*, I had become an honorary Ziegfeld Girl and met Blanche Ring, who had sung "I've Got Rings on My Fingers" and "Come, Josephine, in My Flying Machine." Blanche had been a star in 1906 and was the first celebrity to have an article of clothing, a Blanche Ring blouse, named after her. She was a frail ninety-three when I did her song "Rings on My Fingers" and introduced her from the audience on *The Chevy Show*—until the spotlight turned on her and she became six feet tall, and you could see the radiant star she had been. She had fabulous, almost luminescent skin. I asked her what secret remedy she had used all those vaudeville years of really heavy makeup. "Lard—haven't you heard about us hams?" I watched some television with her. She said, "Look at those people; will they ever learn? They don't know what to do with their hands. You don't put them flat out; you only show them in profile," like a Rembrandt painting. With her gnarled hands she showed me, and she was right; every movement was perfect. There was a lot to be said for old live show business. She still looked magnificent when the spotlight went on.

In July, Braunstein and Chernin again "had to" see us personally. This time they made a special trip to California and came to the Bowmont house to talk to us. This was really a big meeting. They said that since we hadn't cooperated with the IRS, we had to pay the highest tax. The only way we were going to get money fast was a live tour. They had talked to Marty Kummer, and there was no question *if* we were going to do the tour; we *had* to do it, in the fall. They also said that we could not have two residences and pay state taxes in two states: "Decide which is your permanent home." I didn't realize that decision had been made until the van showed up with some of our best antiques from New York: the blackamoors, a four-foot floor-standing globe, the Boulle clock, and two suits of armor Ernie had recently acquired. My nine-foot harpsichord had been delivered directly to Bowmont because there was no room in the New York apartment.

Once it was clear that we were really going to live in Hollywood, I decided to decorate the house with humor, in Art Dreco. According to Dreco expert Paul Drexler of Deerfield, Massachusetts, "There is no room in Dreco Art for mediocrity. In this art form the standards are stringently low. The work should have a certain purity of intent, and an honest lack of taste is needed." I define it as something so awful that no one would dare manufacture it. But somebody did! I went out and bought a polar bear rug and had a grand piano painted white. It looked too passable, like something Fred and Ginger might dance by on the late late show. So I had another piano put together for the family den—an upright guaranteed to get laughs. I had the white keys covered in regular mother-of-pearl and the black keys covered in black opalescent mother-of-pearl. I instructed the carpenter to put every tacky scroll of carved wood up the sides, on the top, around the music stand; there wasn't room left for a piano light, either clip-on or upright. I had him paint the piano part black and the carved wood garbage gold. I waited weeks for my prize to be delivered to Beverly Hills.

When it finally arrived, a crowd was there for the uncrating. After much prying with hammers and crowbars, there it was, my Dreco masterpiece. But nobody laughed. All I heard was: "God, that's beautiful. Wow, it's sensational. Man, what is that stuff on the keys?" I couldn't believe it. To this day I really only warm up to the spirited few people who will ask, "What the hell is that?" This was my version of the stunt pulled by the Ira Gershwins; they had a painting done by a chimpanzee hanging among all their great pieces of art. It, too, was perfectly framed and lighted. Some people they told and some people they didn't.

Also that summer, I did a Hollywood Bowl concert, "The Gay 90s Night," on August 10, using my Juilliard voice. Glynn Ross put the concert together. Later, in the early 1970's, on a live TV talk show that we both happened to do in Seattle, he remembered how surprised he'd been to hear my trained voice. There, on the show, he said, "Why don't you come do an opera for us, at the Seattle Opera?" I said, "Why don't you ask me?" He said, "Okay, I'm asking you right now." I thought it was just idle talk show chatter until he called a few weeks later to discuss which opera I'd like to do. He finally settled on Offenbach's La Périchole, which I didn't know. But, as I learned it, I found was the perfect break-in opera, foolproof. My nightclub agents were furious because I had to turn down two Las Vegas bookings. I was happy because the room's bookers always wanted at least one third of my act to be straight off the pop charts. At that time I was doing a Laura Nyro medley through clenched teeth. So anything that got me out of singing "Stoney End" was all right with me. In Vegas I always felt like a diamond desperately trying to fit into a rhinestone setting.

In August Ernie had to shave his head for his next movie, It Happened to Jane. He was playing the head of a railroad, a character that the writers whispered to Ernie was loosely based on Harry Cohn.

In the summer of 1958 CBS announced its intention to do Wonderful Town as a two-hour television special in the fall.

I was delighted on several counts. It was a part I played for nearly two years on Broadway, and it was now being done in a medium with which I was very familiar. Besides, I would get to work with my adored Roz Russell again. Ernie and I had been seeing her and her husband, Freddy Brisson, socially, at dinner parties at their home, our home, and on the Hollywood "A" social circuit. Roz and I had become even closer friends. Roz and Freddy were going to Europe for the summer, but while they were gone, the network called me. I went in to CBS for fittings and talked to the conductor about restaging my numbers and changing my keys.

Suddenly, one day, someone from CBS called and told me not to come in for my final fitting; Roz had returned from Europe, and her costumes were going to be done first. I was glad to have the extra days off before going into rehearsal, so that I could take some more dance classes and see my vocal coach. I waited a week, and then another week, before any phone calls came. I was told that there had been daily meetings with Roz, the network, the authors and composers, and the advertising agency. Roz had cast approval for the TV version of *Wonderful Town* and had told CBS something to the effect that I was "not right for the part." When she was pressed to be more specific and was reminded that I had won two Donaldson awards as Eileen, she talked vaguely about getting a "new face in the role."

Through two more weeks of meetings the network executives, the show's creative team, and the advertising agency couldn't get her to budge. Finally they asked her point-blank: "What's wrong with Edie? Is she too old, too young, too fat, too thin?" Roz replied, "Well, she just hasn't turned out well." Again they pressed her: "What do you mean?" Roz squirmed and said, "Well, I don't know there's just something about her. I can't—" They kept pushing her to the wall until she finally said, "Well, it's something I truly can't describe. It's something like . . . well, who else could go to Mark Cross and buy an alligator bag in bad taste?"

I was devastated and didn't talk to her for a year, even though she called constantly. We'd go to the same Hollywood parties, even sit at the same table. I would talk to everyone else but never spoke to her once. She'd call up Dean Martin and his wife, Jeanne, and even Ernie, crying and wanting to know why I wouldn't talk to her. I never told anyone the story; I just said I didn't associate with people like that. *Wonderful Town* aired on CBS on December 3, 1958, with Jacqueline McKeever playing Eileen. The reviews were not thrilling; McKeever was too bland, Russell too blatant. I was purring. Only after Ernie died and she was suffering from arthritis did I finally give in and talk to Roz. I was still hurt.

I signed a record contract with MGM but didn't know where to look for material on the West Coast. Dick Quine found me an arranger. "He's a new guy in town, hasn't done much work here, but you'll like him; he's Juilliard-trained." It turned out to be Henry Mancini. Hank, Ernie, and I put together a comedy album that was to feature a talentless starlet who has slept her way to the top without a shred of vocal training. Fearlessly she attacks every type of music: a Piaf-style song in fractured French; "All of a Sudden My Heart Sings," going up an octave but never making the top note; and a country song whose lyrics she forgets—a total satire of all the records currently on the charts. My name was not to appear anywhere.

Paul Horn played the accompaniment to my Florence Foster Jenkins takeoff, where she isn't even close to the key and cries at the end. I sang, as sexily as I could, "He takes me to paradise," followed on the record by a big yawn from Ernie. The musicians were laughing so hard in the studio that you can hear them on the record, too.

For the cover shot I wore a blond wig, gold sequins, and a white fox boa, and I held a three-foot wrench. Unfortunately at the last moment, MGM changed its mind and said my name had to be on the record or it wouldn't sell. Ernie had to throw out his hysterical liner notes about the ambiguous, well-endowed unknown blonde and let somebody else do a straight version. We gave MGM our album title, *Edie Adams Sings Music to Listen to Records By.*

Straight from the recording session, I went to a party at Doris Day's house, with the hot little acetates in my hands. I told everyone it was my latest album. We played about sixteen bars of the first song, "Autumn Leaves" in fractured French, one of my biggies. Nobody laughed. They all said,

"That's delightful. We didn't know you could sing. What a lovely voice." We knew then that we didn't have a hit on our hands. Once more my Art Dreco satire fell on deaf ears. Although it didn't sell well at the time, the album is a collector's item today.

Ernie told Groucho Marx, who had to be in New York for a few weeks, to stay at our apartment. Groucho never got over it. He stayed even longer, he liked it so much. He said, "You're a trusting soul, leaving me there with all those cigars!"

We registered the girls at Bel-Air Town and Country School (later John Thomas Dye), but I thought it was for the fall semester only; they were still on leave from Miss Hewitt's. Their classmates included Pamela Dillman (the daughter of Bradford and Suzy Parker; Tricia Taylor, Robert's daughter; and Debby Boone.

In September I was to do my father's favorite song, called "Home," on *The Chevy Show*. I rehearsed it all week, and on Saturday I heard that my father was going in the hospital for an operation for esophageal cancer. On Sunday, as Harry Zimmerman was rehearsing the orchestra, I knew I couldn't sing that song. I got the first line out and burst into tears. A newcomer to the show, Carol Burnett, learned the song in an afternoon and sang it that night, beautifully. The last Chevy show was September 22; immediately I flew back to New Jersey. Dad was at the Englewood Hospital, and I spent the rest of the week with him. He died on September 26.

I didn't realize how hard my father's death would hit me. In any pain or stress, I'm always the strong one, seeing to it that everything runs smoothly and everyone is comforted, as my father had always done for me. He was the quiet rudder, the one constant and secure thing in my life that I could always count on. He was one man (Ernie was the only other) who always took care of me because he wanted to, not because he had to. Now he was gone. Again, I somehow never got around to dealing with my own feelings until later.

I stayed in the East until October 3, going to Nanticoke with my mother for the funeral and taking care of other details. My mother stayed with relatives, and Ernie and I left for California by train to begin our dreaded compulsory moneymaking tour.

On October 9 we went to a preview of *Bell, Book and Candle*. On October 12 I took an overnighter back to New York to sing at the Waldorf on the fourteenth and do the Pat Boone show on the sixteenth. On October 20, at 12:27 A.M., I boarded the red-eye flight for the Kansas City Kickoff at the great big arena, with a thirty-five-piece orchestra. Ernie joined me there. It would be the first time he would be doing what he did best with no close-ups. Ernie's strength was in underplaying and reacting; an eyebrow on a tight close-up would bring belly laughs in the studio. However, most people in the arena just saw a man standing still. Only my most obvious things done in broad movements with music accents worked, like my Marilyn takeoff, a showstopper geared to any size room. The next two shows, at Lafayette, Indiana, and at the Purdue-Michigan game, met with the same result. By the time we hit the Arthur Murray television show in Chicago, somebody traveling with us said, "You've got to get something for Ernie to do!" We went to San Francisco by plane, which Ernie hated as much as he did the shows. We did several more one-nighters, like a rock band, with the same results.

We were the first act to play Tahoe in the winter, in a nice intimate room in the old Harrah's, across from where the new hotel now is. Ernie was much more comfortable about his performance there because the audience was right on top of us. A magician and his assistant, Chop Chop and Charlene, opened for us. Charlene also served as my dresser.

Ernie had been ordered not to gamble, so the Harrah's bosses took him skeet shooting to keep him occupied. But he didn't want to shoot anything; he just wanted to go home to his new Beverly Hills playroom and play cards. While we were in Tahoe, I had to go to Sparks, Nevada, to take the rabbit test. My God, are there rabbits in every club date? I found out that the rabbit died. I was pregnant, due in June 1959.

Every night I had to hold my stomach in more and more because I got larger and couldn't tell anyone. Charlene helped me get in and out of my fast changes. She'd say, "What happened? What did you have for dinner? Are you gaining weight?" I'd say, "No, no, your fingers are getting fat." Charlene was the first person I told. She said, "I knew it, I knew it." Then you didn't dare tell anyone because no one would book you if you were pregnant. The nesting instinct was really getting to me. I always wanted to go home, but suddenly now more than ever.

However, I had quite a few more stops to make before I feathered my nest and stopped working. I went to New York to do Garry Moore's show. Because my clock was running down, I was in a blur of moneymaking travel, running back and forth to New York City to do shows, right up until Christmas. As I was frantically moving from coast to coast, Mary was moving in for good. The kids had long since decided which coast they were going to stay on: the one that had the Mickey Mouse Club! Annette Funicello was their siren call to Hollywood. As I look back, Ernie had made his mind up on his first trip.

Even after all this 1958 travel and with me pregnant, Ernie decided that he wanted to see Yosemite for the family's Christmas vacation. We all piled into the car, with Ernie driving, Betty, Kippie, both grandmas, and me. That group in the same room is bad enough, but in a closed car, "Don't you wish everyone did?" comes to mind as I remember it. I got my mother into slacks for the first time, not for skiing, but just walking in the snow. Mary wore Ernie's pants, as usual. On the way back we went to San Francisco and ate our way through all those fine restaurants. That, too, had obviously been Ernie's plan all along. I couldn't think why all of us were there otherwise. I remember feeling very pregnant, although I was only four months along. I don't know how we all fit in, what with Mary's food and all the girls' toys. Give me the open road and the one nighters any day; they were easier.

Back home, the house was nowhere near finished, and we had both grandmothers staying with us. The kitchen needed remodeling the worst, but I wasn't really interested, so we always saved it for last, and kept saving it. "We really should remodel the kitchen," I would say, periodically, but Ernie always had a higher priority: a Japanese garden for one party; turn-of-the-century gaslights on the driveway for another party. The salesman had convinced Ernie gas would be cheaper than electricity. However, he didn't mention the installation. Like everything else, these had to be done right away, in two days.

The Japanese garden had to have a waterfall and a pool for koi carp. One hallway outside the girls' rooms was a blank wall, which disturbed Ernie terribly. He had a five-foot well-lit water tank built so he could watch fish going by. The fumigator came to clean the house and told people and dogs to get out. We did, and that was the end of those fish.

While all this construction was going on, there was a green port-a-john seemingly permanently stationed just outside our electric gates. One day the workers put two there. Frank Sinatra, who lived at the top of the hill, had to pass these two green houses and left a message for Ernie: "What's the matter, can't you afford indoor plumbing? Your gate houses are an eyesore to the neighborhood." Ernie took up the gauntlet and immediately ordered two green johns to be delivered and dropped outside Frank's gate. The next day Frank had two large carved wooden cigar-store Indians delivered to our gate to guard the two port-a-johns because, according to Frank, "There were soon going to be four." He was sending his down and we'd need security. For about a week we had four port-a-johns and two Indians at our front gate until Ernie figured out the next gag gift.

Early in 1990 Frank said, "Ernie was ahead of his time, a wonderfully creative, zany character. Our families lived near each other and we learned to expect the unexpected from Ernie. I loved him."

Shortly after we moved into the unfinished Bowmont Drive house, Ernie decided to have a party. "We'll have it outside," he said. I was working in a *GE Theater* trapeze show, "The Fallen Angel," with Louis Jourdan and didn't think we'd be finished filming by the Friday night he had picked; I suggested postponing the party. But Ernie was a creature of spontaneity. So he had his party, for seventy-five people, catered by the Escoffier Room. I got home from work at about quarter to twelve, just as the guests were saying their goodnights. I hadn't talked to any of them, but I did hear that the hors d'oeuvres were lovely. I was hurt. It was our first party,

and I'd almost missed it—my first deeply felt but never expressed feeling that all was not well in la-la land.

Ernie would go to any lengths to create the perfect moment. A favorite trick of his was to have Leonard fill the
Lalique cologne bottles in our bathroom with gin and the
smaller after-shave bottles with vermouth. He'd have ice put
in the powder box, and God forbid that anyone should put
soap in the soap dish; that was reserved for the lemon peel.
This was all prearranged so that he could fix his famous
martinis while I was soaking in the tub and he was taking
his twelve-nozzle needlepoint shower prior to going out to
an important function.

I always had a problem with those late formal European-
style dinners that people used to do back then. Since childhood I had been used to Sunday dinner at noon after church
and a light supper in the early evening. Then, working on
Broadway, I could never eat before the show. I usually ate
something about four-thirty or five in the afternoon in order
to have it digested by eight-thirty. No singer can breathe on
a full stomach, and I can't think well or even run around too
well unless my stomach is empty. In Beverly Hills I did the
same thing; I'd eat a lamb chop or hamburger with the kids
at five o'clock, so that I could survive the long cocktail hour
until the ten-thirty dinner finally arrived. Then I would just
pick at that food. God, did we all really drink that much back
then?

Suddenly we were out every night. We never used our
own dining room except at Thanksgiving. Something was
wrong. I thought we shouldn't keep going out, but Ernie loved
it. The kids had their dinners on a tray; they never left their
television room. We'd come home at two in the morning to
find them watching a movie when they had school the next
day. I would try to send them off to bed, but Ernie would
say, "Oh, let them finish the movie." I tried to get him to
discipline them, but when it was parents against kids, the
kids won. Inside, he was still a kid himself. He let them do
anything they wanted. When he did have time for them, he
was their playmate.

Mia was the most carefully thought-out, wanted child in

history, as was my son, Josh, nine years later. I'd always wanted two children, a boy and a girl, and I got my wish. As much as I hadn't wanted a child before my father died, after he died that's how much I wanted one. I removed my IUD. (I couldn't tolerate birth control pills because they made me very nauseated.) From then on I lived with a thermometer next to my bed. The first thing I did every morning was to take my temperature. When there was a noticeable drop, I was fertile for the next few hours. If Ernie was working, I called him to tell to come home right now. Being a romantic, he liked the mood to be set perfectly, with candles and music, the drinks chilled to the exact temperature. This being on call was not to his impulsive liking. We didn't have to try too hard because within two months of my father's death I was pregnant. Through some happenstance, she was conceived on a transcontinental flight back to L.A. Don't ask me how, but it is possible. Maybe I was the first member of the mile-high club, with my own husband.

I was delighted to be too big for slinky gowns and playing nightclubs. I was thrilled to come home, cozy down, and let it spread. (Later, when I was pregnant with Josh, James Galanos designed a Grecian nightclub dress that made it possible for me to work through my seventh month.) About this time Greg Bautzer, a poker buddy, and Ernie started exchanging crazy gifts. Ernie first sent him some piranhas for his pool, and in return, one afternoon the gate bell rang and somebody delivered a miniature Mexican burro named Piccolo, with two baskets loaded with jugs of Jack Daniel's strapped onto each side. Ernie immediately took to Piccolo, and he became a fixture in his den. However, whenever Ernie wasn't there, Piccolo was angry and lonesome. Sometimes he lowered his head and butted any target he could find. As my stomach got bigger, his target was more obvious. He decided that was what he would aim for. I never went out in the yard without something in front of me, or I stood near a tree in case he lowered his head to charge. Once Piccolo got out of the gate, and all of me jumped into my little MG and tried to race him down Cherokee Lane, to head him off before Coldwater Canyon. I did and had to drive back, towing him with a rope.

Jeannie Martin recently told me this story. She said Ernie

had invited her to lunch by our black pool. She arrived in bathing gear and tanning lotion to find Ernie and me on one of those fifties double chaises longues with a black-and-white-striped canopy on top. The two of us were absolutely white. (I couldn't get in the sun because I burned, and Ernie's spare time was spent playing cards indoors.) We both had on black glasses and black bathing suits. We didn't get up to greet her because draped across both our laps was Piccolo, contentedly snoozing in the sun and happy to be petted by both of us.

As Jeannie settled into her chair to catch some sun, Ernie said, "Remember the party at your house Tuesday?"

"Yes."

"That new couple in town, don't you think they were sort of . . . well, odd?"

Looking at the two of us, a black-and-white study with a donkey on our laps, she didn't know what to say.

Ernie called up Mervyn Le Roy one day out of the blue and asked, "Do you want to go to San Francisco?" Mervyn said, "Why?" Ernie said, "To look at the cable cars, and you're the one who always complains that you can't back out of the driveway at my house. I want to see how they turn around." Mervyn said, "You don't have to go, I know how they turn around; they're on roller bearings and are pushed by hand. You can do the same thing there but I'd suggest a motor to run it." So Ernie installed a turntable which, at the flick of a switch, would reverse your car's direction. But the installer didn't realize that housing for the motor had to be water-free and made no provision for the drainage of the hole he dug under the turntable. Whenever it rained, we had to bail out the motor housing or the turntable wouldn't work.

Even though I had three more TV shows to do in January and two more nightclub engagements in February (Blinstrubs in Boston and with Ted Lewis in Las Vegas), we started to thinking about building a baby's room. We had a lot of rooms, but they all were used; Nan and Leonard had their room and bath, my mother had to be there because I was pregnant, and Ernie's mother was always ghosting. We decided to build the nursery where the skating rink and treehouse were. In classic Kovacs style, Ernie said, "As long as we're building a baby's room, we might as well have a nurse's room, too, with a bath in between." As long as we were constructing anyway, it seemed like a good, cost-efficient idea to me, too.

Since the addition was now going to be thirty-six feet instead of fourteen, I suggested that we could put in my dream back closet along that thirty-six-foot wall in the back of the house. Ernie thought that was a swell idea—for about fifteen minutes. He said, "Well, as long as you're going down the back wall, why not put some stairs and another room on the top, covering all of this? Then you'll have your own sewing room and music rehearsal studio like you've always wanted. We'll put in a wall of mirrors and a ballet barre, and we'll be able to deduct it."

I had a moment's hesitation, but it was beginning to make sense to me. So we were in money trouble already. Why not a little more? Ernie said, "Sure, it's deductible, and it will add to the value of the house. I consider it an investment. Besides, it'll match mine."

I hesitated only another moment and said, "Why not?" He was right. "Call the builder."

What we ended up with was a downstairs suite for Mia and the nurse, including a bathroom, kitchenette, and stacked washer-dryer alcove (the real laundry was at the other end of the house, near the kitchen).

A thirty-six-by eight-foot closet for my costumes and a gigantic studio stood up top, thirty-six by twenty-five, with a slanted beamed cathedral ceiling about twenty feet high, plus its own bath. Mia would have her own small play yard with a sandbox, swing set, and picket fence. I had my sewing toys, including a pullout cutting table, the first of its kind, which could be rolled out twelve feet, then rolled back into the wall, so it looked like a desk. A self-sufficient ivory tower, all mine. All sunshine, light colors, toys, kids, dogs, and music.

A full city block away, at the far end of the house, stood Ernie's mismatched twin tower, a friendly giant castle that was dark and brooding, with its stone, wood paneling, armor, real working guns, massive furniture, and custom poker table and steam room. He usually kept the shutters closed on the windows closed from the inside. Hans Conried called it "not so much a man's den as a grown-up little boy's."

$\mathcal{E}$LEVEN

ERNIE HATED THE ROAD as much as I did. He missed his own studio, the cameras to play with, and the reaction of his crew. That's as live as he wanted to be. He also resented working anywhere or anytime because someone told him he *had* to. But finally, back "home" in Hollywood, outwardly at least, it was business as usual. Ernie had Leonard and Nan to see to his every need and his poker buddies to play with at all hours of the day or night. His daughters were within call, safely on the right coast. And he now had me stashed in my own tower with my toys, sewing, and music. He finally had his entire world under one roof. He was king of his castle, and the newly completed dream den was his throne room. He was happy. I was not. I equated my unrest with the move.

We'd missed the era that everyone on the West Coast referred to as the old days, the golden thirties and forties, old Hollywood, so when Ernie did *North to Alaska*, I was fascinated by the director Henry Hathaway's tales, which he told me over dinner. One vividly stands out about the Jean Harlow-Paul Bern scandal. I had heard the story as the studio released it to the world press: that Paul Bern had killed himself, in remorse, because he couldn't live up to the physical demands of the then-world's greatest sex symbol, Jean Harlow.

255

Henry told me that the real story was that Paul Bern was having a mad affair with a starlet called Dorothy Malotte. Jean came home early one day and discovered them in bed. Paul killed himself and left a note saying something like "Please forgive the charade of last night."

The studio heads felt that Harlow's box office would drop disastrously if it came out that her husband was with another woman, so they leaked it to the press that the charade had to do with Paul Bern's manly equipment (or lack of it). Thus their grosses for the next unreleased pictures not only would not be hurt but would soar to be smash hits. They did.

Dorothy Malotte killed herself three days after Paul did.

In our Hollywood daily visibility in television or movies was essential. Ernie's movie career provided that, at least for him, but artistically he was carrying out other people's visions rather than his own. The studio kept typecasting him in some variation of the captain role he had played in his first picture, *Operation Mad Ball*. In fact, he actually played captains in three of his subsequent pictures, including *Wake Me When It's Over* and *Our Man in Havana*. In four of his total of nine movies, he played captains; in four other films he was cast as a second-lead villain. Even his one big starring part, in *Five Golden Hours*, was a heavy, not really the romantic lead. He finally took out an ad in the trade papers: "Please, no more * # ! * Captains!"

James Bacon of the Associated Press quoted Ernie on being typecast as a comic villain, usually as a stiff army captain: "I don't want audiences seeing my pictures ten years from now and saying, 'oh, I remember him, the guy who always played fat captains.' So I diet between roles. I lost 40 pounds for 'Our Man in Havana.' That shows I can play thin captains, too."

Since he didn't want to go on the road doing clubs or PR (he didn't mind movie locations) and we always needed the money, Ernie looked for television work, this time at home on the West Coast. He did four starring roles in anthology programs in February and March 1959: "I Was a Bloodhound" on *GE Theater*; "Hurrah for the Irish" on *The Ann Sothern Show*; "Symbol of Authority" on *Desilu Playhouse*; and "The Salted Mine" for *Schlitz Playhouse of Stars*.

Sing a Pretty Song . . .

In April 1959, after finishing the Cuban location filming of the feature *Our Man in Havana*, Ernie got to work on his own first network special since *Eugene*, more than two years before. *Kovacs on Music* was an hourlong program for ABC, which surprisingly gave him carte blanche on expenses. Needless to say, he took advantage of that. More important, Ernie began a longtime relationship with the Consolidated Cigar Company that lasted until his death. Not only was he the on-camera spokesperson, but he was to write and produce the commercials any way he wanted to. He had total creative control.

Kovacs on Music, which aired on May 22, 1959, represented Ernie's only shot at sixty minutes of prime time to do with exactly what he wished. It was also his first work with videotape, which gave him the chance to shoot the show in sections and edit them together, a luxury unheard of for this live television experimenter. I was on the show, but very pregnant; Mia was due any day. André Previn, then still a Hollywood wunderkind and not yet known as a world-class symphony maestro, was hired as conductor. André led a sixty-piece orchestra and opened the program playing a few bars of Ernie's theme, "Oriental Blues," loosely based on one of George Gerswhin's first published pieces, a ragtime number called "Rialto Ripples." I was to do one serious spot on the show, Villa-Lobos's *Bachianas Brasileiras No. 5*, scored for eight cellos and a soprano.

André, in those days, recorded as a jazz pianist. Ernie and I had a lot of his records, which we loved. I sometimes had trouble working with jazz musicians, who could improvise but not necessarily read. I was particularly concerned about a difficult piece such as *Bachianas*, with its unusual 7/4 metered phrases. Never having met André before and knowing nothing about his musical background, I asked him, with some trepidation, "Can you conduct a seven-four?"

He looked me right in the eye and said quietly, "Oh, I think I can manage it."

After the first run-through, I realized that not only could he manage it, but he was a musical genius. He made complicated music seem simple. I then understood that he was a schooled musician beyond any I'd ever met before, even at

257

Juilliard. He became one of my best friends and my adviser through later musical adventures. It became evident that he was only one of a few people on the West Coast who could teach me *Lulu*.

André was also sensitive to my obvious delicate condition (I was being hidden behind scenery to disguise my pregnancy) and my limited lung capacity and consequent breathing trouble. I had to sing long, controlled phrases in a high, very soft tessitura voice, the most difficult thing for a singer. Since I could not sustain the long phrases, he had each of the eight cellos bow at different times so that I could take a "catch breath." With his conducting and the cellists "breathing" for me, it sounded like one continuous phrase. Even in my delicate condition, they made me sound good.

I felt classical music was an odd choice for Ernie in his first one-hour special. When I first met him, his favorite composer was Ferde Grofé, and he especially liked his *Grand Canyon Suite*. At Juilliard that kind of music was known as "picture music" and was looked on with great disdain. It was considered a completely unimaginative photograph of what one sees, as opposed to, say, impressionistic music that evokes how one feels after experiencing some emotion. Picture music was so un-Ernie. I couldn't believe it; here was this sophisticated man doing the most spontaneous and original visual effects, listening to picture music on the phonograph.

At the time my favorite composer was still Alban Berg. To me, as an "artsy-fartsy" trained musician, it was as if Ernie had chosen a picture postcard of Atlantic City over the "Mona Lisa" as his favorite work of art. I simply could not understand how a man with his genius and constantly surfacing subconscious mind had not opened the musical door to the back of his head. In my best schoolteacher manner, I started on Ernie's musical training. I made absolutely no headway until I brought him records of three Hungarians, Belá Bartók, Zoltán Kodály, and Ernst von Dohnányi, all of whom had used Hungarian folk tunes as a basis for their heavy, sometimes dissonant symphonies.

After Ernie had listened to all of them carefully and had

made no smart remarks, I felt I had made some headway. He would play Bartók and the others all day at peak volume, dissonance and all. Later, when he had graduated to the intellectually demanding late Beethoven quartets, I would wake up to these cerebral, ponderous works. I couldn't take them before coffee in the morning. Even my mother's Lehár would been preferable. But when the volume on Ernie's new favorites was turned up so high that the needles on the two Macintosh amplifiers never left the red, I knew I had made a dent. Now I could bring him Francis Poulenc's "Conversations" or Paul Hindemith's *Mathis der Maler* and let Ernie take it from there.

In turn, Ernie introduced me to some great popular music. "Our" song back in Philadelphia had been George Shearing's recording of "The Nearness of You." Ten years later, in California, our song was *Gymnopédie No. 2* by Erik Satie. Whenever Ernie and I had words, our peace offering was for one of us to put a record of this mellow work on the stereo system and blast it throughout the house as well as outside by the pool. Satie was the signal to everyone in the house that a party was waiting in the family den: fancy hors d'oeuvres, Ernie's carefully made special chilled martinis for us, Shirley Temples for the girls, and sweet old-fashioneds for the moms.

Because of our giant speakers in each area of the house and outdoors, the entire neighborhood always knew the mood we were in from the kind of music we played. At Christmas, all of Bowmont, Hazen, and Cherokee drives got Christmas carols, whether they wanted them or not. My favorite seasonal album, then and now, is *Joni James Sings Christmas Carols*. Joe Berlingeri, my conductor, had worked with Joni before he worked with me and always thought very highly of her. However, in this album her sibilant s and dentalized t on "Silent Night" are unforgettable. Also, her slur up to "all is calm" is a real all-out guffaw. Much later, before I sold the Bowmont house, I rented it furnished to Sylvester Stallone and his wife, Sasha. I left everything there, books, records, dishes, and silver. The only thing that I requested that the Stallones keep for me, if they could find it, was my prized Joni James record. I hadn't been able to find it to take out with my extra-special valuables. Sly rolled his eyes toward Sasha and said, "A record of Joni James, Edie? Oh, yeah, sure. Right."

Once the musical door was opened to the bottomless well of Ernie's brain, it seemed as if he simply reported on what was going on in there. Once he accepted serious music, he was able to make fun of it for a full hour. As he said in the beginning of the show, "This is about all kinds of music, especially classical music. And since I don't know anything about it myself, I thought I should explain it to you."

Some of the pieces he did on *Kovacs on Music* went further than either of us could possibly grasp. I always had some reservations about imposing just one picture on any given composer's intent. Juilliard taught me that the nature of music as an art form was that listeners formed their own pictures or interpretations in their heads. But I finally decided Ernie's unique interpretation was at least a way to get the masses listening to serious music. At the very least, it was the basic roots of MTV, a mixed blessing.

Kovacs on Music also included Tchaikovsky's *Swan Lake* danced by ten gorillas in tutus. At the end the "prima ballerina" was given a bunch of bananas instead of flowers. The extravagance of the evening was a sketch with Louis Jourdan and me as concert soloists doing a commercial for a gummed label company. As the elaborate takeoff came to a big conclusion, on direction from Ernie the upstage curtain parted, to reveal a fully robed choir that sang only two words: "Buy gum." Then the curtain slowly closed, and the choir was never seen again. A perplexed ABC executive said, "Ernie, you've got to use them in some other bit; you've paid them scale for the full hour." Ernie was stubborn; he said, "No, that's the whole point, to pay all these people a full hour's scale just to sing these two words." When the network executives further protested, Ernie reminded them, "It could have been two other words. Then you'd really be upset."

Meanwhile, Panama and Frank were producing the movie version of *Li'l Abner*, with many of the original Broadway cast. I had been asked to play, and expected to play, Daisy Mae—before my pregnancy. Panama and Frank had agreed to wait until the baby was born, June 1. Every day after

June 1, they called to ask how I felt and find out if there was any news. Ernie would tell them daily, "No, nothing new today. She's still Buddha-size," until he had to leave for London for location for *Our Man in Havana* on June 9. Finally, about June 10, they said, "We're sorry, we can't wait any longer; we've delayed as long as we can. Production is backed up; we have to go on without you." The way I felt and looked in that last month when Mia was three weeks overdue, I couldn't even think of those skimpy costumes. I always felt that the last month was tougher than all eight (in my case, nine) that went before it.

With Ernie gone and Mary and the girls having formed a tight triumvirate (they were furious about the new baby) I felt I needed someone in my corner. I called my mother, who came out immediately and settled herself in my tower. She wanted to be as far away as possible from Mary, who was camping out in Ernie's study in his absence.

I had an easy pregnancy, no morning sickness or silly demands for food. I was happier and healthier than I'd ever been and, best of all, didn't have to go out at night or work or entertain. I didn't have to be pleasing anybody else but myself. I just had to be me and do what my body told me to do. I reverted to a nesting aura that came from I don't know where. I had been reading pregnancy books from Australia and was well aware, even in 1959, that whatever went into my mouth went into the baby's system. I never smoked, gave up even my casual drink, and started on a health regimen. I knew I needed the calcium of a quart of milk a day; I added powdered skim milk to regular skim milk.

But as easy as the pregnancy was, that's how difficult the labor was.

When my water broke on Wednesday evening, June 17, our dear friend and agent Marvin Moss took me to the hospital. I was told to time the labor pains. I had talked my doctor, Stuart Brien, into the Lamaze method of natural birth, then unheard of in the United States. But I ordered the book from Paris and figured that with my singing breathing exercises this would be a snap. I could handle all the breathing by myself. Wednesday night the pains got down to five minutes apart, then stopped completely. Dr. Brien thought it might have been just false labor but kept me at the hospital anyway. The same thing happened on Thursday and Friday, when I was joined by my mother at the hospital for the waiting game. When Dr. Brien came in on Saturday, June 20, he finally said, "We have to do a cesarean, and we have to do it right away." I agreed: "Anything." All thoughts of Lamaze went out the window. I got a spinal, which I hated, because while you can't actually feel anything, you can almost hear or sense that initial cut. I heard the cry, and Stu said, "It's a girl and she's beautiful."

Without my glasses, all I could see was this long (twenty-seven inches), very thin (seven pounds, seven ounces) baby with a head shaped like a cone, much like the Coneheads on *Saturday Night Live.* I said, "Stu, what's the matter? She's got a pointed head." He said, "Don't worry, it'll go away." And in a few days it did. Not only did her head return to normal, but she was beautiful. She looked like a Titian painting, born with an inch and a half of bright red hair. I had to put a flower or bow on a tiny hair clip to show that she was a girl. After eighteen months all the straight burnt orange hair fell out and was replaced by soft, downy white blond curls. She was also smart and could distinguish all colors, including beige, before she was two.

Because she had been conceived on the TWA flight, I had just assumed she would fly out. But Mia and I had the worst of both labor and cesarean. They say that cesarean children have an easy way to go and expect more, whereas labor children have had to fight their way out and so are feistier. Mia was feisty and expected more.

Ernie got the news of her birth at Alec Guinness's country house. It was Saturday night there, and he had been sleeping on the couch, with a telephone and an iced bottle of Dom Pérignon standing by. When the call finally came at 3:30 A.M. London time, Ernie woke up Alec and his wife, Merula, to celebrate Mia's birth with champagne. Alec kept the cork.

Our poor child didn't have a name for two weeks; Ernie and I were phoning back and forth. We had expected a boy from the X rays and settled on Drew, from Andrew, Ernie's father. Since Ernie was in his English period, once we knew it was a girl, he suggested such names as Tracey and Pamela.

We finally decided on Mia, because it went with Kovacs. I had had a girl friend at Juilliard named Mia. The middle name was Susan, after Ernie's grandmother.

With the cesarean I stayed in the hospital for two weeks after Mia's birth. So I had a long time to get acquainted with her alone. I used to stare at her, and when I saw my own eyes looking back at me through hers, I could never understand how anyone could give her own child up for adoption. I hired a temporary baby nurse, Nana Petersen, who specialized in caring for infants their first three months. She was an older, sweet Norwegian woman, who had never remained past infancy. I talked her into staying, and she was with us until Mia was six.

Ernie returned from London and came immediately to the hospital. The head nurse wouldn't let him in to see the baby because he had just come off the plane from overseas and might be carrying diseases. He was livid. When Mia was with me, he had to stay on the other side of the room; a guard nurse stood there to be sure he did. By the time we got home, the hospital had made me so disease nuts that even my dog, Pamela, was not allowed in the room. The dog was so upset that she developed a skin disease, and her fur fell out. The vet said it was brought on by some traumatic change. "What's different?" I said, "The baby." He said, "That's it." Pamela looked so bad and so unhappy that I sent her back to Lillian in New York, where Pamela lived to be seventeen years old.

When we all got home on a weekend, there was no heat in the new baby's wing of the house. Ernie, who could not fix anything, had to crawl under the house, swearing in Hungarian and every language, trying to repair the heating unit. But he did get it working. He wanted to start buying things for Mia right away, but I pleaded with him not to suffocate her with toys. The other girls had had so many things that were just rotting around, and we had given many of them away. I remember a $650 F.A.O. Schwarz furnished dollhouse that had deteriorated in the garden in the rain. I didn't want to make that mistake again.

After four months at home, coping with two grannies and two troubled preteens, I felt the need to get back to work again—and soon. In August UCLA did what was to have been only a reading of Brecht's *Mother Courage* with Eileen Heck-art and Ross Martin. Eileen played Mother Courage, and I played Yvette and a couple of other parts. I had agreed to the reading as a way to ease back into work, but it became a full-fledged production. Eileen was pregnant, not feeling well and didn't want to tell anyone. I sent her to Dr. Brien and made sure she put her feet up and took her chicken soup. In September 1983 a handsome young man delivered a handwritten letter to me backstage in Westport, Connecticut. It was Eileen's son, Luke Yankee, then twenty-three, who said his mother had talked about my kindness during that difficult period. He wanted to say, "Thank you for making me possible. Without you, I don't think I'd be here."

Ernie's answer to my "freebie" Brecht appearance was to pick me up after the last show, with the girls, caviar, and champagne for a surprise trip on a 105-foot yacht he'd hired with a chef and complete crew. We went on a cruise to Baja California for a long weekend.

In late August 1959 I started to work on a new act in order to play the Persian Room at the Plaza. Hugh Martin and Timmy Gray helped me with it, during rehearsals in Los Angeles. Ernie, Mia, and her Nana came with me to New York, where Dr. Fishback baptized Mia at the Central Presbyterian Church. I also did an Art Carney special called *Small World, Isn't It?* with Hermione Gingold. This time I did a slicker act, for four weeks, opening on September 11. I opened with "Autumn in New York" and added to my impersonations another special material number: "You'll See Them on the Late Late Show." Such standbys as my Jeanette MacDonald and Ruby Keeler and, of course, Marilyn were joined by "Shirley Temple" and "Grace Kelly."

Right after my opening, Ernie had to return to California to start the movie *Strangers When We Meet*, with Kim Novak. As soon as he finished that, he had to go into *Wake Me When It's Over* for his buddy Mervyn Le Roy at Twentieth Century-Fox. "After all those years in TV," Ernie told Don Freeman of the San Diego *Union*, "movie work is like having a license to steal. You say a few words and then sit around for an hour. How long has this been going on?"

He also told Don Freeman:

Nothing has changed more in this country in the last five years than comedy. Today we laugh at different things. When George S. Kaufman made his crack that "satire is what closes on Saturday night" he was right. But it's not true anymore; satire is very big today . . . people have grown up. "Maverick," for instance, couldn't have made it five years ago. Witness such satiric comic strips as "Peanuts." Witness how humor we thought was so chic ten or twenty years ago is now considered stale and dated. Today, a pie in the face isn't funny unless it's presented satirically, and how long has it been since anyone put a sign on their cottage that said, "Dew Drop Inn"? Television is the big culprit. Fellows like Sid Caesar stuck their neck out being satirical, and gradually it seeped in. And another big thing is that, today, for reasons I can't explain, people are laughing more at themselves than they ever were.

Consolidated Cigar had been looking for a celebrity to host *Take a Good Look*, the program that it had sold to ABC to promote Dutch Masters. Ernie was an obvious choice, once George Burns and Groucho Marx had turned it down. George still smokes a Consolidated product. He told me recently, "Ernie smoked cigars, and I smoked cigars. I still do. I smoke El Productos. They cost three for a dollar. Now years ago Ernie offered me one of his cigars. I said, 'Ernie, what do you pay for these cigars?' He said, 'They're three dollars apiece.' I said, 'Three dollars! If I paid three dollars for a cigar, first I'd sleep with it, then I'd smoke it.' P.S. If this isn't funny, say Jack Benny wrote it." Ernie's reason for getting up in the morning was to have breakfast so that he could smoke his first cigar. His real reason for all those steam baths was that he could sit in there and smoke a cigar. He once told me that if a doctor ever said he had to quit smoking, that it was a matter of life or death, he'd keep on smoking cigars.

Dutch Masters were meant for the masses, not for connoisseurs like Ernie. During negotiations in his den a roomful of Consolidated executives, including the president, Buddy Silberman, advertising agency people, and Marvin Moss all were on pins and needles, waiting to see what would happen.

Knowing that Ernie smoked only the best cigars, one of the company officers nervously offered him a Dutch Masters. Ernie lit the cigar and puffed it, then took it from his mouth. He looked at it for a second and said, "When I was getting over double pneumonia and pleurisy, my father came to see me and handed me a cigar, the kind he always smoked. It was a Dutch Masters. You know, it's not a bad cigar." Sighs of relief and big grins filled the room. Thus Ernie was able to make the deal with Consolidated, preserving his integrity. He really did smoke Dutch Masters, too.

Consolidated gave Ernie nearly total creative control of *Take a Good Look*, which had been just an average quiz show, cheap to produce, and originally hosted by Mike Wallace.

Ernie was thrilled about his five-thousand-dollar weekly salary and told the press that it was going to take only two hours of a week of his time. However, privately, he told me he had no intention of doing any simple, uncomplicated quiz show. He used it as a means to show obtuse, funny blackouts, which he had the audacity to call "clues." *Take a Good Look* thus became a parody of all TV quiz shows, with his favorite format—blackouts. I was one of three panelists, the girl in the middle, most often flanked by Hans Conried and Cesar Romero; sometimes the female panelist was Zsa Zsa Gabor, Janet Leigh, or Anne Jeffreys. Alternative men were Ben Alexander and Carl Reiner. We were supposed to guess the identities of the guests, who had once been in the news, by means of Ernie's blackout "clues," but God help you if you inadvertently guessed the right answer when Ernie had another three clues waiting to go on the air. Ernie wrote, staged, and usually starred in the clues, along with Peggy Connelly and Bobby Lauher. Later Jolene Brand replaced Peggy.

However, on *Take a Good Look*, the more clues it took for us to guess the guest's identity, the more money he or she won. Guests usually got it all. *Take a Good Look* was on ABC first on Sunday nights, then on Thursday nights for eighteen months, until March 1961.

When we didn't have to make a sweeping walk-in entrance but were discovered already seated at the panel, I wore glamorous beaded tops, exotic court-length gloves, visible above the desk, while underneath I was comfortable in pedal pushers and flats. We now had a wardrobe department, adept at live TV's "fine Italian handwork": no hand sewing—just safety pins, clothespins, or paint. One day, as I was rushing on to get settled before I was introduced, slipping a ring on the outside of one of my long black gloves, I discovered a hole in the glove, with white skin clearly visible. I called wardrobe and, without thinking twice someone grabbed the thick felt pen from the cue card man and simply blacked out my white skin. The hand was still wet as I carefully posed my ringed glove to my chin and said, "Oh, hello." Back again, to live television.

With his altered format for *Take a Good Look*, Ernie was earning a lot of money for a half hour show in 1959. He was putting in at least eight hours a week. More important, Ernie's classic silent Dutch Masters commercials endeared him to Consolidated even after the cancellation of the quiz show. The silent commercials won a Clio Award, the advertising industry's Oscar.

Ernie didn't like the outside PR firm that had been hired to promote the show. Irving Mansfield, one of the producers, called his friend Henri Bollinger, who had worked on other shows and said, "Just come down and observe." Henri did, for a couple of shows, and, as he recently told me, was just about to say, "I can't do this job for you," and quit. Henri said, "I don't even know how to start. Ernie doesn't even talk to me." He and Irving were in Ernie's dressing room when an assistant came in and said, "Ernie, we need you in this next shot." Ernie turned to Henri, tossed him his cards, and said, "Here, play this hand for me." Henri said, "He didn't even know my name, and I didn't even know what the game was." Henri remembered, "I played the hand, and whatever I did I guess was right because when Ernie returned, he told me we'd won." Only then did Ernie say, "What is your name, and what do you do here?" They shook hands, and from then on Ernie and Henri became inseparable, new best friends.

Henri was another of the very few people whose opinion Ernie respected. As I look back in the clip books, it's clear that when Henri took over the public relations for the show, we suddenly had a good shepherd for our visible life. Network publicity, movie company publicity, and sponsor publicity had different ways of promoting. After Henri took over, there seemed to be a guided master plan, where it had been haphazard before. He was soon hired by Consolidated to promote Ernie and cigars in an institutional way and later to do the same for me and Muriel. Henri is still my friend, manager, and public relations person; I could not have survived the last thirty years without his advice. In the face of all chaos, he is the one voice of sanity.

In December 1959 Louis Sobol wrote in his Broadway column from Hollywood:

> . . . the busiest actor here is Ernie Kovacs, working in two studios simultaneously, at Columbia for his chores in *Strangers When We Meet* at 20th in *Wake Me When It's Over.* In between hours, he rushes over to his taping assignments for the weekly TV show, *Take a Good Look.* At night, he has his gin rummy and poker sessions. Ernie insists Hollywood is made to order for him. He has become a personality here—with many friends. "In New York . . . I never quite seemed to make it— they just didn't accept me." On the other hand, his talented wife, Edie Adams, prefers Manhattan, but in a resigned mood asserts: "If Ernie is happy in Hollywood—that's got to be my town too—Ernie's more important to me than any career or love I may have of New York."

In rereading this recently, I wanted to shake me. Outside I was still putting on a happy face. Inside I was really unhappy, but too bottled up to express it. We all were in California, but less of a family than we'd been in New York.

My first movie, *The Apartment,* was even easier for me than breaking into nightclubs had been. Ernie and I were out one Saturday night in late 1959 for dinner at Trader Vic's with Billy and Audrey Wilder. Billy was holding court as usual, and in the middle of one of his witty stories he looked over the dinner table at me and said, "Edie, could you vear your hair up, Svedish style, vit maybe a braid on top?"

I said, "Sure, why?"

He said, "I have a part for you in a picture I'm shooting."

Sing a Pretty Song . . .

I knew all about "the Wilder picture," as we all called it in those Hollywood bravura days, from my friends Jack Lemmon and Shirley MacLaine, but I thought Billy meant the ditzy blond Marilyn type in the bar. I couldn't understand why the hair up in braids. "Which part did you have in mind, Billy?" I asked.

He said, "I'd like you to play Fred MacMurray's secretary."

I was overwhelmed. Until now in Hollywood nobody'd even asked me to be in a four-by-five snapshot. I still thought it was just dinner talk until the wardrobe department called me the next day, Sunday, and told me to bring a choice of several business suits to wear. Even if your agents are still haggling over price, if wardrobe calls, you know you've got the part, even before you've signed the contracts. I did my first scene Monday morning. At least now I was working; it made life in California a little more bearable.

Billy produced the movie as well as wrote the story and screenplay, with I. A. L. "Izzy" Diamond. Izzy, the expert on colloquial Americana, was on the set to monitor every shot. As a young executive trying to get promoted Jack Lemmon allows his company's married senior executives and their girl friends to use his one-room apartment for their trysts. Shirley MacLaine played Fred MacMurray's girl friend. The Apartment won the Best Picture Oscar in 1960, plus two more Oscars for Billy as writer and director and two more for art direction and editing. It was the last black-and-white movie to win the Best Picture Oscar.

I played the secretary to Fred MacMurray's philandering boss. I never understood how Fred, with all his technical training in movies, could film his television show My Three Sons in two days. He explained that he did all his lines to an empty space next to the camera; he never saw the other actors, who came in and shot on other days without him there. This was different from the theater: no possibility of any chemistry between the actors.

I disagreed with Billy during the filming of The Apartment. He saw my character, Miss Olsen, as a flat-out bitter, spiteful bitch. All my Lee Strasberg training had taught me that there's no all-out flat any character. Even Jack the Ripper

269

may have had his good points. Having learned to play Daisy Mae with a few of Strasberg's additions, I thought this was a good place to try it again. I chose to play Miss Olsen another way, outwardly agreeing with Billy, but trying to give her another dimension. It's your duty to provide a subtext, no matter what your lines are in the script. Daisy Mae had taught me: Cartoons and stereotypes belong only in sketches.

Movies for me were like starting all over again. Coming from theater, I was used to learning my part from beginning to end, thus knowing exactly where I was at any given point. Movies might shoot the last scene first and every other scene out of sequence. If you left a scene screaming and running out the door, the scene you might shoot first would be your reaction, coming out the other side of the door. The angry scene in which you left might be shot three months later. If you watch carefully on *The Late Late Show*, particularly in some of the B movies, you will see an actor rush out the door and appear two seconds later twenty pounds heavier. Not only visually, but interpretatively you have to remember how angry you plan to be when you finally shoot the scene coming through the door. It's technically very difficult. In theater the audience tells you how angry to be; there's no planning or plotting. And the audience is always right. In movies technique is all important, even to finding your key light. An inch or two off can ruin the shot.

In January 1960 Ernie and I did the last *I Love Lucy Show*, which was called "Lucy Meets the Moustache." It was difficult for me to be funny because of the obvious tension between Lucy and Desi. They weren't even speaking. He would say, "Would you tell Miss Ball to move two steps to the left?" She would say, "Would you tell Mr. Arnaz that I can't move two steps to the left because I'll be out of my light?" In spite of the heavy atmosphere on the set, the show turned out to be very funny and sparkled, as did all her shows.

I had never worked with Lucy before, so I didn't know how much of a perfectionist she was on the set. She involved herself in every minute detail of anything that touched her in any way. Desi, it was clear, was the overall brain behind the business, production, and three-headed camera technique, not "the bongo player that Lucy dragged into show business." On the first day's shooting my first shot was in the afternoon. I arrived with my hair already done at home by my personal hairdresser, in my usual pageboy style. We all were to go out to lunch, Ernie, Lucy, and I, but at the last minute I saw her whispering to the show's hairdresser. Lucy, it appeared, didn't like my pageboy and decided that I should wear my hair up with a bun in the back. She didn't talk to me about it; I found out when the hairdresser said to me, "I'm sorry, we have to use the lunch hour to redo your hair. She doesn't like it that way."

I said, "But I always wear my hair this way."

At this point, Ernie came in and said, "Come on, honey. Time for lunch."

I said, "I can't go. I have to get my head soaked."

He never missed a beat—"Oh, okay, I'll see you later"—and went out to lunch with Lucy.

Fuming over my tuna fish sandwich, I had my hair washed, set, and dried; that took the two hours. Desi, who had been wandering around the set by himself, popped in to say hello. I started in. "What is this all about?"

He said, "Well, that's how Lucy is. She has to have everything in the show exactly her way." He at least held my hand and commiserated. It was Desi's autobiography, *A Book*, that really got me interested in writing my own. Desi's book was not great literature, but the reader ended up knowing the man. He'd call me up and encourage me to do mine. "You can do it. All you have to do is speak into a tape recorder." I tried it, and that didn't work for me; but it did encourage me.

The hairdresser combed my hair out. Lucy came in and said, "How you doin', Edie?" She and the hairdresser had another long inaudible conversation, and Lucy left, saying, "See you later, Edie."

The hairdresser came over to me and said, "I'm afraid we're going to have to do it one more time. She likes it better the way you had it when you came in."

So once again we had to soak my hair, reset it, and comb it out. My first shot came at about five o'clock in the afternoon. I'd had my hair completely redone three times for that one shot. Whether she knew it or not, Lucy was responsible for my cutting my hair and having it styled in a new 1960's bouffant hairdo, a little ahead of its time. I called my creation the Hollywood bowl.

Even though I was now making movies, I started studying voice with Madame Chamlee, on Hollywood Boulevard early in 1960, to prepare for *The Merry Widow* the following summer. The Metropolitan Opera's Theodor Uppman played Danilo, and David Doyle (*Charlie's Angels*) was Popoff. I played Sonia (in 1986 I did it at the Long Beach Civic Light Opera as Hanna). Madame Chamlee and her husband, Mario, have coached many of the movie sopranos, such as Kathryn Grayson, Jane Powell, and Deanna Durbin. I leapt at the chance to do the Franz Lehár operetta *The Merry Widow* for John Kenley's theater circuit in Ohio. I was to play the same three theaters, in Columbus, Dayton, and Warren, many other times in later years. But this was my first work for the legendary and flamboyant John Kenley. His reputation had preceded him, and he lived up to every outrageous thing I'd ever heard about him. We have since become good friends.

While I was rehearsing, I would bring Mia, who was not yet a year old yet, up to my tower studio, and she would sometimes sing along. She liked to hear me sing, especially when the song told a story. Even in another language, if I could hold her attention, I knew I'd mastered the song. She was already teaching me. During that year and the next, as soon as she could walk, if I had a ballet lesson, she came with me, and the two of us had a private class.

At our first rehearsal, after I was introduced to Mr. Uppman, his first words were: "You're not going to camp this up, are you?" Perhaps he, along with me, had been watching my listing in *TV Guide* change every year. First it was "Edie Adams, singer." A few years later it was "Edie Adams, singer-comedienne." This was the year it had been dehyphenated and said, "Edie Adams, comedienne." It had been so long since the public had heard my real voice.

That's one reason I wanted to do this operetta so badly. It's what I'd really been trained to do. I reassured Mr. Uppman that I intended to have as much fun as possible playing Hanna Glawari in true *belle époque* style because that was the nature of the piece. When we actually started singing, he was dumbfounded. The odd part was that he was the one who got into vocal trouble over the course of the run, while my voice got even stronger. Opera singers rarely did more than four performances a week, but of course, we tough Broadway babies did eight as a matter of course. And how about those fourteen performances a week in Vegas for a month with no days off?

Since I had all the time in the world to prepare for this role, I got a record of a Viennese opera company doing the operetta in live performance. Normally I could understand German, but this all was sung in a Viennese dialect that was not in the libretto. I got my Viennese masseuse to translate for me because one scene got big laughs on the record but was never seen in any German libretto of *The Merry Widow*. When I study a role, everybody's part gets studied. Because we had a comic actor but nonsinger, David Doyle, playing Popoff, the masseuse translated all the low-comedy shtick from the Viennese record.

It provided David an extra comedy scene that he did very well and even improved on. In the second act all the principals sing in a sextet. David insisted he couldn't sing, and I said, "You're going to sing this song, even if you can't sing. I gave you a funny scene. The least you can do is learn your part. The rest of us can't sing this unless you do." I stayed with him after rehearsals every night and hammered it in. My mother would have been proud of me. David finally sang his part in the sextet well enough that he didn't throw the rest of us off. He still says he doesn't believe he did it.

Rudy Tronto, who later did *Sugar Babies*, was the choreographer. He and I restaged some of the stodgier scenes and added more bawdy Viennese scenes, so that the whole production had a special sparkle. Halfway through the two-month run I started to fall for one of the opera singers, so I called Ernie and said, "You'd better get out here; he's a pretty attractive guy." Ernie came running, and I was saved from my romance on the road, Goody Two Shoes that I was. Kenley told me that when Ernie saw me in *The Merry Widow*, his reaction was "untranscribable." Ernie, who had never heard me sing opera straight, stood there with tears in his eyes, saying, "Goddamn, she's good."

Now that I was singing in my real voice and the reviews

were great, suddenly I was getting different kinds of offers. *Merry Widow* at City Center, *The Telephone* of GianCarlo Menotti and *The Fortune Teller* of Victor Herbert, *Lulu*—I was the only nut who wanted to do it.

In July 1960 I went to New York to audition for the upcoming Broadway show *The Happiest Girl in the World*. Since we had given up our big apartment on Central Park West, I stayed at the Hotel Pierre. The accountant Phil Braunstein came to my suite and said, "The IRS man wants forty thousand in cash this year." Things were looking up; we were making more money. Braunstein said that the taxes we owed were about $120,000. With the $40,000 bribe the IRS man would see that our taxes did not run over $20,000, making our total payout $60,000, half. Again, Phil told me to think about it and talk to Ernie. Again, I said that I didn't have to talk to Ernie; we had discussed it, and the answer was still no.

The IRS man's reply to my refusal, as relayed through our business manager, is "forever etched in memory," as Ernie and I often clichéd. "Who does this Kovacs think he is, a goddamn saint? I'll fix his ass." We stood firm, ignored the threat, and the IRS man did just what he said he'd do.

One night in July 1960, after the *Take a Good Look* program, someone from Consolidated came to Ernie and said, "We've just bought a little cigar company from P. Lorillard, called Muriel. Do you think Edie would like to do a commercial for them?" Very few celebrities did commercials in those days, and those who did were stuck with a single image, like Betty Furness with her hand on the Westinghouse refrigerator door. (It took her twenty years to shed that image, she told me later; even after she became a special assistant to the President for consumer affairs, people still thought of her as that girl with her hand on the refrigerator door.) My agent objected strongly since "nobody" did commercials in those days. I said, "Wait a minute, you mean I'm going to be standing there with my hair done, my makeup perfect, in a gorgeous gown and in my best key light, saying, 'Hello, I'm Edie Adams,' on every sporting event for the next two years? Are you kidding? I should pay them. Take it."

The first Muriel commercial, an expensive one that took several days to shoot, was filmed in a silent movie studio on 112th Street in Manhattan that hadn't been used since the silent movies' heyday, about 1911. I was to be put in the back of a Metropolitan Opera scenery truck, the longest truck made, wearing a slinky dress, slit up to there. With my legs carefully crossed, I sat on a girder and was hoisted into the truck. I wore another of my own beaded Marilyn takeoff dresses, cut within an inch of my life, together with the ever-present white fox stole.

The "truckers and scenery movers" stood by ogling me, all done up and selling my cigar. My attitude, from doing the takeoffs on Marilyn and Mae West, was not heavy come-on sex but connecting with a twinkle in my eye: "Ladies, you know I'm kidding, but, fellas, you know I just might not be." Ernie came up to watch us filming one day, complete with his usual tirade against the networks and sponsors, who controlled everything.

The studio was bustling with the usual crew, agency people, dancers etc., rushing around, doing their jobs. Off to one side, standing with two or three other people, was a thoughtful, quietly dressed man with shell-rimmed glasses, very distinguished-looking but obviously having a good time. He was wearing his overcoat and carried two volumes of Bertolt Brecht plays under his arm. He laughed along with everyone else at Ernie's jokes. When I asked our director who the quiet gentleman was, he replied, "That's your sponsor." I couldn't believe it and called Ernie over to inform him that the nice man with the glasses and the copy of Brecht under his arm was from Consolidated, "our sponsor, yours and mine."

Ernie raised an eyebrow in disbelief but ambled over to introduce himself. He ended up talking to the man for most of the afternoon. From my slant board, I noticed that the man went to make a telephone call, and then Ernie went to make a call. When my shooting was over for the day, Ernie brought the man over and said, "Honey, this is Jack Mogulescu; he and his wife, Myra, are coming to dinner with us, and afterward we're going to see *The Fantasticks*." When he told me that we were going to spend the entire evening not only with a sponsor but with the sponsor's *wife*, I was appalled. In those days the average wife was two steps behind her husband, but the sponsor's wife was ten steps behind her.

By the time we ended our cab ride en route to pick up Myra Mogulescu, I had found Jack to be warm, witty, and intelligent. Myra turned out to be an attractive, chic woman, dressed in the latest fashion. She was also very bright and very funny and had just started taking guitar lessons, with no previous musical experience. She was her own woman, a rarity for any wife in 1959. Later, along with Joanne Woodward, Myra Mogulescu became my role model for a wife's being an independent person in what was still a man's world. The Mogulescus became our new best friends, and Jack's was the only opinion other than mine and Henri's that Ernie would listen to concerning his shows. To everyone else with an opinion he said, "Screw."

The last night of this commercial shoot we had to finish before midnight. We finished the last shot at eleven-thirty. Since I had brought some more performing outfits and the lighting crew was still there, I said, "Hey, do you want to try for one more without a storyboard before golden time [midnight]? Can you light that column while I change clothes? Play the voice tape, and I'll show you what I'd like to do." I did a silly but provocative set of poses, peeking coyly around the column. Everybody bought it and went into high-speed activity, lighting the column and setting up camera angles in fifteen minutes while I changed. I came back at eleven forty-five and did another full unscheduled one-minute commercial, which looked pretty good when the company decided to use it on the air in addition to the others. I recently saw it for the first time in thirty years and it didn't look bad at all. In fact, it looked pretty good. Consolidated was delighted to get a free commercial.

After doing the Muriel commercial, I had planned to spend the summer with Ernie, Mia, and Nana Petersen in London and Bolzano, in northern Italy, his location for *Five Golden Hours*. Ernie and I sailed on the *Liberté* on August 6, 1960, with Mia and Nana to follow later, after we got settled. We spent a week in London, seeing everything, including Alec Guinness, wonderful in *Ross*. We ate and gambled at

John Mills's posh Les A (Les Ambassadeurs). John's idea of peasant food was a baked potato filled with caviar. On August 20 we left by train from Liverpool, accompanied by Dr. Rentfrew Salvatore, the international journalist assigned to us for the nonaerial trip to Bolzano.

The people of Bolzano, in the southern part of the Alps, speak mostly German. Bolzano is a resort way up the mountains, with the cleanest, purest air I've ever breathed. There are monasteries and castles with no windows; the locals claimed there was never any dust. The cows grazed on steep mountain pastures, and the unpasteurized milk was very sweet, the best I've ever had. Ernie was happy shooting and visiting all the local wineries. Nana, Mia, and I drove through the Brenner Pass detouring past Hitler's old retreat, Berchtesgaden, to the Salzburg Music Festival. We saw *Don Giovanni* and *The Magic Flute* in the opera house. In the Mozartium, musicians played Mozart on the original instruments, such as the seven-foot-long carved serpentine horn (later to be coiled up in brass as the French horn). From our place in Bolzano we could drive to Verona and even Venice. With Ernie's *Guide Michelin* we'd drive a hundred miles for dinner.

We went from Venice to Paris on the Orient Express. Ernie kept writing "FROY" on the steamed windows, as Margaret Lockwood does in *The Lady Vanishes*. Ernie overtipped, as usual. When one of the baggage handlers objected to the amount and started to make a fuss in loud French, Ernie picked him up by his coat collar and took him to a bank to ask a teller how much it was. It was enough, even for Ernie. The man left. Ernie made a mental note never to go back to Paris: "Why are they so mad at me?" He never did.

When we got to London, I decided I didn't want any more hotels. I wanted to get the currency straight once and for all. The ½'s and ⅙'s were driving us both crazy. But my timing was off; shortly after I got it all straight, the British switched to the decimal system. We took a flat at 1 Hyde Park Street, right across from the park. We paid such an enormous amount in advance for breakage because we were movie people. I should have known when I saw "LC" embroidered on the towels (for Lady Cunningham) that we were in for creative billing. My first clue. Without a hotel concierge, and having to hire our own help and shop for food, we quickly became Londoners. Ernie became even more so than I. He had made the best of English everything, Turnbull & Asser shirts, suits, hats, and shoes. I discovered Fortnum & Mason (caviar at any time of the day and real Stilton cheese), Asprey, which still does my stationery, Hardy Amies and a wonderful perfume called Fun that nobody makes anymore, and all those delicious antique jewelry shops on Bond Street. We moved right in. We saw operas at Sadlers Wells and shows such as *Oliver!* and *Blitz!* John Clements even took us to the Garrick Club to get some theater history to rub off on Ernie. London was and is civilized. I could live there anytime.

Going home, we needed to pick up the *Leonardo da Vinci*, which embarked from Naples but made a stop at Cannes. To get to Cannes without flying, we again had to take a train through the hated Paris. Ernie arranged for someone else to handle our change of trains, and he didn't even buy a newspaper at the station; he went right from one train car to the other. I knew why Ernie wanted to bypass Paris, but I couldn't imagine why he wanted to see Cannes off-season. I'd forgotten about the casinos. Nothing had changed (about Ernie's and my life), except here the gamblers dressed in formal clothes. We stayed at the Majestic. Ernie had seen a gold bidet charm and ran all over town to find it. With his bad command of French, he had trouble making himself understood. The storekeepers kept giving him a john. He thought the bidet charm the funniest thing he could give me (everyone in Hollywood had a real bidet then, and he considered bidets useless); I have it still.

When the *Leonardo da Vinci* sailed through the Strait of Gibraltar, local tradesmen brought out awful-looking rugs in little boats. They were so tacky Ernie loved them and kept buying them. All the passengers were laughing at him and saying, "Ernie, what are you going to do with those awful rugs?" He ignored them. At the costume ball on board I made a medieval costume out of them and won first prize. He had those rugs right in his den. If Ernie liked something, he didn't care if it came from the five-and-dime.

While we were gone, I had my accompanist, Galen Lurwick, coach Kippie and Betty on some of the songs from the new musical *The Sound of Music*. I had a Thanksgiving concert to do in Flint, Michigan (then a booming GM-plant town), on November 20, and the girls were eager to participate. They did very well with "Sixteen, Going on Seventeen," and "Do Re Mi." We sang the title song together, with AC Sparkplugs employees' chorus. Heavy with their success at this first formal concert, they both really wanted to go into show business.

In December 1960, after four glorious months with Ernie on location and in Europe, I returned to New York for another audition for *The Happiest Girl*. I was back at the Pierre and in my room vocalizing for the audition, this time for the star, Cyril Ritchard, when the telephone rang. When the man on the line said that he was Mr. Neimal from the IRS and that he wanted to talk to me, I got physically sick at my stomach, the kind of sick that hits you in the solar plexus when you feel a rush in your ears just before you faint. I told him that I couldn't talk then, I was on my way to an audition; I called Ernie on the Coast and his lawyer in New York. Both of them told me to ignore the tax man, not to talk to him at all. The lawyer said, "It's still in the discussion period." To this day I don't know what that meant.

I went to the audition trembling, was somehow offered the part, but didn't take it. I called Phil Braunstein and said that I was coming right to his office. Walking down Fifth Avenue, I broke into a cold sweat despite the cold December weather. Something strange was going on. When I got to Braunstein and Chernin, both men met with me, very nervously. Phil took his coat off, loosened his tie, and ordered food to be sent in. This was going to be a long one. Phil offered me a piece of paper, saying, "If you sign this now, they'll go easy on you next year." Without looking at it, I asked them what it was about. "Ernie mentioned it to me and looked very worried when he did," I said.

Braunstein and Chernin looked at each other, even more worried than before, and then turned to me. They started on what became a two-hour tirade to convince me to sign that paper. I didn't understand it but deep down in my gut felt that it was fishy, illegal, immoral, or wrong. My pious upbringing would not tolerate that sort of thing. The two men cajoled me in every way they could, logically, angrily, tenderly, and stubbornly, but I flat-out refused to sign. Phil was furious and said that I had to sign it. I didn't.

Back in Los Angeles about a week later Phil showed up at our house one evening and produced for Ernie what looked like the same paper. The two of them had a heated discussion about it in Ernie's outside den. After I heard Phil's car leave, Ernie came in to me and said, "Phil says if we don't sign this tonight, we'll never be solvent again; he's coming by for it tomorrow." Ernie looked at me with the oddest expression I ever saw on his face. The pain in his eyes told me what pressure was being put on him to use this way out. I didn't sign, and we never were solvent again. I still have ambivalent feelings about not having signed that paper, remembering the pain in Ernie's eyes. Phil suffered a heart attack shortly after the incident but recovered and lived until 1988. As predicted, our tax for that year was $120,000.

As recently as January 31, 1979, the IRS sent a man, Richard Carpenter, to ask me about a story I had told the Washington *Post*, alluding to this incident but without naming names. He insisted on my naming names, but I didn't think it was necessary; while Chernin had died in a plane crash Braunstein was still alive then, the taxes had been paid, and it was all long past. However, it didn't make it right.

In a letter to Judge Emanuel Belloff, in November 1960, Ernie wrote: "Someday I'm going to write you a very long letter on what has been my relationship with the tax situation. It has been an appalling one, and while I am not referring to the exorbitant tax percentage I pay there are many other facets of the whole operation which are quite repugnant, and almost make one envy the few who have moved out of the country. . . . Yesterday I was hit with a disallowance of well over $100,000. That means that in addition to the taxes already paid, I will have to pay this additional amount. And when I tell you that it was done as a vindictive reprisal against the fact that I was unwilling to "cooperate," I can only tell you I mean it to its fullest implication. The time obviously is not right for use, at the moment, but there will be someday in the future when I intend to give publicity to this entire thing." Ernie, that time is now.

$\mathscr{T}$WELVE

ON JANUARY 3, 1961, I BEGAN filming *Lover Come Back*, one of the Doris Day–Stanley Shapiro well-dressed light comedies. In this movie most of my scenes were with Rock Hudson, who was a joy to work with. Even when he did reverses (my close-up, his face next to the camera lens, not in the shot), he would carefully hold my arm and inch me into my light. "How can you do that?" I asked. "You memorize your lines and have your light down. How can you find my light for me, too?" He said, "How many pictures have you done?" I said, "Two." He said, "This is my fifty-eighth."

We needed lawyers more in touch with West Coast work and got them in an unusual way. MCA's overseas distribution said they had an offer from Australia for five thousand dollars to show the *Kovacs on Music* program. We said, "Terrific." Then, about a month later, they said we'd have to pay the actors' and musicians' residuals of ten thousand dollars. I'd heard Ernie swear, but I'd never heard language like this before. I said, "Wait a minute. Pull out the sales contract, and find out who the lawyers are for MCA distribution." He did, and instead of getting angry at them, he called them, and we hired them—the firm of Bielenson, Meyer, Rosenfeld & Susman. George Zachary was assigned to us.

Marvin Meyer, Don Rosenfeld, and George Zachary came

281

up to the house on a Saturday because we both were working during the week. At our second meeting, the more serious one, they said, "Okay, you have got to pull back. You are only making nine cents on the dollar." We'd heard that before but were blissfully trying to ignore it. Ernie protested that part of his career was having to be seen, this was Hollywood, his image was bigger than life. We had to spend more. But the lawyers insisted that we be put on a budget, and the government was to take a certain percentage of our incomes. Even at that, only 9 percent of what we earned was truly ours. Our answer to the advice was to change tax accountants. We hired Guy Gadbois, who was also a business manager. But we were committed to listening to these new lawyers because they obviously knew the territory.

When I was working daily, I was thrilled not to be going out at night, just to come home and go to bed early and get up for the next morning's early shoot. Ernie hated to fill out his appointment book, preferring to leave everything to the last minute. With black tie and place card affairs you can't do that. He began to skip some of those formal parties we had committed to. At home, we ate in Ernie's den on special trays. The girls ate in the inside den, around the TV. (Jeannie Martin, who had seven kids of all ages, couldn't keep a cook and butler. She finally hired a short-order cook and everyone was happy.) Slowly the dining room became used only for Thanksgiving, Christmas, and Easter and the girls' birthday parties. For Ernie's birthday, we went to the Luau.

Ernie seemed to be buying more and more "things" for the house. The maids came to me, saying they couldn't keep everything dusted. I went to Ernie and told him that we couldn't keep all this stuff clean and that there was no room for it anyway. I wanted to go on record as saying that I could no longer be responsible for seeing that someone cleaned it.

I would take Nana Petersen and Mia, who was two, to Scandia for lunch. The other two girls had been so hard to table train that I wanted to be sure that Mia knew how to behave in a restaurant. Nana, being Norwegian, could talk to the chef, who would come out to the table with his hat on. Mia could identify a picture of a chef before she could identify a picture of a policeman.

Sing a Pretty Song . . .

Back when Harry Cohn was alive, a dinner at his house had been a big deal, very formal; a swallow-tailed butler stood behind every chair. Harry's wife, Joan, a beautiful, reserved formal woman with aquiline features, set the tone of the whole evening. She orchestrated, in a well-modulated voice—"Would you like some more . . ."—and indicated your butler to serve it. Harry, on the other hand, would say, "Naaahhh, I don't want any of this," and then wave them off. His writers have told me that Harry'd go through their waste-baskets in the Columbia writers' building at night to see if there were any gin scores in the trash. If there were, they would be fired. The writers hated him, but he was always nice to me and was crazy about Ernie. Mother would have loved Joan Cohn's table.

After Harry's death, Joan Cohn entertained but much less formally. Now, when you rang the doorbell, you were greeted not by a swallow-tailed butler but by a touring troupe of Larry Harvey's actor friends. The first time I was taken aback and looked for our hostess. I found her sprawled on the floor with Larry. I said, "Joan, how are you? What's for dinner?" She said, "I don't know, I don't care. It's a buffet. It's in there somewhere." She really loosened up after Harry died. Eventually, before parties she had to hide the light ashtrays, things, as we in the acting profession say, that will travel.

One black-tie dinner Ernie didn't weasel out of was an elegant affair that the Gary Coopers gave for the Earl of Dudley. The same twenty people you saw every other night were there, the same twenty people you saw in Palm Springs, the A troops: the Kirk Douglases, the King Vidors, the Wilders, the Sam Goldwyns, the Goetzes, the Bennys, and the Edward G. Robinsons. Gary Cooper had a personal magnetism that you could spot across the room; it wasn't just a screen persona. If you ever spent five minutes with Gary, you knew he was the second sexiest man alive. I'm not easily bowled over. But he had the most compelling eyes, which looked only at you. He made you feel as if you were the only woman on earth. His eyes never roamed. He had a shy, soft-spoken little cowboy demeanor that was overwhelming. Veronica "Rocky" Cooper had perfect, beautifully appointed dinners, and their Maria was the perfect child. Rocky said to me, "I never had a moment's trouble with her." I envied her because I was having nothing but trouble with my own trio of naughty "children," Betty, Kippie, and our own unique Grandma Mary.

My mother stayed on for a time after Mia's birth. She kept her house in Tenafly but wouldn't rent it to anyone. She had the local police check on the furnace so the pipes wouldn't burst in the winter. (Later, after Ernie's death, Ada came back to visit me and ending up staying for twelve years.)

I tried to block out Mary's unusual behavior, but once in a while it was simply impossible. She'd always changed her hair color when I had to, from green-blond in *Wonderful Town*, to platinum blond in *Li'l Abner*, to the exact same color. But when I did *Lover Come Back*, since Doris Day was a blonde, I had to change my hair to a bright, bright henna red. I came home from the studio the second night to find Mary's hair the identical bright red color. She also copied the way I put on my lipstick.

Mary had a vivid imagination, and I rarely listened to her, especially if she was smiling. Thank you, Grandpa Kovacs. One day I heard her car come in the driveway and heard the car door slam. After a few more moments I heard Mary screaming. I rushed out to find her lying in the driveway and the car down at the foot of the hill. This had happened a couple of times before, with cardplayers; they had simply forgotten to put the brakes on. She was screaming, "The car ran over me, the car ran over me." I knew she couldn't have been screaming if the car had run over her, but I called the ambulance. I took it as just another one of her hysterical fits. When we got her to the hospital, she seemed to have calmed down, and the doctors said that she wasn't hurt. Nothing was broken. I said that the next day I would buy her some nice bed jackets. Later that day Ernie went to visit her. Mary told him, "I don't want any bed jackets. I want that nice soft robe that Edie wears all the time." The next day we went with bed jackets and my robe. As she took off her hospital gown to put on my robe, we all were astonished to see a tire mark imprinted diagonally across her left breast. We all gasped. She said, "Aha, you didn't believe me." The car *had* run over her and hadn't made a dent.

Back at the house things of mine began to be missing all

the time; I never thought much about it until I went to put on my green contact lenses. I opened the tiny case to find them pulverized. Someone had to have done it with a hammer and scraped them back into the case. Although I never confronted Mary about it, I can't think of anybody else in the house from whom I would expect that kind of bizarre behavior.

My own mother continued to be wonderfully inconsistent after my father's death, when I did everything in my power to include her in my life. The first trip we took after she came out to California was to wicked Las Vegas, by train. She was still in her mourning clothes and ever-present hat and white gloves, an unusual sight in Vegas. The first day or so she stayed in her room and read, coming down only for meals. "Don't worry about me; I'll be fine; it's a pleasant room; I have lots to read," she said to Ernie and me. One day Ernie brought her a paper cup full of nickels, and said, "Come on, Mom, let's go down and try the slot machines." She protested at first, but he insisted. So she put on her hat and white gloves and followed him to the big casino. He showed her how to put the nickels in, which fruits were the biggest payoff, how to pull the lever, then left on his own casino business. Hours later, when she hadn't returned, we both went back to the slot machines, to find my churchgoing mother playing not one but two machines at once, one hand on each lever. The white gloves were by now black, and she turned to us with a smile and what I have now come to recognize as a glazed gambler's eye. Underneath all those church years had stood a closet slot-machine junkie. "This is fun," she laughed in a high operatic voice.

The hated show business that she had been so outspoken about when I was a child suddenly became meaningful for her. At age seventy-seven she announced to me that she would like to start acting. She was sure she could do it; could I get her a job as an extra on one of my pictures? I was really thrown by this 180-degree turn. As usual throughout my life, just when I thought I had her figured out, she would change lanes and present me with a whole new set of rules and values. I made a few calls to friends and the studios, but nothing ever came of my mother's acting career.

Ada and Mary were as different as oil and water. Once, in a theater, Mary turned to my mother and said, "I'm having an attack. Undo my bra, undo my bra, I can't breathe." She managed to wiggle out of it, held it up in front of my mother's face, and said, "Ooh, that feels better." My mother, who didn't even want to acknowledge that people wore bras, reacted by getting up and rushing out of the theater.

One day my mother had an angina heart attack, the kind that the doctor explained to me is brought on only by emotion. She had always kept her emotions to herself while Mary screamed hers hourly to anyone who would listen. Mary was the only one who could get Ada going. I called the doctor, and by the time he got to the house with a nurse and EKG equipment, my mother was still lying on the sofa. The machine registered normal. Her shakiness has stopped. He asked what had happened and if it had happened before. My mother said it had been happening many times recently, but she didn't know why. Ernie's mother, who was listening to this from the doorway, asked, "It's not working? The machine's normal? You want to see the heart machine work?"

Then she went over and said to my mother, "I told you a million times, don't put your effing bath mats in the washer. You block the drain every time."

My mother said, "It's not my bath mats; it's your mangy dog towels. And it doesn't block up when I use it, only when you add to it." The electrocardiograph machine was jumping up and down and telling the doctor everything he needed to know.

Mary said, "Was that good for you?" The doctor assured her that it was fine to stop. Mary smiled and left the room.

Our two mothers were competitive about Ernie's and my successes. The dialogue would go something like this. Mary would scream, "Everything my son is I made him." My mother would reply in kind: "Why do you suppose my daughter is where she is today—because of the things we didn't do for ourselves to take care of her? You didn't sacrifice for your boy the way I did." The two of them could really go at each other in an endlessly recurring cycle. I would say to my mother, "Why do you get yourself so worked up like this?

Ignore her." She would say, "Well, I'm right. I won." I had never seen her like that before.

When Ernie got home, and you could cut the atmosphere with a butter knife, he would pull me aside and say of Mary and Ada, "How bad are they today?" I would give him the look that said, "Pretty bad." He would then say, "Well, girls, how about a little drink?" Both would protest, particularly my mother. "Oh, no, no, I don't care for anything, thank you." Then Ernie would say, "But didn't the heart doctor tell you that it was a good idea to have one drink before dinner?" Without waiting for an answer, he'd say, "Don't worry, I'll fix a weak old-fashioned, very sweet, the way you like it." He would put in a few ice cubes, fill three quarters of the glass with liquor, pour in all the sweet stuff he could find, top it with cherries and oranges, anything he had to disguise it, then hand a drink to each of the coy grandmothers. Within twenty minutes they were best friends, giggling, slapping each other on the hand, and having a wonderful time.

Mary, of course, had been mostly responsible for our failure to keep help back in New York, but in California it was even worse. The employment agencies would call the house and ask if Mrs. Kovacs was there. I'd tell them that I was Mrs. Kovacs, but they would say, "No, is Mrs. Kovacs, *senior*, there?" If I said, "Yes, she was," they'd say, "Well, if she's there, we're sorry, we can't send anyone over." For a party I'd have to promise to get rid of Mary for the evening before the agencies would send help.

Ernie's mother had even more influence on our lives in California than she had had in Philadelphia and New York. She wasn't just meddling anymore; she was very much a part of our daily lives, especially of Betty's and Kippie's. Ernie and I were just too busy with our problems to pay too much attention to her. She always sided with the kids. One day when we were out, I returned to find that one of my best designer gowns had mascara smeared all down its front. Mary swore up and down that nobody had been in my locked closet: "The maid must have done it." It wasn't until after Ernie had died that the girls told me that every time I went out Mary took them into my back closet to play dressup.

Mary stuffed and stuffed these girls with food. Kippie, who began to put on weight, asked me to put a lock on the pantry so that she wouldn't be tempted while we were out. Mary insisted that she wasn't feeding them, but the minute we left, she got in her car and went to buy them bagfuls of candy bars, all the while complaining to my mother what a terrible mother I was for locking up the food at night.

The girls went to school at what was now John Thomas Dye in Bel Air, and if there was trouble in school, Mary took the girls' part. The teachers were always wrong; the girls were always right. While most of their friends rode the school bus, Mary decided that this was too dangerous for her grand-daughters. She insisted either that Leonard drive them in the Rolls or that she would, in the big Lincoln convertible that Columbia had given Ernie as a company car. We bought a Corvair station wagon for Leonard to drive the kids to school and back and maybe once in a while to the store.

Max Liebman was doing a one-hour mystery takeoff special, *Private Eye*, in March 1961 in New York. Ernie and I were to play spies. Mary had become so impossible that I convinced Ernie that the best thing would be for her to get her own place and visit only once in a while. The girls, now eleven and thirteen, didn't need her anymore and started complaining about her; she was driving everybody crazy and certainly not obeying the court order. She was indulging the girls' every whim and could not get along with Nana Petersen; Mary was circling her job, too. Nana told me that she and Mia wouldn't leave their end of the house if Mary were at home. It wasn't fair to have them cooped up away from the rest of the family.

Mary was to have been gone the week before we left. The day we were to leave, she was still there. I refused to go unless Mary moved out of our house and into the small hotel room on Wilshire Boulevard Ernie had rented for her. I wouldn't leave with him until Mary was gone. There was this big argument between them, and the next thing I knew she drove away with all her bags to the Cavalier. Andrew Kovacs, who was also concerned about Mary's negative influence over his grandchildren, offered to come and stay while we were gone.

(My mother had earlier returned to Tenafly, where she stayed until Ernie died.)

Ernie played cards on the train across the country. That made me wonder if his fear of flying was the real reason we were always booked on a train, where he was certain to find serious cardplaying friends. Coincidence? In Chicago the luggage was transferred to the train for New York, and you had to go to the Pump Room at the Ambassador Hotel for lunch. Everybody who was in town went there, just to catch the visiting dignitaries on their three-hour layover, although the food and service were great, too. All the columnists, such as Irv Kupcinet, came; it was like the Sardi's of Chicago.

While rehearsing Max Liebman's show, I sang in Carnegie Hall; the show was called *A Valentine for Leonard Bernstein*, and I sang "It's Love" and "A Little Bit in Love" and did some duets with Elaine Stritch playing Roz's part. I didn't have to give her any starting notes. Barbara Cook sang the "Jewel Song" takeoff, Cunegonde's aria from *Candide*, and beautifully.

On the *Private Eye* show I again did a vocalese, this one based on the music of Debussy (including *Afternoon of a Faun*), which prompted Elsa Maxwell (an accomplished pianist who was best friends with Cole Porter and George Gershwin) to send Ernie a telegram: "Thank Edie for the beautiful vocalese of Claude Debussy works, which raises my hope that we can have beauty and truth on TV in spite of idiot producers."

While in New York, we went to see all the shows: *Rhinoceros, Irma la Douce, A Taste of Honey, Do Re Mi*. As we were leaving one theater, I noticed that a diamond pin I had been wearing was missing from the front of my dress. It was a favorite of mine and uninsured, and I wanted to go back to our seats and look for it. Ernie was bucking the crowds and some people who recognized him. He refused to spoil the moment and go back, and did not want me to go back. He said that we'd be right in the middle of the posttheater crowds and pulled me out toward the car. When we got to our destination, El Morocco, I called the theater and asked about the pin, and sure enough, an usher had found it. Only then did

Ernie send the driver back with a reward to pick up the pin. Was he losing touch with reality or did he just hate New York?

We later went to see Jane Harvey at Billy Reed's Little Club. Billy himself was there, doing his usual dance step greeting you at the door, just as always. Nothing had changed. I was "home" in my beloved New York. I was happy. Ernie was not.

Unfortunately we had to go back to L.A. two weeks later. Ernie insisted that I go on the train with him, but I don't know why. We never talked. As usual, he "ginned" his way across the country. The same people were in the Pump Room, and things were pretty much the same on Bowmont Drive when we arrived at 7:00 P.M. on a Saturday. The poker buddies were waiting in the driveway.

My first phone message was to go see Auntie Catherine, headmistress of the John Thomas Dye School, first thing. Mr. Cagle, the principal, had also called several times. Ernie's father said, "This is too much for me, Edie. I'm too old to do this again." He flew back, several hours before we arrived in Pasadena, to take care of the New City house.

I had to fly back to New York on short notice to replace Tammy Grimes on the TV show *An Omnibus of American Song*, later called *The Hundred Years' War Between Sexes*. I had to sing twenty songs, some of which were written by the then-unknown pianist for the show John Kander. But I was back where I belonged, in New York, seeing old friends Hal Prince and Mary Rodgers and Lucille Ball in *Wildcat*. I really felt more at home in New York than L.A. Why couldn't we live here?

I had finished *Lover Come Back* in January and carefully dyed my fire-engine-red hair (my own, not a wig) back to my normal blond color. Mary quickly followed suit. While I was in New York, I was called and told I had to reshoot one scene. The hairdresser even came to New York on a Saturday to color it back once again to the character's Rebel Davis red. Ernie had whispered to me, when we'd seen a rough cut in January, that I was going to have to redo one scene with Doris Day. I asked why. "Because you look too good." (Doris once said to me, "In life I am the hard, shiny apple, and you are the soft, fuzzy peach.'') So in mid-March, immediately after my return from New York, Monday morning at nine, I shot the scene again. The next day, Tuesday, I was back to my regular blond color. This time, Mary didn't have time to make the switch.

After the cancellation of *Take a Good Look*, on March 16 Consolidated offered to finance Ernie in a series of half-hour monthly specials on ABC. These Dutch Masters specials went well beyond his and his crew's eleven years' prior experience of working in television. Now he could indulge to the extreme his fascination with matching visuals to music, such as his synchronizing Tchaikovsky's *1812 Overture* to the breaking of eggs into a frying pan, the snapping of a celery stalk, the spinning of a cow's head, and toy monkeys playing drums. Ernie worked on these shows for up to forty hours at a stretch, paying his crew double and triple overtime. Just when everyone was ready to collapse, he would call Chasen's and order dinners of roast duck and Dom Pérignon, for himself and the crew.

These specials were more conceptual than performance. I couldn't see a place for myself on any of them. I didn't want to take a pie anymore. It seemed to me that he chose more model types, not actors. That way they wouldn't question his direction. "With actors," he always said, "I get an argument." For the first time he didn't ask me to be on his show.

After he had taped the first special, in great secrecy from the press, he came home and said, "There's something wrong with it. I don't know what it is. Would you come down and watch it with me?" It started out with a casual shot of him looking very tired, explaining to the audience how hard he and the crew had worked on the show. I said, "You're feeling sorry for yourself. You know what you've been through the last five days. They don't. If this is the first shot they're going to see, you're going to need something else to keep their attention besides a tired man." When I watched the show, he had matted (key inserted) a tiny moving girl on his shoulder. I began to wonder if Ernie needed me only for help on his shows.

As he had from his earliest TV days, Ernie had the utmost respect for his crew's capabilities, and they in turn adored him. He was a demanding perfectionist, who would accept nothing less than the best everyone had to give. All were pushed to their peak performance. They understood that he was doing something very special and that they were an important part of it. The entire crew chipped in and gave Ernie a party on April 30. I've never heard of that before or since, nor has anybody else.

Ernie directed the show from inside the control room and did increasingly more pieces in which he did not appear. He did the intros from the control room, unheard of at the time. The Hungarian in Ernie was now coming through, in dark, brooding pieces by Bartók and Kodály. The shows had a blacker comedy feel than his previous work. At the time I worried about it because I'd never seen anything like it from him. Before, he'd always done things on at least three levels: The kids could watch the visual, the average adults could see what they'd see, and then the intellectual adult might catch something else. On these, he was digging to a deeper level that I couldn't explain; you got it or you didn't.

The sponsors at first requested that Ernie spend more time in front of the cameras, but he was on a creative high, so he ignored them. Finally, the network, the agency, and even his friend the sponsor, Jack Mogulescu, insisted, so he did bring back Percy Dovetonsils, the poet; Miklos Molnar, the Melancholy Magyar Chef; and some of his other old standbys. My favorite was his takeoff on Sunday morning cerebral shows. He had, as a poet, his poker buddy Joe Mikolas, with his hair parted in the middle and wire glasses, reciting his lifework, a poem called "Dearth . . . the Lack." Joe recited a list of non sequiturs ending with a sly smile and "dearth." My other favorite was "Whom Dunnit," the game show where the contestant is wounded offstage and the cheery panelists question him, hoping to get the correct answers before he expires. Ernie, clutching a bloody wound, says, "Could you hurry it up a little? . . . I don't have much time."

When the first show aired on April 20, we had guests over to watch it in the den. It was the first of what became Ernie's much-in-demand specials parties. He added several television sets around the house. The guests included Jack Lemmon, Felicia Farr, Irving Lazar, Billy and Audrey Wilder, who brought Billy's friend Marlene Dietrich. I had met her during *Wonderful Town* on a publicity tour of the Stock Exchange. I found her very funny, an interesting conversationalist who talked to you directly. I always loved her makeup. She kept the same look, with a line straight out from her eyes. "You must do what you feel. Everything I am is not an accident, my dear. I worked on everything." I heard from the wardrobe department that she came in not only for fittings but also to draw on the dress itself where she wanted darker or lighter beads (before it went to the beader) to further enhance her figure, highlighting the bust and minimizing the waist— something I was to do later in my nightclub act. Hugo Grenada, my lighting man, told me that when she made her Vegas club entrance down a flight of stairs, he had to install a key light for each step. (In movies there is usually only one key light per person per scene.) She got applause on every step, and it was a long flight of stairs.

Much later I was to follow her at the Fairmont (formerly the Roosevelt) in New Orleans. In every hotel nightclub you have to enter the showroom through the kitchen. I know more famous hotel kitchens than I do lobbies. She didn't want to do it, but she was told that was the only way to the stage other than through the audience. Finally, she agreed but insisted on a red carpet's being laid on the white tile kitchen floor and red velvet curtains hung in the service elevator. By the time I got there, after her three-week run, the curtains in the elevator were caked with room service, and the carpets squeaked from the grease. I got rid of them. During her performance she wouldn't let the musicians in the orchestra look at her; they had to look at their music or their toes. When she got older, she wore a specially constructed stretch nude souffle suit that was zipped on underneath her famous nude Vegas dress. No, it was not an accident.

On March 24, at the Writers Guild Awards, I was one of the performers doing takeoffs of movies. I was done up as Suzy Wong, complete with Chinese makeup and black wig; nobody knew who I was. Everybody was making eyes at me, including Ernie. He raised his eyebrows at me. I smiled back as if he knew it was me. When he smiled again and winked, I realized he didn't know it was me. It reminded me of the time the studio wanted him to shave off his mustache for a picture. The studio whited out his mustache on a photograph and he didn't even recognize himself. "If I don't know me," he said, "nobody's going to."

By this time Mary was back, but about to leave again, for an apartment in Westwood. This time it was harder than usual to get rid of her, and I thought I needed a rest. I drove out to Malibu, intending to stay at the Holiday House for a few days. I'd just seen *Psycho*, and in the time it took to drive to my room on the beach from the check-in desk up on the highway, I'd seen someone peering over the fence and got terrified. I got back into my little MG and drove right home.

In April, as we had been ordered to do, we stayed home a lot more—but so did the cardplayers. They arrived earlier, in time for dinner, and stayed even later. They included Sol Schwartz, Monte Friedman, Harold Mirisch, and David Selznick. So many of them came I didn't know who they were or what they did for a living. They were just faceless cardplayers. It was only later, when I was making my own movies and meeting heads of studios, that I would say, "Oh, you're one of the cardplayers; this is what you do for your day job."

When they arrived, I barely said hello and saw if they needed anything. Then I disappeared into my end of the house. As the driveway began to fill up with more and more cars, I learned that I couldn't go out for a drive unless I planned ahead. One time I made them all move their cars. Later, I pulled my car onto the street before dusk so that I could get out if I wanted to. Ernie would ask, "Where are you going to go?" I'd say, "I don't know. I might want a magazine. I don't like being cooped up in that ivory tower." Then he would make a joke about "Rapunzel, Rapunzel, oh, let down your hair." I began to feel like a prisoner in my own home.

Sometimes he'd even pretend that we were going to a movie. We'd look at the paper for twenty minutes to find a movie that we both wanted to see. Somehow we'd always have trouble finding one to agree on. The kids caught on to this ploy long before I did. "Oh-oh, he's picking out a movie;

that means there's going to be a game tonight," one of them would say.

I did make good use of the time up in the tower, learning operas, reading, and sewing such things as ribboned maypole dance costumes for the girls. Mayday, mayday!

Eddie Fisher was crazy about Ernie and Mike Todd, who were both bigger than life. Eddie, who was one of the biggest pop singers of the day, would come over to play cards, and pretty soon he was smoking cigars and hanging out with the big boys. Ernie and I had been to dinner at Eddie and Debbie's, but I didn't know her very well. It was Eddie we saw at our house. I believe that Debbie found out about Eddie's dalliance with Elizabeth Taylor when she placed a call to Eddie's New York hotel room from a party at our house. She rang Eddie's room and got no answer. She said, "That's funny, it's three o'clock in New York and he's not in." Later, at home, she rang Liz's room at another hotel, saying that she was Dean Martin's secretary, and asked for Eddie. A very sleepy Liz answered and said, "Yes." Debbie said, in her best secretary voice, "It's Dean Martin for Eddie Fisher." In a minute Eddie said, "Yeah, Dean, what do you want?"

Not knowing Elizabeth well either, I didn't want to take sides, so when this became public knowledge, it was a surprise that Eddie brought Elizabeth up to our house. There were pictures of Debbie and the baby in pigtails and diaper pins in all the papers. The press couldn't find Eddie and Liz anywhere. They were up at our house. They brought up the papers, which they read, and they giggled over the stories of their high jinks. There wasn't a paper that didn't have all their pictures (including Debbie's and the baby's) on the front page.

Alec Guinness attended our next party to show Ernie's special, along with Doris Vidor, Gloria and Jimmy Stewart, Carl Sandburg, Eden and Groucho Marx, and Marilyn Monroe, who came with Frank Sinatra. Marilyn was talking to Frank. Carl Sandburg, in a wheelchair, looked over and said, "My, what a wonderful piece . . . of Americana." His timing was perfect. When she found out it was Carl Sandburg, she went right over to him and talked to him the whole night long, sitting at a small table, face-to-face. The last thing I

295

remember was her tucking him into his limo with a lap rug and many kisses good-night, as if he were a little child going on a long trip.

Our next party to watch a show got even bigger; we were now up to forty-five people. Peter Lawford said he had some relatives in town; could he bring them? Bobby and Ethel Kennedy turned out to be two starstruck kids (although he was already attorney general): Ethel would say, "Is that really Jimmy Stewart . . . Doris Day . . . ?" They would whisper, like fans. Later, when I visited them in Virginia, I did the same thing: "Is that really Senator Gene McCarthy?" Same wide-eyed stare, stargazing in two different universes.

I was booked to do *Calamity Jane* at the St. Louis Municipal Opera. This again was a stretch for me because I got to wear only one outfit, a buckskin western suit—no rhinestones, no lip gloss, no "clown suit" to hide behind for this one. There was a lot of action and dancing in addition to the ballads in *Calamity Jane*, which had been done only as a movie, with Doris Day. This was to be its world premiere as a stage show. I began to learn the "Whip, Crack Away" song, in which I not only had to crack an eight-foot bullwhip but also had to throw it without cracking and tie up my Wild Bill Hickok. I called my friend Marc Breaux, who had done the complicated solo whip dance in *Destry Rides Again*, had been in *Li'l Abner*, and choreographed our TV shows along with his wife, Deedee Wood. Marc came up our driveway daily, to teach me to crack the bullwhip. The sight of the two of us with eight-foot bullwhips was strange, even for the neighbors and regular delivery people on Bowmont Drive. It was quite a sight, but I did learn to crack the whip and tie up George Gaynes, who was playing Wild Bill Hickok.

The opening featured me driving a stagecoach across the stage, which tells you how big the St. Louis Muni is. It was a tough show to do live because Calamity is on all the time. In the movie it would have been several early-morning calls, but onstage the singers and dancers got to go off and rest up and change clothes while I stepped in front of the curtain and did the ballad solos. They came out in fresh costumes, and I joined them in yet another hoedown number and stayed onstage to sing another solo, while they went off to change again. The first act closed with George, as Wild Bill, stringing me up on a small stage, fifteen feet above the real stage. One day the rope broke and I fell. If you've never heard 12,500 people gasp, trust me, it's a sound you'll never forget. They closed the curtain, and for some unexplained reason, all I got was a bruise. Nothing was broken. At the start of the second act, 12,500 people gave me a standing ovation, just for showing up. Since then when I have to do anything onstage that demands rigging, like riding on and almost falling off the moon in *Mame*, in my contract I insist on having whoever rigs it get on while I watch. Whenever the set was moved, I came in early just to do that. I've never had any trouble since.

I was happy to be working and to be away from playing caretaker. In *The Merry Widow*, only a year before, I had fallen for the leading man and pleaded with Ernie to come save me, and he had. This time, however, I fell for one of the creative team and did not either want or need Ernie's help at all. He seemed to have no room for me in his life anymore anyway.

In the summer of 1961 Ernie's and my financial and tax status became public, thanks to several Associated Press news stories. I was playing *Calamity Jane* when the first story broke. The headline read TAX CALAMITY HITS CALAMITY JANE. The second story told of liens on our property and various complicated loans. Yet another story detailed Ernie's purchase of a $2,000,000 tennis club. (I later found out that it had a $1,950,000 mortgage, a tax write-off, our moneymen said.)

Just before I left for St. Louis, Ernie gave an interview to James Bacon, the Hollywood correspondent for the AP, about the theater. It took place in Ernie's wine cellar, where he took only his favorite people. He was pouring his favorite white burgundy, Bernkasteler Doktor, which we had bought right off the vine on a side trip to Germany from Bolzano. He served it only to people who appreciated it as much as he did. In the interview Jim asked Ernie what he thought of the theater. Ernie, angry that I was going off to do a musical in St. Louis, exploded: "I hate the theater. The limp wrists are taking over Broadway." The story was posted prominently on the backstage callboard at *Calamity Jane* in St. Louis, where everyone was sure to read it.

As good as the specials were, they had to be sandwiched

in among Ernie's other projects, such as his movies for Columbia (he filmed three in six months), TV guest spots, and some more books he was trying to write. *Zoomar* had sold 17,500 hardcover copies for Doubleday, and Ernie was struggling to write another novel, *Mildred Szabo*, a multigenerational story of Hungarian immigrants. A secretary in England lost several chapters of the Szabo manuscript, but he never let up on working on it.

Groucho and Eden Marx took Ernie and me to dinner at Hillcrest with Dorothy Parker and her husband. Groucho asked how the book was doing. "Boy, you've got a lot of sexy girls in that book. Who was you? What about Eileen, Edie? What about that affair in the book? Edie, what did you think?" I said, "It wasn't the affair that bothered me; the idea of an artiste having an affair is not particularly startling. It was the guilty explanation and the stupid excuse that contributed to the only really bad writing in the book." This was the first time I ever saw Ernie nonplussed, without a smart comeback. Dorothy Parker's eyes twinkled back and forth between Ernie and me, as if she were at a tennis game. I looked at her, wondering what was going on in that brilliant and funny head, and asked, "Well, what do you think?" She laughed, and said, "Sorry, I'll have to read the book."

Doubleday turned down Ernie's proposed book of his ballpoint pen drawings of his famous friends, and no other publisher picked it up.

By this time we were incorporated and our company produced the shows. With Ernie now taking care of both above- and below-the-line costs, he exceeded his budget on each of his Dutch Masters shows and blithely ignored anyone who pointed it out to him. One night, at two in the morning, I was fast asleep when I got a call from Marvin Moss. "Edie, you've got to come down here right away."

"What for?"

He said, "Ernie is goofing off, and we're into triple golden time."

I said, "What can I do?"

Marvin said, "At least come down and talk to him and try to get him to finish the show. We all want to go home."

So I got dressed and drove down. Ernie was in the control

room, having a grand old time, playing with his toys. He was surprised to see me, but not troubled.

I went into the control room and sat next to him. Every time he digressed or started kidding and wasting time, I said, "Ernie, which camera do you want lined up? Come on, we have to go home." If he wouldn't answer, I'd say, "line up camera three." That at least got his attention. I stayed at least two hours until we finished the show. Now I could see for myself that things were not going well.

Since I had done my "money show" for the agents and bill collectors, I looked for a show for me. For no money, in a barn seating 450 people, in August 1961, I played Alexandra DeLago in *Sweet Bird of Youth* at Hunterdon Hills, New Jersey. Jed Allen (of *Santa Barbara*) was Chance Wayne. I was much too young for the part of the aging movie star (which Geraldine Page had played on Broadway and in the movie), but I wanted to do it so badly that I accepted it without even discussing it with Ernie. He suddenly decided he wanted to come with me, he said, "to try to get some writing done." I was surprised. It was the first time he'd come along on one of my jobs on his own free will, without my begging him. Could he really be changing? He must have seen a new strength in me that I was unaware of because for the first time in a long while he wanted to be where I was, even if it was in farm country, far from any action. Did he really care? I hoped so.

We rented a house without a telephone in Clinton, New Jersey, far away from everyone else in the company. Once the show opened, we had to get a phone, but for the first few weeks it was like a vacation. I would sit working on my part, while Ernie clackety-clacked on the typewriter, working on a second book, *How to Talk at Gin.* He relaxed in our cloistered house, away from all the Hollywood jazz and baloney, and enjoyed himself writing. He wrote fast and was pleased with what he did.

Like most writers, he didn't really like to start writing. He was always sharpening pencils, clinched Eberhard Faber Blackwing 602s ("half the pressure, twice the speed"); nothing else would do. Given a deadline, he was brilliant. First thing in the morning he would write funny lengthy letters to keep from working. The best things he ever did were spontaneous and fast, like *Zoomar*. When he got a good idea, he couldn't get it on paper fast enough. He wouldn't feel like coming home at night and writing; he'd rather play cards. *Mildred Szabo* had been off and on for years. Now was his chance to work on it for a stretch.

Ernie was the happiest I ever saw him during that last year. We even went into New York to do *I've Got a Secret*, with me playing the tiny John Adams to Ernie's six-foot-plus Abigail.

I had also been going to do *A Streetcar Named Desire*, starting at Warren, Ohio, for Kenley, but once I started working on it, I realized it would be too tough emotionally to do the two Tennessee Williams plays back to back, so I asked Kenley for a postponement. Instead I did *Free as a Bird*, a new play by Richard Derr, at Andover, New Jersey, where I played a guitar as a Russian exchange student in the United States. I had to sing American songs with a Russian accent and accompany myself on guitar. I had never picked up a guitar, so I went out and bought one. I called my teacher Myra Mogulescu; she taught me four chords so well that I could sing four hundred songs in many keys by moving the fret. I went on the Jack Paar *Tonight Show* and accompanied myself on the guitar. I did the big shows for the business manager and the agent and the little shows, paying much less money, for me to learn my craft. Anything I liked doing I did for almost nothing; anything I didn't like I had to be paid a lot for.

All the old gang from my New York theater days came out to see the show, including Marion Javits and Hal Prince. I went out to a club in New Jersey and saw the twist for the first time. I took it back to California before the Peppermint Lounge and taught it to everybody. Hedda Hopper was horrified by this vulgar little dance and said so in her column.

I was now spending so much time in New York that I began to look for an apartment there. On our last big trip to the city, Ernie and I had stayed at the Hotel Pierre—with Mary, Betty, Kippie, Mia, and Nana Petersen—for two weeks. It had cost more than $4,000. I found a studio apartment at the Brevoort on Fifth Avenue in the Village in September, for $215 a month. I could stay there for two years on our hotel bill. Besides, it had a doorman, and I felt safe. The apartment was so small that I painted it all black so I could furnish it with Victorian junk from junk shops. I put the TV set in the fake fireplace, had red beaded curtains made to separate the dinette from the living room. I put the king-size bed in the dinette. It looked weird, but everybody loved it. Once my friends stayed there they wouldn't leave. Ernie wasn't so sure about it. He would send me postcards; one said, "Testing, testing, 1, 2, 3. Are you there?"

From then on I always had an apartment in New York. The next one was on West Fifty-ninth Street, between Sixth and Seventh avenues. Years later my friend Zubin Mehta borrowed it for three days until he found a place to stay while he was conducting at the Met. He stayed the entire season! I would say, "Zubin, I have to come into New York." He'd say, "Oh, that's all right. I'll go to a hotel. For how long?" He went next door to the Hampshire House but left all his stuff in my apartment. It was always like eating at a luncheon bar, with somebody standing, watching me eat, waiting for my seat. One evening, at eight-twenty, he came rushing up to the apartment and said, "I've got to get my black shoes. I can't conduct in brown shoes." I said, "But it's eight-twenty." He said, "I'll make it"—and he did."

The government was now in the act. The IRS said that I had to take any legitimate job offered me. When word got out to the bookers, I was offered only a third of what I had made before. I signed for the Thunderbird in Las Vegas for seventy-five hundred dollars a week, to substitute for Gogi Grant, who was expecting. My new act included the first twist number on a Vegas stage, complete with my newly designed fringed twist pants, which I had put together in one afternoon and worn on Jack Paar's Tonight Show. Within one week they were in the stores. By the time I got to the Thunderbird I had done the outfits in Vegas glitz, with gold beaded fringe trim. I played for two weeks in November. This was the first opening of mine that Ernie did not attend. Instead, he sent a stuffed antelope head, from the lodge in Ketchum, Idaho, where he was ostensibly hunting with "Pat" DiCicco." (Pasquale DiCicco was linked with mobsters, including Lucky Luciano, and married Gloria Vanderbilt when she was seventeen. Previously, he had been married to movie star Thelma Todd, and was implicated in her death.) Ernie was traveling with a faster crowd. He wanted to buy a leopard to go with a coat he had bought me earlier. He brought the leopard onstage in Vegas, but I was terrified that it would bite Mia, so I wouldn't let him keep it. Also, when I saw the live leopard next to the leopard coat, I decided to sell the coat. I wasn't too pleased with the stuffed antelope either. Things were really getting out of hand. He didn't seem to care about anything.

Ernie was experiencing periods of depression, probably intensified by all the effort it took to hide the extent of our troubles from me. One day in 1961 the game was up. Two IRS men showed up to say that we were being put on a strict allowance. Our relationship was really, really bad, and neither of us had the time to stop and figure out why. The pressure of our increasingly frantic life-style and constant working was overriding our basic love for each other.

However, with Meyer and Zachary's help, we were now incorporated, considerably reducing our taxes for future years, but still leaving this mammoth bill to pay. When Ernie shot *Sail a Crooked Ship* in 1961, the government attached 90 percent of his salary, which in the old days (91/9) would have been only 9 percent, or $9,000, of his paper salary, $100,000 per picture. He was so depressed during filming that he carried a large glass of Jack Daniel's around with him on the set, something he had never done before.

Nan and Leonard were preparing ever more elaborate parties. Denise, the wife of Vincente Minnelli, was the new girl in town. I met her at Joan Cohn's when Ernie and Vincente both were late, and she was so funny. Denise hadn't seen enough of the seedy side of Hollywood, so Ernie and I took the Minnellis to the Pink Pussycat with Groucho and Eden Marx. Groucho said of one of the strippers, "She looks like Marshal Tito." Vincente was so proper and soft-spoken; Ernie could imitate him perfectly, directing a picture: "That's quite lovely, but I think the little white collar . . ."

Denise gave several dinner parties, including one elegant

black-tie affair at Romanoff's, which Ernie canceled in order to play cards. The next week he canceled the Edward G. Robinsons, again in favor of a card game. I went alone to the Minnellis; Ernie was supposed to come late but never showed. He did go to the Sam Goldwyns, after which we took Vincente and Denise to a Venice coffeehouse with us, for a beatnik poetry reading.

After I closed at the Thunderbird in the hated Las Vegas (I took my sewing machine with me) on November 20, I was looking forward to a family Thanksgiving dinner at home in our very own dining room, always an island of tranquillity in whatever turmoil was going on. After all that room service, I wanted family at home for the holidays. At least for Thanksgiving we'd have a nice holiday dinner. But for some unknown reason, that year we went to Scandia for a "family" meal with both Mary and Andrew Kovacs and Ada Enke.

Grandpops had had a few Old Granddads and was feeling good and magnanimous, the way Hungarians get just before they cry. Mia was saying grace, but Andrew couldn't hear her, so he started getting weepy and sorry in a loud voice, accompanied by sobs, wailing about how he had neglected Ernie all his life. Mary shouted, "Shut up, Andy, don't you have any manners at all?" Ernie whispered, "Quiet, Pop." When Mia's grace ended, my mother looked up at the ceiling. Betty and Kippie looked as if they were about ready to cry, Mary was still swearing in her loud rasp, and Ernie had left the table after a few choice words to his father. Andy still didn't understand what he'd done wrong. He blew his nose. Nobody spoke. There was nothing left for us to do except laugh and drink the champagne that Ernie brought back with him to the table. That is, everyone except my mother.

Perhaps because Christmas was coming, Ernie tried to attend as many functions as he could, but by mid-December he was back playing cards. He did make it to the Upper School Christmas Carols at John Thomas Dye on December 17, but they were over at 9:00 P.M., so he could still play cards. We went to the *Lover Come Back* preview at the Academy and the premiere of *The Children's Hour*, in black tie, on December 21.

On Christmas Eve we had our usual open house, with all

the regulars popping in, the Lemmons, Minnellis, Janet Thomas, and her new date, Fred De Cordova. For Christmas Ernie bought me, among other things, a classic 1937 Bugatti. I'm a car nut, but this gorgeous car exceeded anything I'd ever dreamed of. The worse things got, the more he seemed to spend. I had been going along with everything, making personal concessions, such as going to New York and leaving everybody else at home. In true gambler's style (when you're down on your luck, bet everything you've got), Ernie was spending money we really didn't have. It took me back to the week after I'd met him in Philadelphia and he'd spent his life savings, "so you won't have to take a cab." I had mixed emotions. As much as I loved the Bugatti, I hated driving it. It was difficult to drive; you had to push buttons to shift gears. If we went to a restaurant, one of us had to park it because nobody else knew how to work those buttons. I understand that people in Europe today who own fully restored 1937 Bugattis keep them in their living rooms next to their Renoirs. I felt that's where mine belonged.

I never knew until Nan finally told me in August 1989 that Ernie had said something to them during this Christmas week 1961 that so chilled them that she and Leonard decided not to discuss it with me. "Mr. Kovacs bought me and Leonard a certificate for a record player and radio console. We had one already and told him that what we really needed was a television set but it was too expensive. He paused, gave us an odd look, and said, 'Go ahead and get them both. I'm never going to pay for this.' " It started me wondering what had really been on his mind during that period.

Our new business managers made a deal with the IRS to pay off all the liens. Ernie and I each had to earn five thousand dollars a week for five years, and then we would be clear. Although I was pregnant again, from then on I had to take every job offered to me. There were no good or bad career moves, just the need to earn that money. Whatever I was offered at whatever reduced price I had to take. It was then I learned the unwritten rule of the movie industry: "Never let them see you sweat." Hollywood will tolerate rape, rampant dishonesty, even incest and ax murders; the only thing you can't be is without funds, "hungry."

For Christmas 1961 the financial clamps were really on us. Ernie had always spent lavishly on every expensive gift in sight for all of us. Now even he knew there was no kidding. We told the kids that it wouldn't be our usual crazy Christmas, that they would have to make presents for us and each other. We even economized on the tree, as silly as it seemed; instead of spending the usual seventy-five dollars, we got one for thirty-five. Ernie tried to go along with it, even saying, "Finally Christmas is what it's supposed to be," but he was visibly depressed. On Christmas Eve he made eggnog, took his ritual single sip, and switched to Jack Daniel's.

We went for a drive in the Bugatti on Christmas Day, and Ernie was in a good frame of mind. At the kids' urging, he made the exhaust sputter and cough and seemed to be enjoying himself.

The night after Christmas we went to the black-tie opening of *A Majority of One,* starring Rosalind Russell and Alec Guinness. In the middle of the picture I suddenly felt very ill and went into the ladies' room, followed closely by two women reporters. They were the first ones with the news that I was on my way to the hospital in a cab. They also got the scoop that I had a miscarriage the next day. Ernie always said it was because it was in the middle of Roz's picture.

On the twenty-eighth Rosenfeld and Zachary, the lawyers, and Guy Gadbois, our business manager, had us in for a long meeting, at least a couple of hours. I had been offered the *Today Show* and the stage show *Venus at Large,* and the lawyers and Gadbois said I had to take them, commuting weekends again, since both jobs were in New York. Even Ernie now realized that I had to go. It was the second time I'd seen him speechless. He said quietly, "I hate this. I don't know how I'm going to do it, with you there. . . ." He really was bewildered. He even said, in jest, "I'm worth more dead than alive." (He did have some life insurance.) His world was crumbling. His toys, his playpen, his life in California were falling down around him. I didn't see how I could go to New York with Ernie in this frame of mind. I'd try desperately to find something in Hollywood. The next day I taped a Muriel commercial, then I went to Delbert and Ann Mann's party—alone.

Ernie gambled even more, slept even less, and otherwise escaped from reality. By the end of 1961 I was at the end of my rope, although still in love with him. I began to wonder how I was going to survive in New York worrying about his excessive gambling and his outward denial that anything was wrong. What would the girls do without a mother figure? It was an untenable situation. I even threatened to divorce him if we didn't straighten out our lives together. "I know, I know," he responded. "I'll do it. We've got to build it back up to what it once was because it was good." Then Ernie broke down in tears. He was so troubled. I hated to see him this way. I felt sorry for him, and really didn't want to leave him alone in the middle of all this.

On New Year's Eve, at a big WAIF benefit ball at the Beverly Hilton, Ernie and I vowed to make it work out. For the first time, I said, "Ernie, you've got to stop gambling." He promised, in tears, that he would. I was going to try my damnedest to get out of my commitments in New York. I didn't know how I was going to tell Gadbois and Rosenfeld and Zachary. But we *were* going to work it out.

$\mathscr{T}$HIRTEEN

FOR THE FIRST WEEK OF 1962 Ernie did not gamble and was making a heroic effort. We had quiet dinners at home two nights in a row, a record. On the third we invited the Goldwyns, Wilders, Minnellis, Janet Thomas and Fred De Cordova for Louisiana bouillabaisse, one of Nan's specialties. The next night Ernie surprised me and bought tickets himself (I was always the ticket buyer) to a Bach aria group. It was a sweet gesture and proved to me that he really was trying. He was wearing his famous vicuña network exit coat. He seemed to be enjoying the concert.

The tall soprano had done her solo, the ample mezzo had done hers, the short wide bass sang his part, and the rather attractive Nelson Eddy look-alike baritone sang in an easy manner. Things were going well until I looked in the program to see what the last solo was. I nearly passed out when I saw that it was to be a solo sung by a countertenor (who sings about an octave above a regular tenor, in a kind of high soprano falsetto—think BeeGees). The man stood up; he had to be about six feet six, and he was very muscular and imposing—until he opened his mouth.

I was at least prepared and had an idea of what to expect. But Ernie, who was somehow sitting with his coat on his lap and his chin in his hand, stared straight ahead at this high-decibel sound. His hand dropped, his chin dropped, and his eyebrows went up in the middle. I pretended not to be watching Ernie because knowing him . . . He must have stared for about thirty seconds in disbelief and looked around him. Nothing. Everyone around him was just sitting quietly, looking at the stage. I had just said to myself, "Phew, he made it, he got through it without . . ." when I felt his shoulders start to go, then saw his hand slapped on his mouth to suppress the laugh that was now totally out of control. I gave him a sharp elbow in the chest. He stopped, for all of five seconds; then again the shoulder and hand-over-mouth routine repeated, he bent forward, shaking with laughter.

Still looking straight ahead, I gave him another shot in the ribs, and whispered, "Ernie, come on!" After two or three of these rib breakers, I felt him getting up. I finally looked at him and he had the vicuña coat stuffed in his mouth, and the tears were streaming down his face. He was gone, I mean gone laughing, and ran up the aisle completely convulsed. When I caught up with him in the outer lobby after the piece was over, he was still laughing. I must admit, so was I. All he said was: "That's a hell of a sound coming from a guy who looks like that." As miserable as Ernie was, he could still laugh.

Gordon and Sheila MacRae gave a party on January 5 for Gary Morton and Lucille Ball, to celebrate their recent marriage. It was an outside party with an orchestra and a tent. I was afraid somebody was going to riffle the cards (a sound which to a gambler is the same as an alcoholic hearing liquor poured over ice) after dinner when the men and women separated. But no one did. On Sunday we stayed home because we both had a full workweek coming. Ernie was doing two shows, a pilot for ABC and his own special. He had started keeping a typewriter in his portable dressing room, so he could work on two things at once.

I had to go see Mr. Cagel at the girls' school again on January 8, a Monday. I taped a Lilt commercial at NBC at seven o'clock that night, then rushed home. When I got there, my heart sank when I saw poker cars blocking my entry. The game was on again.

Sing a Pretty Song . . .

On Wednesday, January 10, I took Mia and Kathy and Mary Frances Crosby to Marineland, getting back in time for Joan Cohn's informal (slacks) buffet, for Laurence Harvey and the other actors in *Summer and Smoke*. I went alone because Ernie was working on his show, or so I thought. When I got home, the cardplayers were there again.

On Friday, January 12, 1962, I taped the new game show *First Impressions* at 11:00 A.M. We were to be at the Wilders at 7:30 that night, in cocktail dress, for a baby shower for the Berles, who had just adopted their son, Billy. Ernie said he wouldn't finish his taping until about 9:00, to go ahead without him. He would come later.

Ernie got up early to drive, in the Rolls, to the Griffith Park location. He was shooting the pilot *A Pony for Chris*, playing an old western snake-oil salesman with Buster Keaton as his silent Indian sidekick. After the day's filming, at about 6:30 P.M., Ernie had to drive to ABC-TV in Hollywood to edit his own show, his last Dutch Masters special. After three hours of adding music and making minor edits with Gene Lukowski, Ernie left ABC for Beverly Hills. By then it had been raining for three hours and the streets were getting slick. Ernie never liked driving and had always had someone drive him in New York. In L.A. Leonard drove us only to formal openings or the Oscars. Ernie drove himself in his big, bad, beautiful black-and-white custom-built 1952 Rolls Mulliner with separate headlamps, the only car that suited him in Hollywood. It had been owned by a Middle Eastern potentate and had right-hand drive with the gears on the left and was supposed to be driven by a chauffeur. People would yell at Ernie, "When are you gonna defrost that thing?" The car's weight also made him feel relatively safe. When we went to look at cars in London, I had wanted him to buy the Bentley shooting brake. The Bentley was the same ostentatious Rolls except for the grille on the front and countrified wooden panels on the sides, for grouse shooting in Scotland. There were even fewer of those shooting brakes than of custom-built two-toned Rollses.

Although both of us had taken lessons in London to master the right-hand drive, Ernie was hard on cars. He really didn't pay too much attention to traffic and lights; his attention span was short. He'd get good ideas and write them down while driving and smoking.

Jack Lemmon told me that the most scared he'd ever been in his life was when he was driving down from Bowmont Drive to Coldwater Canyon with Ernie in the Rolls. Ernie turned to Jack and said, "How much do you wanna bet there's no traffic on Coldwater?" Jack said, "*What?* I don't want to bet anything." Ernie: "Ten bucks there's no traffic on Coldwater." Jack: "No, are you crazy?" Ernie charged ahead, went straight out onto Coldwater; luckily for both of them, there was no traffic. Jack never forgot it.

When I rode with Ernie, I had to half drive the car and always keep an extra eye on the road. I'd light his cigars, so he wouldn't keep his focus on the cigar lighter. When he switched to the more difficult matches, which took both hands, my automatic response was to grab the wheel, while he tried to steer with his knees. We did this little ballade without even thinking about it, while talking and planning shows. We never discussed my copiloting, and I was never a backseat driver; but I was always more aware of the road than he was, no matter who was at the wheel.

Ernie arrived at the Wilders' apartment, at the corner of Wilshire and Beverly Glen Boulevards, at about 10:00 P.M. I was already there, as we had arranged, and so were all the other twenty or so guests, among them Kirk Douglas, Yves Montand, Dean Martin, and Lucille Ball. Ernie looked tired but drank very little and was his typical life-of-the-party self. Jeannie Martin sat on the couch with Ernie at one point. She recalled never having seen so much love in Ernie's eyes. "He told me that he felt exhausted and was depressed about his finances, especially because Edie *had* to go to work. He didn't mind her working; it was just that she *had* to."

When the party began to break up, at about 1:30 A.M., Ernie asked Milton if Yves needed a ride. Milton said that Yves had decided to ride with the Berles because they lived closer to the Beverly Hills Hotel, where he was staying. As Ernie and I waited for our cars, the drizzle had lessened to merely a mist. My MG was being fixed, so I had brought the Corvair to the party because it was the only car available. The first car the valets delivered was Ernie's Rolls. Knowing that I had never liked the Corvair, he told me to take his car. As I got in, he closed the door after me and said, "I'll be right there. Be careful. The streets are very slick."

I arrived home within fifteen minutes and after another twenty minutes began worrying about what was keeping Ernie. Whenever we took separate cars, he always beat me home. My first thought was that he had stopped to pick up a pizza because he had missed the food at the Wilders. After another half an hour I called the Wilders and was told that Ernie had left just minutes after I had. I walked outside on the front lawn, something I never did, and paced up and down on the wet grass, waiting to hear his car in the drive. I tried to convince myself that everything was all right, that he'd be along any minute. But down deep inside my gut feeling was the same as when my father had gone in for his final operation.

Then the telephone rang; it was a reporter asking for Ernie. When I told him that Ernie wasn't at home, the reporter asked me if I knew anything about an accident. "No, I don't know anything," I said.

"Excuse the call," he said.

"What do you mean?" I asked.

"Excuse me," he said again. "Why don't you just call the West Los Angeles Police Department?"

"Why?" I asked.

"Well, there's been an accident."

"What do you mean, an accident?"

"That's all I can say."

I telephoned the West Los Angeles police, but they would only confirm that somebody had been killed in an auto accident. My first thought was: Oh, my God, he's hit somebody. Then I walked outside again, into the cold, wet grass, and looked up at the sky. "My God, my God, where is he?" In spite of my heaviest New York fur coat, I still couldn't get warm. I began to feel that sickening sensation in my stomach and buzzing in my ears that I'd known from childhood as the signal that I was going to faint. The phone rang again. It was another reporter, and he said, "Is Ernie Kovacs there?"

I said, "No, but I expect him any minute. Who's calling?"

He said, "Ignore the call," and hung up.

Now I was frantic and called the police again, but they still wouldn't give me any information. This time I said, "This is Edie Adams Kovacs, please don't put me on hold, please tell me what's happening."

The policeman put his hand over the mouthpiece, and I heard him say, "It's Mrs. Kovacs. What'll I tell her? Jesus, God, he's on his way to the coroner's office." Lifting his hand off the mouthpiece, he said to me, "Gene Dolson is coming right over to see you, Mrs. Kovacs." Gene was a Beverly Hills policeman who had become a friend of Ernie's and mine, often stopping by for coffee and to gossip about whose car was parked in back of whose house in the afternoon. Then I knew. If Gene was coming over, it had to be serious.

When he arrived at the house, I said, "It's really bad, isn't it?"

Gene said, "Yeah, it's bad." He looked at me for a moment, then said quietly, "He's gone." I wouldn't believe it. I had just been with him an hour and a half before, although it seemed like seven years. I didn't do anything, cry or scream. It was as if I weren't there, as if I were in somebody else's dream.

I refused to accept the fact that Ernie was dead until Jack Lemmon called me from the morgue, having identified the body. The horrible thing is that I couldn't cry. All I knew was that I had to call Ernie's father, even if it was dawn on the East Coast. Only Gene was with me when I called Andrew, waking the poor man up. Because of a bad connection, Andrew couldn't hear me as I kept telling him, "Ernie has been killed." Finally the operator, who had been listening, came on and said, "She's trying to tell you that your son is dead."

I broke down completely then, spent. Ernie's mother stood on his balcony, howling and yelling; I couldn't make out what she said. Friends began to pour in, among them Billy and Audrey Wilder, Felicia Farr and Jack Lemmon, Mervyn Le Roy, Richard Quine and Kim Novak. They all were great and tried to take over and comfort me. They called my doctor, Stuart Brien, who arrived at 4:00 A.M.

According to Dr. Brien, he found me in a state of "dry hysteria," in which I wasn't able to cry. He sent everybody out of the room, then out of the house when they started drinking in Ernie's den. He gave me a sedative and tried to put me to bed in our master bedroom, but I just couldn't get into the empty bed. I went into the office and lay on the daybed there for a few hours. Dr. Brien called Dr. Charles Markman, the girls' pediatrician, who arrived before the girls woke up. He came into the office and said that he and Stu had talked and decided it was best that I break the news to the girls; it had to come from me. I sent somebody into their room to unplug the phone so that nobody would wake them up and say their father was dead.

The two older kids, Betty and Kippie, were awakened at about eight in the morning and were told to come into the office, that I had something to tell them. They came into the office and saw me sitting up in the fully made daybed, with Drs. Markman and Brien standing by. The girls knew that something was wrong, but the sweet thing is that they were concerned about me; they thought I was sick. They asked, "What's the matter? What's happened? Are you all right?" When I finally told them what had happened, they didn't believe it either. "No, he's not dead, he's not dead, he's just hurt badly." The girls broke into tears, and I cried again. We tried to comfort each other, and Kim Novak, who became our personal nurse, gave us cold compresses. Other friends came by to take care of Mia, Kippie, and Betty. I ended up in the girls' room, too. I just couldn't go back in that bedroom.

Brien advised me to tell Mia, who was then only two and a half, that her father was on a long trip and wasn't coming back but that he was in a very nice place and was safe and happy. It was crucial that I not say he was gone only temporarily.

Mia noticed the flurry of activity and that I was sad. Because she was usually at my end of the house and rarely near the poker-playing den, it was a couple of days before she even asked me where Dada was. I didn't know how to explain the finality of death to a toddler. She couldn't yet comprehend even the death of a pet bird. Mia had a child's-eye view of animals. At Christmas we'd had ice cream molded in the shape of bunnies, kitties, and doggies. She was squealing with delight until we started to put our spoons in and eat them.

Then she started to cry. She couldn't watch us eat the ice-cream animals and had to go to her room. She loved animals. How could I explain death to a child who couldn't bear to see her ice-cream kitty melt?

I could see that it was important to tell her that he was gone permanently, that he would not be back, but that he was very happy and had everything he wanted around him. At one point Mia asked if Dada was in a nice hotel; even at that age she knew that would be very important to him. I said, "Yes, but Dada misses you." From then on, when any of us left the house, Mia asked, "Where are you going? When are you coming back?" She watched very carefully as we told her exactly how long we'd be gone. When I went on the road, I told her exactly where I would be and when I'd return. Since she didn't yet have a real concept of weeks or days, I left a pile of little notes and drawings for Nana to give her daily. I left some from Ernie, too. I made a point to call her daily from the road; from then on she knew always that I was coming back but that Ernie was not. I'd take great care to make plans with Mia for things we would do when I got home.

I had always said to Ernie, "I want to grow old with you. I'm looking forward to that." Ernie had often said that he was never going to live to a ripe old age: "It's not in the cards, baby." We often laughed about it. He seemed anxious to go on expensive ocean voyages, eating and dancing and otherwise enjoying himself. He reminded me every day on shipboard that this was important to do it all now, while we were young. He'd say, "Look at those old people, trying to have fun. Do you want to wait until you're in a wheelchair? Nah, come on, live it up."

But his death in a car crash just ten days before his forty-third birthday was truly impossible for me to accept. I would never have believed that he was really dead unless I had seen him one more time. I had asked for a closed coffin at the funeral because I didn't know the extent of the injuries. However, I made them open the casket for me and Pop so that I could give Ernie his rose, because he had always given one to me. I put a cigar in his hand because I knew he'd need it. He looked so different in death, and I was sorry that I had asked to see him. He felt so cold, but that became the way he would appear to me in dreams for a few years after.

We never would know everything that happened because Ernie was alone in the car and there were no witnesses at that hour of the morning. Kirk Douglas often said he was the last person to see Ernie alive. Ernie got in the car and turned and waved good-bye to Kirk. Never one to pay much attention to the route he was taking, Ernie apparently had got into the right-hand lane on Beverly Glen, so he couldn't turn left on Wilshire, as he should have to go back to Beverly Hills, and found himself heading toward Santa Monica Boulevard. This was not unusual for Ernie; he was always preoccupied while driving. According to the newspapers, by the time a passing motorist came upon him, Ernie had died, with his left hand stretched out toward his unlit cigar.

Apparently he had hit the brakes suddenly and the Corvair had veered out of control on the wet pavement. We found out fifteen years later that the back wheels on all Corvairs left the ground whenever you put the brakes on. The car wrapped itself around a utility pole on the driver's side. The passenger's door was open, and Ernie had sprawled out. His head had hit the steering wheel, causing a hairline fracture to his skull. The death certificate said he died instantly of "a fractured skull and ruptured aorta." Chillingly, twenty years later, just a few days short of her twenty-third birthday, our daughter, Mia, was killed instantly on a rainy night when her car hit an unpaved shoulder on Mulholland Highway. Her death certificate said she died instantly of "a fractured skull and ruptured aorta."

Ernie would have preferred no funeral service at all, and at first I tried to suggest a memorial later. However, so many of his friends were there in the house for days, and they said, "We need to have something to say good-bye to Ernie." I tried to keep the service, at the Beverly Hills Presbyterian Church, brief and simple. His friends expected something a little more colorful and Kovacsian, but I knew that since Ernie didn't like fusses and tributes when alive, he surely wouldn't want anything like that now.

The burial, at Forest Lawn, was private, with just me and

the children and a few very close friends. Dick Quine, who was supposed to have been a pallbearer, had to stay back at the house to calm down Ernie's mother, who was truly out of control. Mary had threatened to throw herself into the grave: "If he's gone, I'm going, too." She'd have done it, too, especially if the press was there.

The pallbearers included Frank Sinatra, Jack Lemmon, Billy Wilder, Dean Martin, Mervyn Le Roy, Joe Mikalos, and Dom from Dominick's. Barry Shear and Jack Lemmon put two more cigars into Ernie's coffin before they closed the lid for the last time. He was buried on a green hill called Remembrance. His grave is marked by a reproduction of his signature, the dates of his life, and the inscriptions "Nothing in Moderation," his motto, and "We All Loved Him" underneath. Twenty years later, on Mia's gravestone, right next to Ernie's, we put "Daddy's Girl. We All Loved Her, Too."

For a while I couldn't even talk about anything. My whole life had revolved around Ernie and his needs. I really didn't have an opinion of my own. I had pronoun and tense trouble: I couldn't say "I" when for ten years it had been "we." I said this "is" Ernie's favorite chair when it should have been "was." Betty and Kippie and I slept together in their rooms for about three months after Ernie's death. I finally said, "That's it. We can't do this anymore," and we stopped. When I returned to Ernie's and my bedroom, with its outsize California bed, what I first missed was reaching out at night to touch his back. He had slept on his stomach, usually spread-eagled, and I could always find at least one foot and his large, smooth back. Suddenly our bed seemed vast.

I had to learn to sleep on the right-hand side of the bed, where our telephone was and is in most hotels, the side usually reserved for the right-handed man of the house. My automatic side of the bed remained the left side, even when I traveled alone. At first it seemed unnatural for me to sleep near the main line of communication with the outside world. From childhood I had felt that was clearly a man's job but I finally had to, when I found myself the sole support of six people.

Three days after the funeral Dean and Jeannie Martin gave us the keys to their Palm Springs house. Even though he was gone, Ernie's presence filled the Bowmont Drive house. We all needed a change. All of us—two grandmas, three kids, Nana Petersen and I—went down there to stay for a few days. The change of locale was good. We tried to busy ourselves. I bought everybody muumuus, and we did a lot of walking around and sightseeing. After five days there I was going out of my mind. Everything was hanging, six people's lives. Kippie, Betty, and Mia were looking for me to set an example, so I knew I had to go ahead. We left sooner than expected. We arrived back home one day before Ernie's last TV show went on.

Nice people still came by to comfort me. Charlton and Lydia Heston brought me a Bible. The nights were the hardest, but the Wilders, Berles, Lemmons, and Groucho Marxes visited me often, cheering me up. Shirley MacLaine couldn't have been more generous with her time. While she was working on *Two for the Seesaw*, keeping long hours at the studio, she would call and ask, "Busy tonight? I'll come over after I finish work." She'd walk in about nine o'clock, with her makeup still on. She must have exhausted herself talking to me. One of the points she kept making was that Ernie went the way he wanted to go—fast. Later on he might have had a long illness. Ernie, she said, knew when to get off. He always felt he would go fast.

Ernie's last show was aired on his forty-third birthday, January 23, 1962, at 10:00 P.M. Mia had gone to bed, so the two grandmothers, Betty, Kippie, and I watched, quietly and tearfully, what had turned into a tribute. We all tried not to cry, but before the show was halfway through, we were passing the Kleenex.

That same day I had had to deal with the money people, the unholy trio Rosenfeld, Zachary, and Gadbois; they recommended that I declare bankruptcy. I said, "No, that will never be an option for me. It's not in my family heritage."

While I was still in Palm Springs, some of our friends began to organize a weekly anthology series of television shows as a benefit for me and Ernie's three children. "The whole thing started spontaneously," said Jack Lemmon, "a bunch of us started talking about it—guys like George Burns, Jack Benny, Dick Quine, Milton Berle, and Mervyn Le Roy

—that there had never been a top-notch anthology show; we thought it was a good thing for Edie to participate in. We kept talking and talking, and soon there were thirty-nine people who had said they would do it. They included practically every top star in the business."

As touched as I was by the concern of friends such as Frank Sinatra, Dean Martin, Kirk Douglas, Lucille Ball, and Kim Novak, I'm sure it would have embarrassed Ernie. We had a pact that if anyone called from Ralph Edwards's *This is Your Life* for either one of us, the other would say we had left the country. He always felt uncomfortable at roasts.

So in my first interview after Ernie's death, with the AP's James Bacon, I had to put a public stop to the anthology show. I was sure that even with all his debts and tax troubles, I could earn enough to take care of the children's upbringing and education. If Ernie's friends wanted to go ahead with a tribute of some kind, they could give the money to cancer research, the Motion Picture Relief Fund, or some other need.

Henri Bollinger, who by now had been hired by the cigar company for institutional public relations, also advised that this was not the kind of person I was or image I wanted to project. People in Hollywood may have been surprised by my sudden initiative and forcefulness since I had been in Ernie's shadow, but nobody back in Pennsylvania was—especially anyone who had known my father.

After Muriel renegotiated my contract for six figures and more active participation, I was sure I could take care of us.

The incident did give rise to a joke printed by Walter Winchell. After hearing about the offer of a benefit for the estate, one of Ernie's admirers said to another, "Quite a story, isn't it?" "Yes," agreed the other. "Imagine anyone in Hollywood having thirty-nine friends."

Yet much as I was intellectually prepared to start a new life, my emotions had to catch up to my decision. I would spend hours trying to focus on the future only to come across an old letter of Ernie's in a drawer and have the nightmare come back to me again. I would give long pep talks to Betty and Kippie only to have Mary show up and wail never-endingly about "my baby." She started on public personal tirades against me. She went to the AP and UPI offices to tell them that I was stealing her inheritance, then went on live TV to say that she had been locked out of her apartment because I hadn't paid her rent, which I had. Mary began her long series of drawn-out, silly, expensive, and completely unfounded lawsuits, first claiming that I was an unfit mother, then saying I should adopt the girls, and finally accusing me of stealing her insurance policy from Ernie.

Kathy and Bing Crosby were among the first to visit me a lot in the early dark days; they had given Ernie and me a Labrador retriever that they had bred when we lost a dog. Bing came not only to offer condolences, but real TV work. He said he was doing a special with Bob Hope in May, and did I want to be on it? I certainly did.

The turning point in personal terms came the day that eight strange men, IRS bill collectors, sat in my living room, carving up our assets. As they were tagging the furniture for its imminent sale and that of the house itself, I asked meekly if the kids could keep the horse they loved so dearly. The IRS men said no. Something snapped in me, like a cold shower. Suddenly I thought: Hey, whoa. This is negative. I'm taking away the only security the kids have left. I turned into a tiger and shouted at the men, "Just wait a minute. Don't sell anything. Give me a month." They left. I called up George Zachary and said, "This can't be. I've got to save the house. How you can you get them to give me more time?" When I was a child, my family had had no money, but a lot of pride. When Ernie's death hit me, I also had no money, but I still had a lot of pride. I jumped back into show business with both feet. I didn't care a lot about what other people might have done or thought of what I was doing. I did what my instinct told me to do: Go back to work. I never wanted anybody to say, "There goes Ernie Kovacs's widow . . . the poor thing."

Ernie's den was another big challenge because we had always eaten out there. About two weeks after his death, when I was trying to feel functional again, I said, "Okay, kids, this is it, now or never, get your trays. We're going to eat out in the den." As festively as possible, Betty, Kippie, Mia, and I went into the den and sat down around the ship's-plank coffee table. We picked up our forks without a word. We suddenly put the forks down simultaneously, looked at one another, and, with tears in our eyes, picked up our trays, walked back into the house, to the regular den, and blew our noses. So much for that idea. We made tearful jokes but, with smiles on our faces, put on the family TV and finished dinner. We just weren't up to it yet.

I had to take on so many responsibilities for which I wasn't ready that I needed professional guidance. We all did, Betty, Kippie, and especially Mia. I didn't want to make any mistakes with her. During this time I had to be so many things to so many people, especially at home, where I was a major general, mother superior, and a few other things besides. Everyone made demands on my time, and everyone was entitled to it. There wasn't really enough of me to go around. I needed help to face the reality of Ernie's death and the problems it raised for me and the children. Stepparenting was the hardest thing I ever attempted in my life and the one thing at which I failed miserably. I did give it my best try. No matter how much you do or how much you try you are the one blamed for everything, especially when both natural parents are absent. Today I feel bad that Betty and Kippie are still estranged from me.

I read a book called *Beyond Laughter*, by a psychiatrist who treated mainly comics. I was delighted to find that he practiced in Beverly Hills. In the middle of March 1962 I started seeing Dr. Martin Grotjahn, who had written the book. What psychiatry did for me, at least at first, was to help me cope a lot more easily. I finally had a male adult that I could trust with my innermost feelings and problems. The ultimate care giver needed some care herself.

Comforting people is an art, I came to find out. You must appeal to their strengths, not their weaknesses. What I needed was reinforcement in my new role as tower of strength, someone everyone draws strength from. What I did not need were tearful reminders of the circumstances and that I was a fragile rock. On the outside I was a rock, confident, encouraging and full of hope, but on the fragile inside, emptiness, loneliness, and hollowness were what I was feeling. All through that period I kept hearing inside my head a phrase from a poem

I had learned as a child: "Life must go on, I forget just why."
I needed to say that to myself many times a day.

After I tried to put my life back together and keep everybody on an even keel, I went to a formal dinner party and was seated at a table with Kay Spreckels Gable, Clark's outwardly fragile widow (in contrast to the also newly widowed Rocky Cooper, who was a pillar of strength). Kay kept leaning across her male dinner partner to say, "Oh, isn't it terrible, there will never be a man on God's earth to compare with that man," referring to both Ernie and Clark.

At first I tried to say, "Yes, but we must get ahold of ourselves and get on with our lives."

But two courses later she was leaning even further over her companion and wailing even louder, "What are we ever going to do without them? Our lives are over. It'll never be the same. What are we going to do?"

I didn't want to be part of this duet, so in the middle of the veal Oscar I retreated to the ladies' room for a breath of fresh air. I sat there regaining my composure, and looked up to say, "Oh, Ernie and Clark, if you find humor in this, please find a way to help me. Because right now I don't." By the time I got back for dessert, the other guests at the table had calmed Kay down. I was spared more tirades on the perils of being a lonely widow. Kay remained a professional widow until she died. That's just the kind of stuff you don't need to hear; it doesn't reinforce your new image of yourself. It only chips away.

It took some time for the enormity of the job facing me to sink in. I was now completely responsible for nine people: two teenagers, one toddler, one mother, one mother-in-law, three live-in servants (Nana, Leonard, and Nan), and myself.

In my daily meetings with George Zachary, he was so patient, saying "Call me anytime if you don't understand anything." I called him a lot. George's advice, since by choice I had been mostly a hausfrau the previous year and earned only twenty-six thousand dollars, was to declare bankruptcy, take Ernie's insurance money, and go live in New City, New York. I found out quickly that at that point Ernie and I did not own anything. The government had liens on everything

—house, art, cars, furnishings, and television shows. If I didn't pay what was owed, the government would take everything.

I began to try to sort out Ernie's messy estate and figure out exactly how much he owed and to whom. He kept a lot of things in his head that he didn't tell business managers on either coast. Even with Guy's and George's help, this was going to be a monumental job.

Proving that I could get back to work again and earn meaningful money was my next priority. I started by shooting my postponed Muriel commercials; it was good to be back at work since it took my mind off everything else. It was another step in the right direction.

Henri insisted that if I intended to get back in show business seriously, I had to start to promote myself. He suggested I start vocalizing, wear a pretty dress, get my hair done for photographs, and go to as many Hollywood functions as I could. This meant I had to get my hair done every day, sometimes twice a day. Robert Russie came to comb me out nightly, in my new big teased hairdo. Henry's advice was partly the usual Hollywood syndrome of being seen night after night in order to get work, but as always with Henri, it was also a gesture of friendship. He thought I should get out more.

On February 12, another stormy night identical to the one we all didn't want to remember the month before, at the same location, the Beverly Hilton Hotel, the Directors Guild gave Ernie the award for outstanding directorial achievement in television. The citation was for *Eugene*, the Silent Show redone as one of his own company's productions, this time in color, for ABC. He got standing ovations from both the New York and L.A. directors; he would have liked that. Jack Mogulescu was in California for the commercials, so he took me to the Directors Guild and to Frank Sinatra's and Juliet Prowse's engagement party on Valentine's Day night. It was an elaborate black-tie dinner with many elegant courses. The dinner was longer than the engagement. It was my first big party out after Ernie's funeral.

While he was in L.A., Jack offered, and I signed, a beautiful new contract with Consolidated. I redoubled my efforts for

Muriel cigars as the first lady of put-on commercial sex and began to reassemble my nightclub act.

The Bowmont Drive property (including the den, which Ernie had thought we could always live in if we lost the house) had been attached—along with everything else. George thought we might have to move to New City, which I had thought we owned free and clear, and I told the girls that this was a possibility. (Even the IRS wouldn't leave you without a small place to live if you were really trying.) They hated that idea, and as much as I would have liked moving to New York, I was determined to try to stay in L.A. and in the house all three girls thought of as home. Once I started to make some money from the cigar contract, I was able to buy back the house and its contents. With Ernie gone, it was way too big, but by closing off some of the rooms and moving things around, we made it cozier.

Lover Come Back was released to rave reviews and record-breaking business on February 17. My fourth lead, to Rock Hudson, Doris Day, and Tony Randall, as a feather-brained café performer and Rock's girl friend was praised.

I held my own party on March 2, my first time entertaining without the master. I had the usual troops: Groucho; the Wilders; the Lemmons. Outwardly I was doing just fine, but inwardly I was still treading water. I felt empty, like half a person, in spite of the surface strength I was putting on for family and friends.

About three weeks after Ernie's death things got about as low as they could go. Though inwardly strong, I was beginning to wonder myself if I could live up to the mother-father role of being all things to all people I suddenly found myself playing. On top of everything else it had rained hard and steadily for two weeks. Coldwater Canyon was a surging river, Bowmont Drive only slightly less submerged. That Saturday it poured again, and Sunday morning Nan woke me up and said, "Oh, my God, Mrs., there's a foot and a half of water in the basement." That was where I stored all my costumes.

Because no cleaners were open on Sunday, Nan and I, with help from Betty and Kippie, put sheets down on all the linoleum floors, in the kitchen, dinette, entrance hall, and lanai. In our jeans and sneakers, soaked to the knees, we proceeded to drag upstairs my velvet and fur capes, rhinestone Vegas dresses, and even the Nairobi Trio overcoats, whose cheap purple dye (for the color version of the Silent Show) seemed to have soaked off on everything. We wrung out each garment, wrapped it in a sheet, so that it wouldn't rust or run on another costume, and stacked it safely on one of the floors. The rhinestone gowns went in the kitchen, where we hoped that the heat from the now-open oven doors would keep them from rusting and the cloth from molding. The fur and velvet capes went into the hall.

I was struggling with a wet, very heavy full-length, full-circle black velvet cape with a hood and white mink trim all around, trying to wrap it in two sheets. The cape, which I called my *Tosca* misery cape, was giving me a big fight, and it was clearly winning. I was so upset I didn't know what to do. I had an overwhelming urge to laugh. I don't know why, except that everything was just so bad that it couldn't get any worse, or so I thought. I started laughing uncontrollably and hysterically, with tears streaming down my face. The kids and Nan joined in, and we couldn't stop. We laughed and laughed and laughed, and cried and cried, until we were exhausted. Five days later things did get even worse; while I was in New York, shooting a Muriel commercial, the hot-water tank burst, and there was another foot of water in the basement. Luckily, by this time the costumes were at the special cleaners recommended by the fire insurance company to deal with water damage.

Packing to go on the road was difficult because Ernie and I always had had the same dialogue going. He'd ask me if I were going to use the shoe bag; I'd always say no. I knew he liked it, it was his favorite bag, but he always asked me first, so I could say no. Then he'd ask me again if I was *really* not going to use it. I'd say, "No, you take it." I used heavy-duty Seventh Avenue fiber packing cases for my costumes; they are indestructible but very difficult to pack and get the tight-fitting lid on evenly. And every time I'd say to him, as he was helping me get the lid on, "You have to get all four corners set before you can close it." I didn't realize I was saying it so much until he started saying it before I did. The first time I packed after his death, it came back to me. As I said it to myself, he wasn't there to say it first.

The toughest of all things to deal with after his death was certain pieces of music, such as Erik Satie's *Gymnopédie* and George Shearing's version of "The Nearness of You," which were hard to listen to without tears.

The one thing I could not bring myself to do was to empty Ernie's drawers and closets. I couldn't even open them. Maybe like Mia, I felt somehow he might return. So long as his clothes were there, he was there, and I was not all alone with the responsibility.

It took almost two years before I could get rid of Ernie's little things from the bedroom. With Nan's help I threw out his socks, shirts, underwear, little scraps of paper with notes on them, keys that fit nothing, dried-out cigars, and restaurant receipts. It was another year before I moved out Ernie's shoes, suits, ties, hats, and overcoats. I think they'd still be there today if Nan hadn't pointed out that since I was getting married soon, I "must clear out his things. Your new husband's gonna need some drawers and closets, too."

Since I had never had to budget a household income and it had been eleven years since I'd watched my mother's careful shopping, I didn't know what an average family spent for food—or anything else. I had never seen the bills. Now that I was beginning to see them, I couldn't figure them out. I did go buy a budget book; when in doubt, I'd buy a book or take a course. I even asked Gadbois to send to Washington for a pamphlet about what the average family spent for food and essentials. I started with the hardware store, whose average monthly bills ran fifteen hundred dollars. I couldn't figure it out. What was it? Hammers, nails? Nobody fixed anything at the house, certainly not Ernie, and even Leonard knew only whom to call.

Nobody checked the bills; they went straight to the business manager. It was the same with food. Whatever anybody in the house wanted, they simply called up and had it delivered. One day a small order arrived with the bill on top, $56. I called the store and asked what it was for. The clerk said it was a case of dog food. I said, "Fifty-six dollars?" Silence. Then the clerk said, "Oh, we made a mistake with the decimal point." It should have been $5.60. It happened all the time. The cleaners, everybody, took advantage of us because they knew nobody in that house looked at the bills. I was being told I had to cut down, but I had to ask, "from what to what?" I didn't know the boundaries. That was one thing that Ernie had never taught me. At the time the going price for anything you wanted done at our house was $1,500: the roof repaired; the plumbing fixed; the driveway repaved; a heating system replaced. The bill always came to $1,500.

Every day agents met with me, trying to help me out of this maze. Now my personal diary contained everyone's appointments, mothers' and children's doctor's visits, ballet classes, and school events. I also wrote down what everything cost and kept going over all the bills. At least now the merchants knew someone was watching the store.

Ernie had a concealed safe in the floor of his den. He'd always said, "There's fifty grand in there if we're ever in trouble or need it." I did not have the combination. I told George Zachary about it. He said, "You need a witness. That'll be me. I'll find a safecracker." He did, and we all met at the appointed hour. The safecracker drilled away, in his protective helmet, as George and I sat, anticipating our newfound treasury for paying some of the bills. The safecracker finally broke through the lock, opened the safe door, and there was absolutely nothing there. Not even a scrap of paper. I guess he'd had a recent marathon card game. George said, "Well, we gave a try." The safecracker said, "Maybe next time."

Ernie's estate had been valued at $2,100,000, but the gross "value" didn't present a true picture of the estate. We owed the IRS around $200,000. ABC-TV presented a bill for $220,000, which Ernie owed for his overtime costs on his eight specials. I knew there was a lot more owing that I hadn't found out about yet.

George and I were in daily contact about the money problem. Since I didn't know what he was talking about, I took everything down on a secretary's steno pad and called him again the next day to clarify what I'd underlined. The terminology was beyond anything I'd had to deal with before. George said, "Edie, why don't you take a course at UCLA? I don't mind explaining it to you, but I want you to understand everything I'm saying." I went out to register, and the beginning and intermediate courses seemed too elementary for me. To take "Advanced Federal Tax Accounting," you either had to take the beginning and intermediate courses as prerequisites or prove that your circumstances qualified you for its equivalent. I needed the consent of the instructor, and when I went to see him, he said, "You certainly qualify." I started the following Thursday. Not only was I the only female in the class, but all the men were working lawyers and accountants. It felt to me like an old movie, *Maisie Goes to College,* a dizzy blonde in the midst of all these black suits. While I never intended to work as an accountant, I learned enough to understand the terminology and at least be able to ask the right questions of my tax accountants and lawyers.

In the midst of all this, anticipating returning to work, I decided to take ballet lessons at Tanya Lichine's. I took individual lessons so Mia could come with me, whether she wanted to or not. I outfitted her in Capezio leotards and ballet shoes; Capezio had everything for the toddler ballerina. I wanted to spend time with her alone, and since my time was closely budgeted these days, it was easier to take her with me. It was also better for her to get out of her tower.

The first thing to go was my Christmas Bugatti; Bill Harrah came, looked at it, and bought it for his car collection, which later became an antique auto museum in Reno. The little Bentley went next, and we put the Rolls in storage. I was advised to rent an unpretentious car; Gadbois chose a clunky secondhand greenish yellow Thunderbird, not the cute classic 1950's model with the porthole on the side, but everything awful. It was big and overblown and only pretended to be a sports car. I hated that car.

It was curious to me who came to the house demanding immediate payment for what—and in cash. A fellow fixing my MG came to my house one night and said he had to have cash that minute or he couldn't give me back my car. That was out of the realm of my experience. I never had much cash on me or paid any bills, certainly not in cash. Ernie, the gambler, felt secure only when he had a wad of hundred-dollar bills in his pocket, as had his father before him.

The people who came to give me cash were from all the

unions Ernie belonged to. I didn't even ask them; they just showed up with cash. If that hadn't happened, I don't know how I would have paid these people who demanded cash. Robert Wagner showed up with ten thousand dollars in cash, saying he owed it to Ernie from a poker game. I said, "Thank you very much, but I have no way of knowing who owed him or whom he owed. That's very sweet, Bob, but no thanks." He never got over it and told everybody about it.

I didn't have any idea of gamblers' winnings or how IOUs worked. Since I knew nothing about cards, I would just forget about it. (There was nothing in writing.) Strangely enough, the only person who insisted that Ernie owed him a considerable amount was the very wealthy and social John Hay Whitney from New York. He demanded, without an IOU or other marker, immediate payment of thirty-five hundred dollars he said Ernie owed him. I paid Whitney off as soon as I could, but I never got over the fact that he was the only one of Ernie's poker-playing "buddies" who ever asked for money.

The term "head of household" did not exist for women until the feminist movement of the 1970's but in 1962 that's exactly what I was. Yet I couldn't deduct the cost of child care when I worked. If I had been a man, I could have. It also bothered me that when I was traveling, I could not write off the cost of a secretary because I might secretly be using her for child care. Every businessman I met on the road accompanied by a very attractive "secretary" was allowed to deduct her, wine her, dine her, and use her for whatever else he had in mind. The Diners Club and all the other credit card companies cut me off; in those days the widow was always cut off. Thank God, the women's movement changed all that.

I kept taking voice lessons, with a coach in Los Angeles and another in New York, because I still wanted to be a serious singer. I had no ambitions as a dancer but took ballet classes to develop grace in movement and for exercise. Since I had been the first to introduce the twist to L.A., I used it for exercise for an hour at a stretch, losing as much as three pounds per session. It became a Sunday afternoon ritual for my mother, Mia, and me. Nan was the one who really taught us to "get down" when we did the twist. Even my mother, who would never have done such a thing in public, was all for "getting down" for exercise. She certainly had come a long way from Tenafly.

Milt Hoffman and Al Wein, who had worked on Ernie's show, came to the house to tell me that ABC was using the Kovacs tapes, taping over them to do the weather and the news. All the people on the crew were upset because they had worked so hard on them. Wasn't there anything I could do? I called George Zachary, who made a deal with ABC to buy the tapes back—one whole wall that said "Kovacs." They were put into Bekins film storage in 1962, uncataloged but temperature-safe. I know that Ernie would have approved of this use of his insurance money. He had a policy in Canada that I hadn't known about.

Now that our household was all female, with my three daughters, my mother, and me, we began to dress up more and use the dining room for elaborate celebrations, even when it was "just us girls." As a tax write-off I made a $25,000 down payment to buy back the California Racquet Club (now the Beverly Hills Country Club), which the government had also seized; then I went all out. Nan put out my best Irish linen tablecloth and napkins, glistening china, and silver candelabra. I dressed myself, Betty, Kippie, and Mia in long dinner gowns, and we swept into the dining room. I looked over the spread and proposed a toast: "This is a big celebration for all of us. We've just made our big payment on your father's tennis club. Now there's only one million, nine hundred forty-nine thousand to go."

Instead of unloading all of Ernie's toys and investments, no matter how foolish they seemed, I began to push my own career to salvage some of our life-style as well as to pay the bills. My mother had closed up her house in Tenafly, although she didn't sell it, and moved in with us. She was permanently entrenched in my upstairs workroom. Kippie, who was a lot like Ernie when it came to spending habits, uncharacteristically came to me one day and asked how much her horse was costing a month. When I told her, she said, "Let's sell it. It's something we can do without. We can grow up." We all grew up a lot in those months.

*F*OURTEEN

ONE DAY WHEN MIA AND I were at dance class, Roy Gerber called to say that Consolidated had bought the half hour immediately preceding the Academy Awards. (Roy had recently moved to L.A., and after Ernie died, Marvin Moss refused to handle actors and became strictly a literary agent.) Consolidated was thinking of doing a fashion show; would I like to host it? I said of course, I would if I would be allowed to sing a song or two. Roy said he'd work on it.

He did, and not only did I get to sing one song, but I got the whole half hour to do whatever I wanted. I made a list of everything that I'd like to do, and Barry Shear called to say he'd like to direct. Why I felt I could handle Barry when Ernie couldn't (Ernie had fired Barry from *Take a Good Look*, because he couldn't get along with the crew), I don't know. But I did hire him as director. Ernie had also barred him from the poker games because he never brought cash, only items, like watches and cameras, to bet, and Ernie wouldn't have it.

For months I had kept Ernie's den, which was also our office, locked up and never went in. But now that I had my own show, it was time to open up our production office again. Ernie had built it as a corporate room with corporate funds, and if it wasn't used as such, we couldn't deduct it. I didn't want to change the den, but the paneled walls, heavy furniture, and armor collection were oppressive. I took out the poker table and replaced it with my white grand piano. I added brass and Lucite tables for everybody to work on and flowers in season. Now I could get down to work.

For the special, which was on a tight production schedule, I revived a few impressions from my old nightclub act: Jeanette MacDonald, Marilyn Monroe, and Shirley Temple. I desperately missed Ernie's criticism in preparing the show. Even when he wasn't involved in my work, he had been my chief sounding board. This would be the first performing I had done in eleven years without his help and guidance.

Peter Matz and I revived our Gershwin vocalese; in the middle were eight bars from *Porgy and Bess*—no words, just the melody of "My Man's Gone Now." David Oppenheim, whom I'd hired because of his fine work on the *Omnibus* special I'd done, told the press I was going to close the show with "My Man's Gone Now." I knew he wasn't going to be my producer long.

I taped the first part at ABC on the West Coast, with Dick Shawn playing a rock star. I wanted André Previn to play the piano for my Gershwin, and since he had to go to New York for a Carnegie Hall concert, I took the rest of my show to New York. Consolidated gave me free rein over the music, so of course, it turned out to be a musical special. I sang two Kurt Weill songs, "My Ship" and "Bilbao Moon." The latter was currently a pop hit as sung by Andy Williams, so I decided to do it in the original German. I got an introduction to Lotte Lenya, who lived in New City, and she carefully coached me in the stark original Brechtian style. When the advertising agency people heard the advance tape, they were furious: "My God, she's singing a German song in prime time; she can't do that." The vocalese they didn't understand at all.

I held firm and must have been doing something right because *Here's Edie*, which aired on April 9, 1962, had universally fabulous reviews. The show did for me what Ernie's Silent Show had done for him five years earlier. There was a lot riding on that show, so it was a good thing that the critics loved it. *The New York Times* said: "Edie Adams came back to television last night to demonstrate triumphantly her talents as a singer and comedienne." The Detroit *Free Press* said that *Here's Edie* was "a stylish half hour of variety with more entertainment in thirty minutes than the Awards had in four times that length."

The place to be for the Academy Awards that year was Doris Vidor's party. I was there early to watch the special. When it finished, everybody applauded. The Hollywood movers and shakers never do that. I had finally made it in in Ernie's town on their terms. We got two Emmy nominations, one for the special and one for my performance. That show established me as myself in big-time show business without Ernie. I was no longer the magician's assistant. I was *it*. This was the first time that I was allowed complete artistic control, and I had learned Ernie's lesson well: There can be just one opinion—right or wrong—on what goes into a show. I have been forever grateful to the Muriel sales team for their faith in my judgment, for letting me have my own way.

After the special Muriel signed me as star and my own newly formed production company (put together by George Zachary), Ediad Productions, for eight half hour shows. I was to produce the shows through Ediad. Consolidated also tore up the contract we had just made in February and gave me an even brighter financial future as its spokesperson. I found that when I was busy working on the show or commercials, I had less time to be devastated by Ernie's death.

Even at my lowest, in those first few months, I had a lot of energy and loved working, even though some thought it was too soon. Because of my responsibilities, I now understood, for the first time, why men always worry about having to work. It was only the men in those days who had total financial responsibility. I didn't like my new head-of-household spot. As a kid I'd even had sympathy for the guys at age eighteen, having to face a lifetime of providing. I'd watched my father work hard all his life with no personal reward. Suddenly I was in that position. In my dealings with the tax people, I felt like the man in a divorce case, with the IRS playing the role of the gold-digging blonde trying to separate me from my funds.

Muriel treated my commercials as an art form; sometimes we spent as much as a week filming one sixty-second message, and usually the production values were so great that the company spent more on the one-minute commercial than on the budget for my whole show. Commercials were the toughest thing I ever had to do in show business. Both product and performer must appeal to the viewer and stand the test of time. As in the movies, every tiny flaw is magnified. And the ultimate test is, Does it sell the product? You're selling two things, personality and commodity, and too much personality overpowers the product. Too much product without getting the viewers' attention doesn't sell either. Muriel sales increased tremendously, from four million to forty-four million cigars in just that one year. Muriel and I were a match made in heaven. That year, 1962, I was named Commercial Spokeswoman of the Year by the advertising industry.

Once I got the show, I reinstituted my old routine of cross-country commuting, staying at my little apartment in the Village. I went out a lot in New York. My first public performance there was singing along with Danny Kaye at a fund-raising dinner for Senator Jacob Javits at the Waldorf. I was and remain a notoriously liberal Democrat, but not where Senator Javits was concerned. He was a special kind of Republican. I felt the same way about Nelson Rockefeller and later campaigned for him.

The big puffed hairdo had just come in as I was beginning my cross-country personal appearances under contract to Muriel. In 1962 you got dressed up to go first class on an airplane. Because of the time change, in order to get to New York before evening, I had to take a 6:00 A.M. flight. That meant that at 4:00 A.M. the hairdresser had to be at my home, where he pumped and pushed and squeezed and teased until I had the new lady of the 1960's bouffant hairdo. I had to sit erect in the plane, without a pillow, so my hair wouldn't bend or flatten. Every time the flight attendants passed hot towels around I'd look on enviously as everyone around me washed their faces, knowing I couldn't. I had to get off that plane hours later with every teased hair in place for the photographers, who were always waiting there.

I decided that there wouldn't be much comedy in my television shows because I'd always felt more at home in music and I still wasn't feeling very funny. I was afraid to do comedy unless I had a comic editor nearby, and Ernie had always done that for me. The guest on the first of my new series was Duke Ellington and his orchestra, which backed me while I sang a duet with Johnny Hodges. I planned to feature jazz more than I had in the past since, along with the Navajo blanket, it was the only true art form that was peculiarly American. In Europe jazz performers were treated much as classical concert performers are in this country. I wanted to be one of the first to give American jazz artists their due. Besides, I didn't know much about jazz and I'd be learning something, too. Also, my budget wouldn't allow fancy big stars, but it would allow the best jazz artists available: Count Basie, Stan Getz, Woody Herman, Lambert and Hendricks (I did Ross's part), and Bobby Darin. I was right: The shows are timeless, and the music still holds up.

I met with a boardroom full of GAC (General Artists Corporation) executives. I told them I had to make lots of money fast; I didn't need the star treatment and didn't care what the dressing room looked like. I'd dress in a closet if the numbers were right. "Don't turn down anything," I told them; "advise me of any and all offers." I tried them out, and they were fine. Among the first things GAC got me was a recording contract with Decca Records. My first album was called *Edie Adams Through These Swinging Doors*, a series of old saloon favorites done in a new way.

Eddie Fisher was my escort in May 1962 for the Emmy Award ceremonies, where Judy Garland and I lost out to Carol Burnett but Ernie won a posthumous Emmy for Outstanding Electronic Camera Work. Eddie told the press that our relationship was one of "mutual sympathy" since he had also lost a spouse when Elizabeth Taylor ran off with Richard Burton. For me he was simply another of the series of lost souls who seemed to find me for comfort and nourishment. Sam Goldwyn saw the pictures, and at a party he and Frances gave, pulled me aside and said, "Vat's da matter vit you, you going out vit actors? You don't go out vit actors; you go out vit the producer or director." (He didn't consider Ernie an actor.)

Inevitably, going out as much as I did caused the press to link me with a variety of male admirers. The ones I was photographed with weren't the ones I was really dating. I loved Rock Hudson, and he was my public date for a lot of these events; but I was actually seeing Clifford Odets, an angry, angry man, or writer Cy Howard, who really made me laugh—something I desperately needed to do.

Clifford, who I was to see a lot of for the next year, interested me from his first invitation: He wanted to take me to a concert of Paganini quartets and cook dinner beforehand. He was a fascinating conversationalist who could talk about anything. Even the bad dinner (he was an even worse cook than I but didn't know it) and the fact that we never got to the concert didn't bother me. He was a brilliant, troubled, and unusual man—right up my alley. Clifford was more interested in me than I ever could be in him, but I did enjoy his company. He made me think. He also encouraged me to write, which nobody had ever done before. I took him things to look at, now that I was writing my show. He also knew music, so he made a good editor. He was interested in me, not in the Kovacs mystique, and said so. "You're living in the shadow. You've got to get out of it."

Odets did not want to go to a lot of parties, but since I had to, I managed to get him to a couple. He did want to live in Beverly Hills and on a grand style but was reluctant to play the social game. At a party given by movie mogul Joseph E. Levine for Sophia Loren, I taught the very serious Clifford to do the twist. He finally caught on and did it quite well.

He asked me if he could write a humorous monologue for one of my TV specials; his only stipulation was that he get to direct it. Naturally, I said yes, but fast. He also helped me condense a speech I had to make at a tribute for Ernie.

The one form of work I did have to turn down during this period was Broadway musicals. I was set to play the part of Belle Poitrine in *Little Me* opposite Sid Caesar. I didn't want to uproot the girls and take them to New York. Also, the stage didn't pay as well as other forms of entertainment, and I was still in need of making as much as I could in as short a time. Besides, artistically I wanted to play both female leads, the older and younger Belle. After all, Sid was playing seven parts. The producers wouldn't go for it, so I optioned *Oh Captain*, in order to try to produce it as my own property, first live, then shot for TV. I would play the two ladies' parts, a sexy nightclub singer and an uptight British wife. I had it for a year, but it never got off the ground.

My first movie role after Ernie's death was in Stanley Kramer's *It's a Mad, Mad, Mad, Mad World*. It was made in Southern California, so I got to stay home with the children. Before filming began, Stanley invited the cast, including Milton Berle, Phil Silvers, Sid Caesar, Jimmy Durante, Spencer Tracy, Buddy Hackett, Terry-Thomas, Ethel Merman, Jonathan Winters, and Mickey Rooney to a lunch at the studio to get acquainted. Stanley also wanted us to see the second-unit aerial footage of the car chase shot in Palm Springs. Buddy Hackett said, "You got funny cars. They're funnier than us. What do you want, funny cars or funny people?"

I tried to tell Stanley, whose five previous pictures had been serious dramas, ending with *Judgment at Nuremberg*, that comics were different from actors, that he might be in for a few surprises. He said, "No, no, I can handle it." Before the end of the picture he came over to me and said, "Dammit, if Clyde Beatty can do it, I can do it, too."

This comedic chase picture, which was originally five hours long and filmed in the single-lens Cinerama process, had been bought on the basis of a postcard-size résumé from the writers, William and Tanya Rose. It was Kramer's attempt to revive silent slapstick comedy (Buster Keaton was among dozens of guest stars) in a modern, more violent chase setting. It became such a big thing among comics that if you weren't in it, you asked to be. The Roses wrote in cameo parts for Jack Benny and Jerry Lewis among others.

Before *Mad World*, my movie parts had been bits; this was my first full-sized role. I played Caesar's wife and the part *was* beyond reproach. We were one of the nutsy teams looking for buried treasure in the desert. I was nervous in my first scenes for *Mad World*; the first day's shoot on the whole movie was Sid and I in the hardware store when he blows it up. On top of that, Spencer Tracy showed up to watch Sid and me work. I apologized for my jitters, but Spencer said, "If you weren't nervous, you'd be tuning up for a lousy performance." Even later he continued to be helpful to me.

As far as I was concerned, with the funny people and

laughter around, I should have paid them. I liked working with all those good strong comics. I understood them. Being out there by myself is what would have scared me. Teamed with a strong comic such as Sid, I had no problem. I was comfortable working with him and enjoyed the frantic atmosphere on the set. The off-camera action with this extraordinarily talented troupe was as funny as that on-screen. Here were all these great comics doing what they do best, each trying to outdo the other.

No professional still cameras were allowed, but I was there with my Minox and captured all the food fights during lunch breaks. Spencer Tracy never joined this madness and lunch; he and Katharine Hepburn went off on a quiet picnic with a basket she had prepared at home, complete with linen tablecloth and fresh flowers.

On location around Palm Springs in the summer, I learned that moviemaking wasn't as easy as I had thought it was back in Hollywood. It's very hard to be funny in 120-degree heat. No matter what action Stanley gave the actors, they tried for top position in the shot. In one scene fifteen of us funny people get out of one cab and rush toward the buried treasure. Every time we shot the scene, Milton Berle ended up on camera last (so he'd have more footage). Finally, Stanley gave everybody a number to get out of the cab and thence out of the shot. Milton was number five. We shot the scene, and the next day Stanley came in and said, "I don't know how he did it. I saw him get out number five and leave number five, but on the dailies, after everybody had left, there was Milton, number fifteen, the last one in the shot."

I immediately took to Terry-Thomas. He showed up first in Palm Springs at the pool in a Mexican hat with a five-foot brim. He was totally crazed. I felt right at home. He liked caviar with a spoon and had a maroon Bentley like mine, except his was a convertible. When I was in London, he took me to the premiere of *Mutiny on the Bounty* in November, wearing a huge bearskin coat with the car top down in what I remember as a freezing snowstorm. The next night he took me to a remote comedy club, Hockney in the East End, where you stood up in a pub to see the latest unknown kookie comic. He, Sid Caesar, and I made an unlikely trio. We once went to a party at Dean Martin's house. Jeannie Martin said we all three marched in together, sat on a bench in a row together, and then left together as a set. One evening he and Jonathan Winters came to a party at my house dressed as Canadian Air Force officers. I asked why, and they said they were passing Western Costume and it seemed like a good idea at the time.

Another time I asked the whole cast to a party at my rented Malibu house. Terry, who was a good swimmer, said he could see something out on the ocean horizon; would I like to go out and explore? I said sure, and the two of us swam out to a Coast Guard raft and discovered some basking seals. We were sitting out there resting when the Coast Guard stopped by. "Are you all right?" they asked. We said, "Certainly." They said, "Well, you'd better come back in with us. Sid Caesar said you disappeared from view and told us to come rescue you."

In the midst of the movie, and as I was recording my Decca album, Judge Belloff called me in a recording session to say that Ernie's first wife, Bette, had resurfaced. He was just warning me that there was a lawsuit pending and that she had gotten herself "a real tough lawyer, a barracuda, an ambulance chaser. Get yourself Murray Chotiner at this number because you are in for some heavy trouble." Bette filed in July to sue me for "her" portion of the estate, five hundred thousand dollars and custody of her daughters, in that order.

I hired Murray Chotiner (who later was famous for being close to Richard Nixon and who died under suspicious circumstances). Bette's lawyer chose to subpoena my psychiatric records from Dr. Grotjahn to prove that because I was in analysis, I was not a fit mother.

Grotjahn was on vacation. When he came back to his office after a month, while going through his accumulated mail, he was served with a summons. All his psychiatric records were impounded. "Ach, Gott," Grotjahn exclaimed, "half of Hollywood is in there." On the stand Chotiner chose to say my life was an open book. If Dr. Grotjahn on the stand even once referred to his notes, they would become the property of the court. Since these were his personal notes that he took during all his patient's sessions, a lot of secrets could have been let out. Grotjahn was magnificent, giving all his testimony from memory. So Hollywood's psychiatric problems did not become an open book, and Bette lost this rather sensational public hearing.

I took the beach house in Malibu for the month of August because I didn't want the girls glued to TV sets. Even Mia at age three had a social life: She attended Merle Oberon's pink and blue tandem birthday party for her children, Bruno and Francesca, without me because I was working. Among the other guests were Michael Reagan and Tyrone Power III, who looked just like his late father. We lived right next door to George C. Scott and Colleen Dewhurst, who left a pile of beach toys for the kids when they moved back east.

Jack Lemmon and Felicia Farr finally got married, in Paris, in September 1962. When they returned, I decided to give them a dinner party for two hundred at Ernie's and now my famous tennis club. At the party Ethel Merman congratulated Roz Russell on the movie *Gypsy*, and Roz congratulated Ethel on *Mad World*. The day before the party, I'd won my custody battle over Bette Kovacs, so it turned out to be a joint celebration. Rock Hudson again was my date, and Patricia Kennedy Lawford wore an Oleg Cassini gown, to do the delight of Oleg, who was also there. I soon began doing the town with him whenever I was in New York.

In my regular shows, beginning in September 1962, I wanted a mood variety program with a little theme running through it. I felt that the low-key approach was good for a half hour. I wanted to throw in an art song once in a while, not because I preferred serious or classical music to popular but because I felt there should be a place for it—even if I had to sneak it in.

We began to hold our regular production meetings out in Ernie's newly lightened-up den. Billy Morris was the set designer, and Ret Turner was wardrobe. In all the initial creative meetings Billy and Ret both would be there. By the time we discussed the show from top to bottom, I never had to explain the theme of the show or ask for anything specific for the sets or costumes. Billy and Ret always knew what I wanted. I never saw a sketch until airtime.

As the producer I hired myself as costume designer, using the credit "Costumes by Enke." (I still didn't feel confident enough to use my stage name; Enke could have been a man.) With the budget for three shows I could buy Jimmy Galanos's entire sample spring or fall collection, which I could amortize over all eight shows. Whenever I was seen singing, it was always in a three-thousand-dollar beautifully designed Galanos gown. The actual costumes, for guests, were easy for Ret to whip up. It was a cost-efficient thing to do. All the glitz, feathers, and maribou were in my back closet. The look of the show holds up even today because of those Galanos dresses and Billy and Ret's fine work.

After a few shows Muriel began to use some of my musical staging ideas and specific looks in numbers on my show for the commercials. While I was quite happy singing and not talking much or doing sketches, there was one whole show that Ernie had completely mapped out for his series of specials, which never got on the air. At first I could see myself doing it, but the show was so peculiarly Ernie that I thought I'd better not attempt it with anyone else, even though Sid Caesar sometimes works the same way Ernie did. I tried a few of Ernie's sketches on the air with other people, but the sketches never worked.

I was signed to costar with Bob Hope and Anita Ekberg in *Call Me Bwana*. Originally the movie was to be filmed in Africa, so I got every shot against tropical diseases. The first clue I had that we weren't going to Africa was when I said to Bob, while doing his special, "Weren't those shots terrible?" He said, "What shots?" We ended up doing the whole picture in London. I was hired to play a nearsighted spy. When I got on the plane to go over the pole to London, Mort Lachman, Bob Hope's writer, told me that I wasn't going to play the spy. Anita wanted that part. I said, "Well, who am I?" He said, "I don't know." The next day in London I was in the first shot with Bob. We were photographed getting off a plane together. I kept asking the director, "Do I know him, do I hate him, do I love him, are we married, what?" He said, "We don't know yet." So we shot half the picture without me knowing what character I was playing.

I tried to read my lines in an offhand, noncommittal way. When I saw my double throwing gangsters over her shoulder and doing karate chops, I discovered I was a CIA agent. I said,

"Fellas, I know we can't go back and reshoot, but at least let me redub. This is a tough lady I'm playing." So back we went, and if you ever see the picture, you will see me with an innocuous face barking out lines like a marine sergeant.

The movie's ending is one I'll never forget. Since Mort Lachman and Bill Larkin were writing this movie (without screen credit, as a favor to Bob) only one day ahead of the scenes being shot, the movie took on a life of its own. Three quarters of the way through the picture, I am tied up and buried in the sand up to my neck. When it came to the end of shooting time, I still wasn't out of my sand pile. I said, "Mort, we can't leave yet. What happens to me at the end?" He said, "See the picture." Months later I did. Someone asks Bob, "What happened to Agent QXB [me]?" Bob says, "We had a call from her. She's all right!" Every time I see Mort I say that line to him, and he says, "What do you want from me? We weren't supposed to be writing it in the first place. We just wanted to go home!"

I was asked to do a Royal Command Performance at the London Palladium for Queen Elizabeth and Prince Philip. I was disappointed that I wasn't going to sing a real song, just play a ditzy talking woman to Bob Hope's jokes. We tried it out in Manchester and Blackpool. Bob and I did the traditional royal family jokes. I asked him, "Why do they change the guard at Buckingham Palace every day?" And he replied, "It's a strong union." Oh, I wished I could have sung just one song.

I did one *Here's Edie* in London while I was making the movie. My whole family—Betty, Kippie, Mia, Nana, and my mother—was there for thanksgiving, and since I had a service flat, I was able to accommodate all the other stray Americans working in London on Thanksgiving. The English, naturally, don't observe the holiday, so when my mother carefully explained to the disbelieving cook that we wanted "sweet potatoes" made with brown sugar, molasses, and marshmallows, the cook said, "On potatoes?" My mother said, "Yes, sweet potatoes, of course." We all had a big laugh when the cook proudly brought out a bowl of white potatoes prepared with molasses, brown sugar, and marshmallows.

I was to do a second *Here's Edie* in Salzburg, after the end of the picture. However, I had to cancel everything to return to L.A. for another one of Mary's many mandatory two-day depositions. Mary's machinations even delayed my opening at the Riviera Hotel in Las Vegas until the following February.

Ralph Nader, then an unknown, called to ask me if I wanted to sue General Motors because the Corvair in which Ernie was killed had some structural faults. I declined because at the time it seemed everybody else was suing me— Bette and Mary among others. I'd had it with lawsuits. Years later I met Nader at a party and he said he had figured that I hadn't sued because General Motors had paid me off. I couldn't believe my ears. Since then Mr. Nader has not been one of my favorite people.

My TV show in January 1963, the fourth edition of *Here's Edie*, capitalized on the then-current bossa nova craze. Stan Getz, Laurindo Almeida, and the Roger Wagner Chorale were the guests. I sang "I Wish You Love" and "Something's Coming" with a bossa nova beat, and an unbilled Don Rickles and Cesar Romero danced it with me. I cut the comedy completely except for the opening bit, where I played a frustrated senorita to Don's stomping flamenco dancer. In spite of his hatchetlike comedic tirades, I find Don to be one of the sweetest and most sensitive people I ever met in show business.

When I finally resumed my nightclub career in February 1963, at the Riviera in Las Vegas, I probably held the record for the most postponements, thanks to Mary. This was my big Vegas act, with four boy dancers and four girl dancers. I never liked to do an act with dancers because (A) I couldn't dance and (B) I had always done takeoffs on that peculiarly cute style of Vegas act, usually geared for movie stars who didn't dance or sing. I tried to talk the bosses into hiring Stan Getz at the height of the bossa nova craze, but they said, "Nobody's heard of Stan Getz [he was then number one on the charts]. Let's try to get Charlie Barnet." They did, so instead of doing the very contemporary bossa nova with the boy dancers, I did an old big band number, "Skyliner," with Charlie Barnet.

Groucho Marx hosted the opening night party. He introduced me by saying, "There is nothing that Edie can't do; there are some things she won't do, but nothing she can't do." Not everything I did worked. I tried an avant-garde comedy trio, the Munchkins (Alan Sues, Paul Mazursky, and Larry Tucker), in the act, but while they were on doing chic Second City–style humor, the bosses were telling Roy Gerber, "Get 'em off the stage right now." Roy said, "I can't do it in the middle of the act." "Get 'em off the stage!" They were lucky to finish that first show, and they were gone before the second show. I replaced them with Rowan and Martin the next night. Paul and Larry later told me I had bought them their first and only tuxes for that debut.

Since I was Jimmy Galanos's best customer for my TV show, when he designed his only collection of furs, he offered me the entire set of samples at a price so ridiculously low that I couldn't afford not to buy it. But in order to deduct it, I had to appear in all the furs, as part of my costumes in the act. There was no way for me to squeeze them all in except during Dick and Dan's turn. At odd times I would roller-skate through in a sable jumpsuit, a sable housecoat, and seven other fur pieces.

Business was so good that I was invited to return to the Riviera later in the year at twenty-five thousand dollars a week, a raise of ten thousand dollars. Even if most of it was going to the IRS, I would make enough to keep the wolf from the door and be able to do one of my *Here's Edie* specials from Vegas.

George Masters came to Vegas to do my face for my TV show, with a new kind of Marilyn makeup. Later I told Tommy Kearnes, the makeup man at NBC, about it. I carefully described it. He said, "That's a pretty big departure. I'll have to ask them about it." I said, "Who is 'them'?" He said, "Why, the producers." I said, "My company, Ediad, is producing. I is them." He excused himself, went out, checked, and came back to say, "Okay, anything you want." The reviews said I looked especially good in my new glamorous eye makeup by Tommy Kearnes. I believe he later won an Emmy for makeup. It was fun being the producer.

I turned down three firm movie offers because of my television show, but I did manage to wedge in *Under the Yum Yum Tree*, in which I played a Ph.D. and *Love with the Proper Stranger*, in which I played a stripper, in the spring of 1963.

Freddy Brisson, the Lizard of Roz, came back into my life while I was still at the Riviera, as the producer of the movie version of the hit play *Under the Yum Yum Tree*. David Swift would be directing Jack Lemmon, Carol Lynley, and Dean Jones in the comedy. Roz Russell, in an incredible turnabout, told her husband to hire me. But Auntie Mame's magic spell was everywhere. She had told the makeup department that my blond hair should be toned down. We tried on innumerable wigs, and they finally settled on an uncharacteristic dark maroon wig, styled in a nondescript teacher hairdo. The severe wig was topped only by the dowdy, ill-fitting costumes. I was almost unrecognizable. That was okay with me because I didn't like how I looked. Although Mary was no longer living with me and I was confronting her monthly depositions, she nonetheless attempted the maroon streaks, with even less success than usual.

Because *Love with the Proper Stranger* started filming on location in New York only a week after finish of *Yum Yum*, Alan Pakula and Robert Mulligan had to shift all my scenes to the studio at the end of the picture.

Only Robert Mulligan, who had been a theater director, took the time to rehearse us scene by scene on *Love with the Proper Stranger*. The picture starred Steve McQueen as a trumpet player and Natalie Wood as a working girl with whom he has a romance. I played Steve's occasional girl friend, Barbara of Seville, a stripper who lives with many yapping lapdogs. My own Cardigan Welsh Corgi, Morgana, loves to watch *Wild Kingdom* and dog and cat food commercials on television but for some reason doesn't like Phil Rizzuto. One day, while we were watching *Love with the Proper Stranger*, she began growling at the scene where the yapping dogs are eating dinner. When the camera panned up my legs to reveal that it was me feeding them, it stopped her cold.

We learned between twenty and thirty pages of script at a time, then did them in sequence with the camera crew standing by. Everybody contributed ideas to the filming. I'd say, "Gee, Bob, can we try it this way?" And then we'd all do it that way. Steve would say, "I like it this way." Then we'd do it Steve's way. We'd all decide which was the best way. The crew, without cameras or lights in their hands, knew exactly what to do, whichever version was chosen. But that was an unusual luxury in movies. I've never heard of it before or since.

Merv Griffin was the emcee for a White House press photographers' dinner on May 24, 1963, at which I sang. President John F. Kennedy was there, and I was introduced to him by Merriman Smith. During JFK's speech I peeked through the curtains from backstage to watch this handsome, charismatic man. As I stood there, I was almost tackled to the ground by an FBI man, pulling me away. He said, "Don't ever peek through a curtain at the President. When we see that from across the room, we ask no questions. We all have orders to shoot to kill." Later Merriman came up to me and asked if I would like to meet the President for a private drink after the dinner. "He'd really like to see you; there won't be anyone else there." In Hollywood we'd heard all the rumors, so it took me only a little while to figure out what he meant. I may be the only shapely blond female then between the ages of fifteen and forty-five who said no to JFK, but it wasn't because I wasn't asked.

About this time I had a weird dream, which I can remember today. It had all sorts of symbolisms and wombs; it was so bizarre I couldn't figure it out. I went to Dr. Grotjahn and described it to him in great detail. He went through the classic Freudian dream analysis, but he couldn't figure out the meaning either. Before I left his office, I said, "Let's get back to this dream; haven't you anything more to say?" He smiled and said, "Well, perhaps you have a schizophrenic vagina." I laughed but went straight to Dr. Brien's office. I explained that I had absolutely no symptoms, I felt fine. But would he do a pelvic exam because I felt something was wrong? Something was wrong. The next day I was in the hospital, where I had my left ovary and my appendix (OB's blue plate special) removed. I was in the hospital for one week and was scheduled to tape a special two days after I came out.

Barry Shear was doing another show and refused to come to the hospital to work on mine. I said, "If you don't come, I will have to hire your assistant because we have to deliver the show on Saturday. He said, "Use a rerun." I said, "No,

Consolidated has already told me as the producer they will
not accept a rerun. They want a new show. I have to start
without you." He hung up, and that's the last time I ever
spoke to him. I hired Steve Binder, who had been directing
Steve Allen. Binder designed a chairlike contraption that was
attached to the boom camera because I still couldn't stand or
walk for any length of time. Bob Hope graciously filled in as
guest star on very short notice.

During my first show of the new season Binder and I
disagreed about how the program should be run, and I retaped
a portion of the show that he had done. Joe Behar replaced
Binder as director.

I decided to do Somerset Maugham's Sadie Thompson in
Rain in summer stock for John Kenley's circuit in Ohio. I
wanted to buy the TV rights for a ninety-minute special. Rod
Serling came out to Ohio to see me in Rain and was enthusiastic about the putting the package together. Clifford Odets
wanted to adapt the script and direct and was all set to visit
me for the opening but never showed up. He wrote saying
he wasn't coming but never mentioned that he was ill. I closed
on August 4, with Rod in the audience, and drove on to New
York. Clifford had his nurse call the house in L.A. to try to
reach me. I flew back immediately on the tenth and saw him
every day at his house until he died, on the fifteenth, of
cancer. The funeral was the next day. With Clifford gone and
other projects coming up, I dropped the idea of adapting Rain
for television. I was always sorry never to have worked with
Rod Serling or Clifford Odets.

I did my fourth movie in a row, The Best Man, based on
Gore Vidal's hit play about presidential contenders. I played
Cliff Robertson's wife, a character originally based on Pat
Nixon but with a lot of Ethel Kennedy thrown in. Gore
thought that combination showed both sides of the totally
devoted political wife in 1963. Haskell Wexler was the ci-
nematographer who did extraordinary work matching the
new hand-held camera footage with real convention footage,
the first time it had been attempted. I began to notice these
technical aspects of moviemaking. Before now I had been too
involved in learning the techniques of acting in film. Franklin
Schaffner directed the movie, which starred Henry Fonda as

the party's leading aspirant, Margaret Leighton as his wife, and Ann Sothern as a party organizer.

I returned to the Riviera for a four-week engagement in November 1963, with Rowan and Martin again, for even more money. Now that I was becoming a regular in Vegas, I briefly tried to become one of the swinging new liberated women. As I look back, it was clearly just another link in the chain of what was fast becoming my obsessive compulsive behavior. I had to have excess in everything—buying, eating, even sex. However, it just didn't work, although I gave it a good healthy try.

Whenever people ask, "Do you remember where you were when Kennedy was shot?," I do. On November 22 I was playing the Riviera and doing a takeoff on Jackie Kennedy in a pillbox hat: "Is it Onassises or is it Onassi?" This new impersonation was in the act only four days. All casinos went dark the night of the twenty-second.

Judy Garland was working at the Cocoanut Grove. Ernie had played poker with her husband Sid Luft, and I always found her to be very pleasant and funny. Later I was to meet her to go see Buddy Rich with some friends. She sat right in the front row, joked back and forth with Buddy, and even sang a song. She left before the rest of us did, and we waited for Buddy to pack up the band. When we went out at about 3:00 A.M., my car was gone. The attendant said "Miss Garland took it." I had to call a cab. Puzzled and angry, we all were stranded. The next morning I called her house. "Judy, that's my Bentley. Why did you take it?" "I don't know. It looked so pretty there I told them it was mine." I couldn't get angry with her. I just told her I'd come over to pick it up.

Another time I went to a party with Guy McIlwaine, then Judy's publicist, at Norman Jewison's. Judy was there, looking wonderful, and sang a song. The next afternoon we were to go to a party at 3:00 P.M. for her and Mickey Rooney. Guy called me at 9:00 A.M., saying Judy'd had her stomach pumped at UCLA the night before and was still in the hospital. We decided to go to the party anyway, both assuming Judy wouldn't be there. As we walked in, fashionably a half hour late, Hollywood time, we saw her looking radiant, hair done, makeup on, and holding court, making everyone laugh, as if nothing had happened.

I was interested in bridging the gap between comedy and music and drama, perhaps because of my opera training. I was now in a position even to encourage the community at large to expand its cultural horizons. Los Angeles, where it now looked as if I were going to be living, was just about to open its Music Center, close on the heels of New York's Lincoln Center.

I hosted a black-tie party for Leonard Bernstein at the Beverly Hilton for 162 guests. I wanted to bridge the culture gap between New York and L.A. Lenny, who had written the music for only one movie, *On the Waterfront*, said he'd never do another film where the music was "incidental." But he did want to write a musical picture. Eddie Sauter conducted his "Focus" with Stan Getz on saxophone and backed by twenty-four of Hollywood's top studio musicians. Among the guests were Johnny Mercer, André Previn, Jule Styne, Julie London, and Mark Taper. Taper, who came with Ann Miller, had given millions to the Music Center, and I was also honoring those people who had made it a reality.

The champagne and caviar flowed freely during the cocktail hour. A huge birdcage hanging from the ceiling of the hotel's grand ballroom contained masses of chrysanthemums and cooing white doves. Fountains of fresh carnations were spiked with Joy perfume. Zsa Zsa Gabor, in a black and gold brocade dress and a rope of pearls, was too awed to try to shuffle the place cards. For dinner we had frog legs in tomato sauce, squab with wild rice, artichoke hearts with tiny peas, and a gorgeous dessert decorated with pianos and ballerinas. Ernie would have been proud.

My date that night was again Cy Howard, who had been a companion of mine long enough for people to start talking of my remarrying. I got madder at Cy than at anybody in the world and would say, "That's it, I don't want to see you again." But just as it had been with another funny man earlier, all of a sudden I would look around and he'd be back in my life again, all smiles and making me laugh. That was his charm, his wit, and his ability to make me laugh in any sit-

349

uation, even making love. But I never knew whether he and I were off or on at any given moment.

Our final parting came when Gloria Grahame, who had been divorced from Cy for six years, showed up unannounced in his office with her newly born son by third husband Tony Ray. Gloria was divorcing Tony, the son of Nick Ray, who had been her second husband. She was also accompanied by her and Cy's daughter, Paulette. "Don't marry Edie Adams," Gloria said to Cy, "I'm back." I couldn't figure the whole arrangement out and began to feel that Cy was not for me, after all. Every time I was seen talking casually to a male the columnists played it up big. But I wasn't ready to think about marriage with all that was going on in my life. Also, Ernie had spoiled me by not being afraid of my strength. Mine was an opinion he consulted and respected. The men I was seeing now, including Cy, seemed to be threatened by it. Once I had the firm contract for ten more *Here's Edie* shows, it made sense to put a down payment on a studio of my own, instead of renting space. Besides, I could rent it out to other people and make money. But Cy ran to my shrink, Grotjahn, and said, "What's the matter with her? She's going to buy the effing studio." It was a good idea, but I was talked out of it by both of them.

Meanwhile, my new date in New York was Billy Rose, who lived in the Rothschild mansion off Fifth Avenue, which he had bought from Bernard Baruch. It was as big as the New York Athletic Club. His cozy dinners were served in an elaborate dining hall, with more servants that I'd ever seen, even at Harry Cohn's. Billy was a feisty little man and reminded me of all I'd ever read about Aristotle Onassis. Rose was a workingman, originally a speed typist, who by sheer determination and hard work had pulled himself up to this place of incredible power. He seemed to know everybody of international and historical fame, he was funny and witty, and I was very impressed.

I spent many hours in his upstairs office just off the bedroom, watching him read his own ticker tape machine. One evening he said, "Wait a minute, I want to show you something." He went into the bedroom, opened a walk-in safe, and came out with several velvet jewelry boxes. He opened them all and showed me the most incredible set of matched diamond and sapphire necklace, earrings, pins, bracelets, and rings. As a new amateur jewelry collector I'd never seen anything like that, even at the Victoria and Albert's royal jewelry collections in London. Billy said, "Wouldn't you like to try these on?" I said, "Oh, no, I can see that they're gorgeous." "I'd really like you to wear them out one night; maybe if you get used to them, you'd like to wear them permanently." I later found out that he had given this set to all his wives. However, when he divorced them and gave them each a hundred thousand dollars—no more, no less—he took the jewelry back.

The one gift Billy Rose did give me was a touchstone in a little velvet jewelry bag. We went out a lot, to all the hot New York places, but during one of our quiet dinners he asked me, unexpectedly, how much money did I actually owe. I said, "I don't owe anything. I have some money I'd like to invest. Billy, please, you know all about the market, please invest this for me in whatever you like." He said, "No, I can't take that responsibility; whatever extra money you have should go into tax-free municipal bonds." No matter how much I pleaded to help me to invest, he wouldn't relent. "No," he said, "just remember, tax-free municipal bonds."

I was on this work whirlwind and watching the IRS and accountants smiling. I did it without any shred of ego, doing my makeup on the plane. I was in and out so fast I didn't need a dressing room. All I really cared about was the money; being a star and having the temperament to go with it could come later. By this time I was doing okay, getting twenty-five thousand dollars a week in Las Vegas, and thirty-five thousand dollars per supporting role in pictures. My television show was picked up in August for nineteen episodes instead of the original nine. I was finally in a financial position to go for quality along with quantity. Now I was allowed to do something for me.

It was a big moment when I finally could get rid of that hated pea green Thunderbird and buy myself the car I really wanted. Driving past the Bentley dealership one night I had seen a beautiful maroon Bentley Continental in the window. The next morning I called and said, "I'd like that car in the window." The salesman sniffed. "Oh, that's a special Mulliner model, and it's thirty-four thousand dollars." I said, "I'll take it; deliver it to two-three-oh-one Bowmont Drive." He said, "But madam, we have to teach you how to drive it." I said, "No, you don't. I took lessons in London. Just deliver it." He did insist that I be there when he did deliver it, because he didn't believe me.

In spite of Billy's good advice, I decided it was time to buy myself something else nice. From California I called my friend Abe Blumstein, who had offices right in the diamond market on Forty-seventh Street in New York, and said, "Abe, I want the biggest, gaudiest, heaviest carat-weighted diamond bracelet you can find. Call me when you've got something."

He said, "What type do you want? Antique, Deco, contemporary, mounted in platinum, white gold, yellow gold—with or without other stones—what?"

I said, "I don't really care, as long as it's big and weighs a lot."

Several days passed. Finally Abe called. He said, "I've got something here that's big, but I don't know whether you'll like it or not. It's kind of dated, about fifteen or twenty years old, and it's kind of, well, bulky."

I asked, "Are the stones fairly good?"

"Yes, but the design is kind of—"

"How wide is it?"

"About an inch an a half."

"How many carats does it weigh?"

"Ninety-seven."

"I'll take it."

"Don't you want to see it?"

"No, just get it appraised and send it out."

"Edie, you're nuts."

"Yes, I learned from the master."

I simply had to prove mostly to me that I could do it on my own. Later I wore that bracelet everywhere with other smaller real ones I had acquired along the way (bought and paid for by me in several of my manic buying binges) to many Hollywood parties. I felt they were like my stripes—hash marks for services rendered. They looked suspiciously like all the fake ones I had used in my takeoffs on Marilyn Monroe and all the other beauties.

One night Groucho's wife, Eden Marx, asked me, "Edie, why do you wear all that tacky junk jewelry?" I just smiled and said, "I don't know. I just like it. It's just fun." To this day I don't think she knew it was real.

Despite all my activity, I never caught a cold while I was working; everyone else did, but not me. I waited until the day after I was home.

Dr. Kantor, my throat doctor, is still laughing about the time years later, when I came back from the road in my seventh month of pregnancy with Josh—obviously not going to work again until after he was born. I had absolutely no voice at all and for no other reason than I didn't have the responsibility for two shows a night. I used to get home and have what I called a beautiful cold. It never failed; after a long tour it always happened. It was delicious; I could lie in bed all day and not feel guilty.

There was one other great part to this luxurious cold. I didn't have to apply makeup, put on my eyelashes, have my hair teased, or be wonderful for anyone. The procedure was always the same. I would sleep late, tell Nan I was ready for my breakfast in bed, then put on my favorite scroungy but comfortable old terry-cloth wrapper, and go back to my safe in the back closet. Since I never took my good jewelry with me on the road, I now would put two or three rings on each finger and all my diamond pins on the lapel, collar, and even the belt of my faded aqua shmatta. I put on all the earrings I could clip on my ears, bottom, sides and top; I could even put the pierced ones through my robe on my chest and with a little practice make them twirl like a stripper. The bracelets went from wrists to elbows on both arms. My unteased hair was covered with the pins that were left.

There I would sit in bed, with my glasses (no contacts) on a red, dripping nose, not an inch of me exposed without some sort of diamond or other precious stone on, eating Nan's famous Mexican eggs—a no-no on the road. Nan would always bring the tray in, singing, "There she is . . . Miss America."

After three years of phone book-size depositions, the judge dismissed Mary's senseless charges in fifteen minutes, and she was told by court order never to bother me or the children again.

My trips to New York for work got to be on a tighter and faster schedule. It got so that I always arrived at 6:00 P.M., after the stores had closed. I always asked the limo driver to slow down as we drove up Fifth Avenue so I could at least look in the windows. I never had time to shop because of early rehearsal or shooting calls. In L.A. I had little shopping time, too, but to get to the studios, I had to drive through the Valley with its neat little houses. All of them seemed to have boats or recreational vehicles parked in the drives. How I envied them their time to play.

By 1964 I had "paid off the farm." In eighteen months I had made five movies, filmed nineteen half hour television shows, done Muriel commercials, made three records, done two plays in summer stock, and spent sixteen weeks headlining nightclubs in Las Vegas and New York. I had met a man I would soon marry, a father figure for Mia.

Once again it seemed I finally had it all . . . or had I?

INTERMISSION

$\mathcal{I}$NDEX

355

Index

Index

Index

Index

Index

Index

Index

Index

Index

Index